Professions in Government

Professions in Government

edited by
Frederick C. Mosher
Richard J. Stillman, II

Transaction Books
New Brunswick (U.S.A.) and London (U.K.)

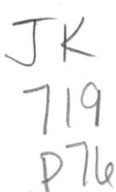

Published 1982 by Transaction, Inc. New Brunswick, New Jersey 08903. This material was originally presented in *Public Administration Review*, Vol. 37, No. 6 and Vol. 38, No. 2. Copyright © 1977, 1978 American Society for Public Administration.

All rights reserved under International and Pan-American Copyright Conventions. No part of this book may be reproduced or transmitted in any form or by any means, electronic or mechanical, including photocopy, recording, or any information storage and retrieval system, without prior permission in writing from the publisher. All inquiries should be addressed to Transaction Books, Rutgers—The State University, New Brunswick, New Jersey 08903.

Library of Congress Catalog Number:79-93072
ISBN:0-87855-863-2
Printed in the United States of America

Library of Congress Cataloging in Publication Data

Main entry under title:

The Professions in government.

   Articles previously published in Public administration review.
   Includes bibliographical references.
   1. Civil service—United States. 2. Professions—United States. I. Mosher, Frederick C. II. Stillman, Richard J., 1943-   III. Public administration review.
JK719.P76   353.006   79-93072
ISBN 0-87855-863-2

Contents

PART I

Introduction	1
Frederick C. Mosher and Richard J. Stillman, II	
Military Professionals in Changing Times	3
Colonel William J. Taylor, Jr.	
Foreign Affairs Officials: Professionals Without Professions?	11
William I. Bacchus	
Educational Administration: An Ambiguous Profession	21
Edith K. Mosher	
The City Manager: Professional Helping Hand, or Political Hired Hand?	29
Richard J. Stillman, II	
Urban Planners: Doctors or Midwives?	41
William C. Baer	
The Professionalization of Police: Efforts and Obstacles	48
Richard A. Staufenberger	

PART II

Introduction	57
Frederick C. Mosher and Richard J. Stillman, II	
Lawyers in Government	57
Laurin A. Wollan, Jr.	
Economists and Policy Analysis	64
Steven E. Rhoads	
Professional Accountants in Government: Roles and Dilemmas	72
Ellsworth H. Morse, Jr.	
The Professions and Government: Engineering as a Case in Point	78
Richard L. Schott	
Scientists and Government: A Case of Professional Ambivalence	85
W. Henry Lambright	
Conflict and Convergence: The Mental Health Professional in Government	91
Saul Feldman	
Professions in Public Service	96
Frederick C. Mosher	

PART I

INTRODUCTION

Frederick C. Mosher, *University of Virginia and U.S. General Accounting Office*
Richard Stillman, Jr., *California State College, Bakersfield*

Many months ago Dwight Waldo, then editor-in-chief of this journal, suggested that we develop and organize one or more symposia on the subject of professions in public administration — upon their nature, strength, and impress upon public policy and its implementation. The topic itself is by no means new. But the pervasiveness and the importance of professionalism in the conduct of American government may not be fully appreciated.

The proportion of professional personnel in the American labor force has of course increased enormously since World War II, and the most spectacular rise has been in the public sector. Between 1960 and 1976, the number of persons who worked directly for governments and whom the Census classified as "professional, technical, and kindred" ("ptk") doubled (from 2.6 to 5.4 million).* In 1976, two of every five "ptk" workers in the employed civilian labor force in the United States worked for federal, state, or local governments. The Census enumeration of employment does not include military personnel, but if one were to add to the government "ptks" military officers and those employed indirectly by governments on grants and contracts, the proportion might well approach one-half. The "ptk" workers in government are more than one-third (36 per cent) of all governmental civilian employment, about three and one-half times the comparable proportion in the private sector. In relation to levels of government, the proportions of "ptk's" to total employment were 21 per cent for federal, 39 per cent for states, and 42 per cent for local units.

More than half of the professional civilians in government are in the field of education, ranging from pre-kindergarten to university presidents and adult education. Thus, the statistics above may skew one's impression of the importance of "ptks" in non-educational governmental employment. However, if one omits educators from both sides of the ledger, more than one-quarter (26 per cent) of all government employees are the "ptk" category, more than double the comparable proportion (12 per cent) in the private sector.

The phenomenon of professionalization in our society — and of other societies — has been widely treated in social science literature, particularly in the field of sociology. But the sociologists have given minimal attention to the impact of the professions on government and professional performance related to governmental purposes. Most of them have ignored the demonstrable facts that: a great many professions are almost exclusively governmental; some of the others exist by virtue

---

*These data are based upon the 1960 Census and unpublished data of the Bureau of Labor Statistics for 1976. The Census definition of "professional, technical, and kindred" includes occupations which some might not construe as professional, such as applied scientists, athletic coaches, surveyors, embalmers, writers, artists, and entertainers. On the other hand, it excludes some that might be considered as professional, including all of those who described themselves as "managers and administrators" (of whom governments in 1970 employed 822,000), military officers, and police. All of the current statistics in this and the following paragraph are based on BLS estimates for 1976 except the percentages on the different levels of government, which are drawn from the 1970 Census.

of governmental authorization and operate within the constraints and delegations of government; and many exert vigorous and sometimes monopolistic influence upon those powers and contraints. Only a tiny number of the sociological studies have delved into the impact of professions upon public policy and its effectuation.

Those interested in government and in public administration have been comparably deficient though in different ways. They worry that public administration is not in itself recognized as a profession, even while they know full well that the great majority of public administrators are lawyers, businessmen, military officers, doctors, educators, social workers, engineers, etc. Much of the doctrine and litany of the old public administration, like that of business administration, assumed a two-tiered organization of management and workers. Later were acknowledged the participation of educated professionals, usually described as "staff," advisory to the "line." Only recently has it been widely recognized that much of the line, both its managers and its workers, are also professional. And there has been insufficient concern about the impact upon public policy and administration when management, workers, and staff are all or mostly professionals. There are some notable exceptions in the rather brief history of public administration, but until the last decade or so there were rather few efforts to understand, let alone influence, the nature of preparation and the nature of practice of professionals in these other fields which in fact populate so many administrative posts in government.

The articles in the symposia in this issue and in a later issue of PAR undertake to enlarge understanding of the basic features of about a dozen different professions that contribute to the practice of public administration. They do not include Public Administration itself, and we are consciously finessing the question of whether it is or is not a profession.

Indeed there is no agreement as to what a profession is. For purposes of these symposia, we have described, rather than defined, a profession in terms of characteristics commonly associated with it; a more or less specialized and purposive field of human activity which requires some specialized education or training (though this may be acquired on the job), which offers a career of life work, and which enjoys a relatively high status in society. It normally aspires to a social, not selfish, purpose. Usually, but not always, it requires a degree or certificate or credential of some kind. Often its members join in a professional organization, local, state or national, which enunciates standards and ethics of professional performance, sometimes with powers of enforcement.

Few, maybe none, fully live up to all the prescriptions of a "true" profession. It is probably more appropriate to consider professionalism as a process in a direction rather than a description of a status. In the development of these symposia we have discouraged the authors from trying to evaluate the field they were describing against someone's criteria of a profession and urged greater emphasis upon the directions and influence in governmental terms of the field of activity they were describing. More specifically, we asked that they consider, in relation to the profession they were analyzing:

- The kinds of positions and the kinds of agencies filled
- The degrees of dominance in policy and administration in those agencies
- The degree and manner in which professionals were equipped to make decisions and manage their agencies
- The distinctive features of the profession in regard to professional ethos, values, perspectives, and methodology
- The channels of entrance, including requisite education, credentials, etc., and the degree to which they are relevant to job responsibilities
- The influence of professional organizations and, where relevant, unionization
- The degree of individual autonomy on the job
- Responsiveness to changing scientific knowledge and technology, expansion of public problems beyond the normal boundaries of the profession, political pressures, encroachments of other professions
- Directions of change in the profession and their impact upon public policy.

The authors of the articles in the two symposia were given wide latitude to discuss these questions and/or others which seemed to them relevant. Obviously, none could treat all of them. And obviously we could not cover more than a small sample of the professions.

The symposia are divided in two parts. The first, which follows in this issue, concerns the public service professions — those employed exclusively or primarily by governments — military, foreign service, educational administration, city management, city planning, and police. The second, which will be published in a subsequent issue of this journal, will deal with professions employed in both the public and private sectors: law, economics, accounting, engineering, applied sciences, and mental health. All of the authors are distinguished governmental practitioners of the profession about which they write or scholars who have studied it in some depth — or both.

Military Professionals in Changing Times

Colonel William J. Taylor, Jr., *United States Military Academy*

The military has long had many of the same characteristics as the other professions,[1] but, times are changing. Many of the traditional characteristics of the military profession are subject to the influence of societal trends.

The dynamics of change are several. First, the continuing social revolution in the United States has had an important impact upon the military. The reappearance in the mid-1960s of virulent anti-militarism expanded significantly the number and difficulty of the problems with which the professional military officer was confronted. Drugs, racism, and dissent impacted upon the military, raising challenges on moral, philosophical, and ideological grounds to established traditions, policies, and practices.[2]

Second, the gradual emergence of "worker democracy," the amilitarism of the 1970s, and the demise of military conscription have changed the character of the personnel resources available to the military and raised new challenges for the leadership of the armed forces.

Third, the continued technological advance that has been reshaping American society has had its impact upon the military services. Technological advance has increased the number of specialities and subspecialities required to handle new bodies of knowledge. This, in turn, has led the military services to turn toward greater specialization to develop and maintain essential military expertise. Increasingly, these considerations have derogated the traditional concept that every officer must be a generalist and, to the extent that this is true, have necessitated fundamental changes in officer education, career patterns, and management.[3]

Impacts of Change

The impact of societal change on the military profession has been real. Clearly, technology has had enormous impact on the weapons components of force structure. However, the major effects of change in the context of this article relate to people in the profession.

High Defense Costs

The All-Volunteer Force (AVF) was proclaimed a reality by the Secretary of Defense in January 1973. In the intervening period of almost five years since that time, military personnel costs have increased rapidly, now constituting 56 per cent of the total defense budget. The two primary reasons for the increase have been the additional costs involved in attracting personnel to volunteer for military service and inflation.

Given a relatively healthy economy in the first three years of transition toward a volunteer force (1970-73), the armed services found themselves in competition with civilian industry. The rationale for a volunteer force had been established explicitly in the Gates Commission Report, which "... placed primary reliance to recruit an enlisted force on monetary inducements determined by the prevailing market-place economy, and thus emphasized the 'occupational' aspects of military duty."[4] Thus, military recruitment efforts fo-

---

The views and conclusions expressed herein are solely those of the author and do not purport to represent the policy of any government agency of the United States.

Colonel William J. Taylor, Jr., is the Permanent Associate Professor for National Security Studies and Director of the Debate Council and Forum at the United States Military Academy. A frequent contributor to various journals and books, his recent articles appear in the forthcoming fourth edition of *American Defense Policy.* He is currently co-authoring a text, *The Elements of National Security,* and co-editing a book, *Military Unions for the United States: Issues and Alternatives.*

cussed on creation of personal incentives – higher salaries, combat arms bonuses, educational opportunities, and military working and living conditions more commensurate with other walks of life. The associated increases in manpower costs were real. The rapid inflation from 1973 forward accelerated growth of all defense costs.

Search for Cost Reductions

Both critics of large military spending and congressional and defense budgeteers interested in holding the line on rapidly escalating manpower costs have sought ways of cutting costs. One means has been a relatively rapid reduction in force (RIF) from a high of 3.5 million during the Vietnam War to 2.1 million by 1977. Following the departure of those who left military service voluntarily, many officers and enlisted personnel were forced to leave the service involuntarily with attendant publicity concerning insecurities of service commitments and vagaries of military personnel policies.

A recent cost reduction proposal has focussed on the military retirement system. One of several schemes debated would offer retirement with some benefits at earlier stages in military service, rather than the present minimum requirement of 20 years. One might suggest that such a provision for entry and early exit from the active-duty military would create a perception of the military as an "occupation" rather than a "calling" or profession, detracting from the traditional military ethic of unlimited, long-term commitment to public service. The military retirement system poses problems for the military profession not shared by most other professions.

Many of the measures for cost reductions studied or adopted have impacted upon military benefits. "Military entitlements" such as shopping privileges in post exchanges and commissaries at prices below the local civilian retail market, free medical benefits for service personnel and their dependents, adjusted active duty pay scales for comparability with civilian pay scales, educational opportunities, retirement pay, and post-service employment opportunities: all these are being scrutinized by civilian defense management and various congressional staffs. The extent of "erosion" of military pay and benefits is an issue of debate. However, there exists a widespread perception within the military that such erosion is significant.

Perceptions of "Service"

Extant societal trends toward "industrial democracy," "co-determination," or "worker democracy" are not new. Their underpinning is the general historical shift in the Western World toward democratic and egalitarian principles.[5] Made possible in large part by the trade union movement which preceded it, the movement has accelerated over the past 10-15 years, manifesting itself in growing employee perceptions of arbitrary treatment at the hands of management, and discontent with dehumanized working conditions and meaningless work.[6]

The most fundamental aspect of the "youth revolution" of the late 1960s was a shift in approach to authority ("The Establishment") in both governmental and private sector managerial forms. Many of those in or influenced by the period of the youth revolution constitute a large part of today's work force and military personnel pool. The approach to organization per se has been changing. Increasingly, organizational goals command allegiance only to the extent that they coincide with personal career goals and self-fulfillment.[7]

This shift applies more to age groups under 35 and far less, if at all, to higher-ranking military professionals now in government, most of whom are over age 35. However, other things being equal, those who rise in rank and to the more influential positions related to government in the near future will not be immune to the trends of the society from whence they came. "Professional commitment" to military service may be no less in the future, but it could be qualitatively different. The change need not be detrimental to the public interest, as long as those responsible for planning, programming, and budgeting for defense understand the implications of societal change for the professional military and reflect that understanding in defense management.

The Officer Education System

As they have evolved, the services' educational systems can be described structurally as a combination of generalist and specialist subsystems. The former category comprises three types. The first type includes preprofessional schools – ROTC and the service academies. The second includes entry schools or basic courses for military job training, as opposed to education. The third type includes "professional" schools and civilian schools. The professional schools are the career courses for retraining and doctrinal update at approximately the fifth year of service, command and staff colleges at mid-career for about half the professional officers, and senior service colleges for more than 1,000 senior officers and government officials each year at roughly their 18th year of service. Graduate civil schooling is provided for some officers who are to be assigned to positions requiring graduate education.[8]

Given the inherent tendencies of large bureaucratic organizations to respond slowly to fundamental change, the military services were surprisingly quick to recognize the implications of technological and social change. The services' educational programs required to provide the skills needed to keep pace with technological innovation have been broad indeed. And, an assumption of an increased requirement for officer involvement in the politico-military dimensions (both domestic and international) of the nation's security tasks has led to an increasing emphasis upon officer education in liberal arts fields. In the 1960s, for example, the number of positions in the services defined as "requiring" civilian graduate school preparation in the social sciences nearly quadrupled. By the mid-1970s, the percentage of active-duty officers with graduate or professional degrees was impressive indeed.[9]

The requirements of military specialization and the education system which supports it have continued to increase. However, as part of escalating military personnel costs since 1973, the officer education system has come under increasing scrutiny. Despite sound arguments to support full-time officer graduate civil schooling, the education programs of the 1960s and early 1970s are falling increasingly under the meat axe of cost-benefit analysis. The monetary costs are relatively easy to quantify, but otherwise clear benefits resist quantification.

Specialization

Although all the military services have developed personnel management systems to support the requirements of specialization, most are of recent vintage. For example, the Army's Officer Personnel Management System (OPMS) is a creation of the early 1970s. The underpinning of OPMS is the recognition that the day of the military generalist is past. The basic concept seeks to increase professional competence, improve productive competition, and provide greater satisfaction by encouraging officers to focus their careers according to individual talents and interest.

Officers may focus on command and spend a large share of their time serving with troop units. Those who perform best with such units are selected for successively higher commands. Other officers focus their careers along functional lines, e.g., personnel, operations, plans, recruiting, project management. Still others eventually become specialists along such lines as ADP, R&D, logistics, or information.

The long-term impact of specialization is unpredictable. It is possible that, as greater numbers of military personnel specialize, they will identify more with a narrower group of specialists and subspecialists (both military and civilian) than with the larger corps of military professionals. This could impact upon professional group identity and corporateness, and reinforce what some view as a trend in military service toward an occupational model.

Unionization of the Military

Recent studies identify several variables which may be leading toward unionization of the active duty armed forces:[10] (1) the trend toward "worker democracy" or "co-determination," (2) emphasis on monetary inducements for recruiting enlisted personnel for the AVF, (3) publicity given to measures studied or adopted to reduce military personnel costs, (4) widespread perception of eroding pay and benefits among military personnel, and (5) the growth of public employee unions in the sector of the labor market with the greatest potential in the next decade.

Despite the confluence of these variables in establishing "a trend" toward military unionization, which some suggest is "inevitable," it is not at all clear that there is significant support for unions of active duty military personnel within the military, within public employee unions, or within the attentive public.[11]

There are hypothetical dangers that the establishment of military unions would strengthen the shift toward military service as an occupation, undermining some of the important dimensions of military professionalism indicated by the diagram on the following page.[12]

It might be suggested further that union membership could involve some commissioned and noncommissioned officers as well as enlisted personnel. Where the line might be drawn between "the bargaining unit" and "management" remains

CHART 1
THE OCCUPATION-PROFESSION MODEL

Dimension	Occupation	Profession
1. Theory, intellectual technique	Absent	Present
2. Relevance to social values	Not relevant	Relevant
3. Training period	A. Short	Long
	B. Nonspecialized	Specialized
	C. Involves things	Involves symbols
	D. Subculture unimportant	Subculture important
4. Motivation	Self-interest	Service
5. Autonomy	Absent	Present
6. Commitment	Short-term	Long-term
7. Sense of community	Low	High
8. Code of ethics	Undeveloped	Highly developed

problematical among those who have addressed the many issues of military unionization.[13] Wherever the line is drawn, there would be significant impact upon several traditional characteristics of the military profession — group identity and corporateness, a hierarchy of offices and legally defined structure, and members' commitment to unlimited service.

Military Professionals and Public Policy

Not all military professionals in government are on active duty. Military professionals with influence upon public policy cannot be neatly categorized. Who are the military professionals?

Non-Active Duty Professionals

One should be concerned most with identifying those of the active duty professional military who serve in government positions which impact upon the conduct or planning of public policy. However, there are other groups of "military professionals" who impact upon public policy.

Clearly, there are *retired* military professionals who impact upon public policy in a variety of ways. One recent study shows that, as of June 1975, there were more than 141,000 people who had retired from active military duty working for the federal government. They were employed by every federal agency. Most, over 78,000, worked for the Department of Defense.[14] Another recent study concludes that one of every seven retired military people now holds a federal civilian job. In the mid-1960s approximately eight per cent of all retirees worked in state or local government jobs.[15]

Many other retired military personnel are employed by firms engaged in defense contracting. Estimates of the numbers involved vary widely in a large number of studies dealing with various aspects of "the military industrial complex."[16] Such studies have made interesting headlines periodically. However, beyond pointing up the fact that many ex-military are employed by defense contractors, and that some of them might have some influence in defense procurement, few definitive conclusions have been drawn. Certainly there has been little to suggest widespread impropriety related to employment of retired military people.[17]

Many thousands of retired military people hold memberships in military associations which represent the interests of individual services, various categories of military personnel, or of the armed forces generally. Examples of approximately 24 such organizations are the Association of the United States Army, the Fleet Reserve Association, the Marine Corps League, and the National Association for Uniformed Services.[18] These organizations perform a number of services for their separate constituencies by many means, one of which is lobbying in both the Executive Branch and Congress.

There are many, both officers and enlisted people, among the Reserve and National Guard who are no less "professional" than active duty personnel. In many cases, their impact upon public policy at the federal, state and local levels may be significant. Many hold appointments to governmental executive positions and many are members of Congress and state legislatures. Many more are in private industries which impact on public policy in a variety of ways.

Active Duty Professionals

The total number of active duty military involved in the planning and conduct of public policy is large indeed. The entire active duty military force of 2.1 million is involved in the United States and abroad in the daily conduct of a broad range of public policies, the most obvious of which are categorized as defense policy or national security policy. Far fewer are involved in public policy planning, and most of these are commissioned officers.

CHART 2
ACTIVE DUTY MILITARY PERSONNEL ASSIGNED TO DOD BY ORGANIZATIONAL COMPONENT

Office of the Secretary of Defense	620
Org. of the Joint Chiefs of Staff	1,126
Army	767,037
Navy (including Marine Corps)	718,203
Air Force	599,066
Other Defense Activities	6,946
Defense Communications Agency	1,506
Defense Civil Preparedness Agency	1
Defense Intelligence Agency	1,897
Defense Investigative Service	1,036
Defense Mapping Agency	748
Defense Nuclear Agency	545
Defense Supply Agency	1,079
Office of Information for Armed Forces	81
Defense Security Assistance Agency	21
Defense Advanced Research Projects Agency	32

Clearly not all public policy planning is done in the Nation's Capital, but most of the major planning decisions are made in the various Washington agencies with the assistance of information from agencies in the field. In early 1976, military personnel in the Department of Defense (DoD) were assigned as shown in Chart 2.[19] Of those assigned to DoD, several thousand served in support of non-DoD functions in almost every federal agency. Several hundred were assigned to agencies outside DoD. In 1976 there were 60,738 active duty military personnel working the Washington, D.C., metropolitan area.[20]

Clearly, most of the direct military influence on public policy planning derives from the officer corps and, given the hierarchical structure of military authority and responsibility, only a limited number of higher-ranking officers can be thought of as influencing public policy directly. To be sure, generals and admirals lean heavily on the analysis and information provided by hundreds of their subordinates on various staffs, but it is from the general or flag officer ranks (and generally from the higher general officer grades) that influence on policy decisions emanates. In early 1976, the number of generals-flag officers, the majority of whom were serving abroad or in positions distributed across the United States, was as follows:[21]

CHART 3
GENERAL AND FLAG OFFICERS ON ACTIVE DUTY BY GRADE

	Army	Navy	Marine Corps	Air Force	Total DOD
General of Army - Fleet Admiral	1	–	–	–	1
General - Admiral	10	10	1	13	34
Lieutenant General - Vice Admiral	32	37	8	43	120
Major General - Rear Admiral (U)	182	97	22	112	413
Brigadier General - Rear Admiral (L)	211	133	37	189	570

Active Duty: Roles and Functions in Government

The formal roles of the professional military in the conduct of public policy are defined by the chains of command. The operational chain of command established by the National Security Reorganization Act of 1958 flows from the Commander-in-Chief through the Secretary of Defense to the commanders of the unified and specified commands worldwide (e.g., Commander-in-Chief, Pacific, or "CINCPAC"). The Joint Chiefs of Staff (JCS) serve formally as the principal military advisors to the President, National Security Council and the Secretary of Defense on operational matters, and have authority to translate policy directives into military operations. Although it has been debatable whether the JCS are in the formal chain of command, it has become the practice (with exceptions) for operational orders to be transmitted through the JCS to commanders in the field. The chain of command for all management and leadership functions other than military operations flows from the Commander-in-Chief through the Secretary of Defense and the civilian service secretaries to the individual service chiefs of staff.

Military professionals are charged not only with the command and management of the armed forces, but also with advising the Secretary of Defense and the President on strategic and structural decisions in defense policy. Strategic decisions are focussed worldwide. They concern the composition, readiness, deployment, and use of military forces. Structural decisions are focussed domestically. They deal with procurement, allocation, and organization of the people, money, and materiel which make up the armed forces.[22]

The degree of military influence on foreign and defense policies has been a traditional issue of debate. Prior to World War I, the military significantly influenced the formulation of public policy in only exceptional cases. There was a recognized division of labor between civilian authority in politics and diplomacy and military professionals who fought wars relatively free of civilian interference.[23]

World War II and the immediate postwar years marked a total break with the past. The military's responsibility for policy execution was deemed to provide them a unique perspective for policy advice. They were accorded extensive politico-military roles in developing war termination and postwar occupation policies. The period of the Cold War expanded the range of policies for which military advice was sought. The National Security Act of 1947 formalized the expanded roles of the military in policy formulation. A series of national security reorganization acts and revisions of the national security system further elaborated the formal military positions in and the flow of military advice through an ever-expanding public policy bureaucracy.

The degree of military influence on strategic and structural decisions in defense policy in recent years has been conditioned by four general categories of variables: (1) national perceptions of threats to U.S. security interests, (2) weapons technology and force inventory which largely determine "the possible" in U.S. security policy, (3) the nature and degree of competing domestic program claims for defense funds, and (4) the status of U.S. alliance capabilities. The extent to which military advice is considered appropriate or necessary at the National Security Council (NSC) level, by the Congress, and by the attentive public is conditioned by the interaction of variables within and among these broad categories. The general prestige accorded to the military in given periods is also a function of the same interactions. The degree of military influence depends periodically on the personal prestige of particular military figures who attract public attention and confidence — a Marshall, Eisenhower, Bradley, MacArthur, or Ridgeway. The Vietnam era produced no such military figures.

Military Influence: Nature and Means

The formal processes for military inputs to routine national security decision making are defined by the NSC System and by the budgeting system which underpin management and orderly processing of the annual defense budget through the Executive and Legislative Branches. The NSC System also provides for crisis decision making. In both routine and crisis situations, the systems provide for military inputs at every organizational level.

The formal NSC and budgeting systems do not account for the specifics of organizational process and political bargaining which condition information, information flows, and positions advocated at most levels of the federal bureaucracy. Military professions necessarily are involved in the pulling and hauling involved in decision making within large bureaucracies. However, the extent to which they are involved is sharply circumscribed by institutional structure, and by the political mandates and professional military ethic of civilian supremacy.

Civilian control of the military, a cherished American tradition, has evolved to produce significant institutional changes since World War II. A gradual shift in authority began with the creation in 1947 of the Office of the Secretary of Defense (OSD) and a small policy staff under James Forrestal. The National Security Reorganization Acts of 1949 and 1958 made the Secretary of Defense clearly the central figure in the management of defense matters. By 1977 the Office of the Secretary of Defense had grown to include 2,700 civilians. Twenty-six of these civilians are appointed by the President to administer major OSD offices and there are 24 admirals and generals assigned to support them. There are 181 civil servants of two, three, or four-star military rank equivalency, 37 of whom are Civil Service Grade Step (GS) 18, equivalent to four-star military rank.[24]

Some have argued that the bounds of intent in the concept of "civilian supremacy" have been overstepped and that appropriate *authority* has been wrested from military professionals who have been given increasingly broad politico-military *responsibilities* since World War II. The suggested result is that, like all professions, quality personnel will not be attracted to or retained in a military profession largely divested of authority.[25]

One might argue the contrary, suggesting that the role of force in the international system has changed so significantly since World War II that the job content of defense management has expanded well beyond traditional military expertise. The technological and information revolutions and the growth of bureaucracy mandate a different kind of management expertise which inheres more closely in civilian business academic training and experience than in military training and experience. Thus, the evolutionary expansion of civilian management reflects only natural societal trends, was inevitable, and is desirable.

Approach to Public Policy

Some have been concerned that military professionals *en genre* have a "military mind." The literature on civil-military relations abounds with debate on this topic.[26] Some advocate the existence of a military mind; other argue that it is a myth. Some suggest that, to the extent it exists, the military approach to policy supports core American values; others take alarm at such characteristics as military nationalism, political conservatism, and authoritarianism. Still others conclude that military professionals are heterogenous in their views on and approaches to public policy issues. One recent study finds increasing heterogeneity to be largely a function of the military education system.[27]

Over the years there have been general criticisms of the practice of appointing professional officers to civilian posts in government — danger of parochialism, possible limited viewpoints, possible susceptibility to pressures from the military, and dangers to civilian control of the military.[28] However, the demand for their services has been relatively high.

In addition to three *professional* officers (Taylor, Grant, and Eisenhower) and eight non-career officers (Washington, Jackson, W.H. Harrison, Pierce, Hayes, Garfield, B. Harrison, Roosevelt, and Carter) elected as President, many have been appointed to high civilian posts. Four generals — Grant, Sherman, H.L. Scott, and MacArthur — served as Acting Secretary of War. Several others served in the 1930s in high positions in the National Recovery Administration, the Public Works Administration, and the Works Progress Administration. General George Marshall served as both Secretary of Defense and Secretary of State. Five of the last 11 Directors of Central Intelligence (DCI) and six of 11 Deputy DCIs have been military officers.[29] And many have served in Assistant or Deputy Assistant Secretary positions in DoD.

As a result of the high productivity of the officer education system at the graduate level in the 1960s, professional officers of higher rank bring to their jobs in government a relatively high degree of expertise in diverse public policy fields of study. Many of these officers, educated full time, fully funded for two years on civilian campuses, have acquired a far greater understanding of the values of the society they serve than might have been typical of their professional military predecessors.

Future Directions

Whether or not straight line projections of current trends augur well for the vitality of a corps of military professionals in government service is problemmatical. The requirements for increasing specialization through education and training and the dictates of industrial democracy run counter to increasing pressures to reduce military personnel costs. The All-Volunteer Force is in a state of flux. Alternatives to the Volunteer Force deserve serious consideration in the very near future.

The soundness of advice from high-ranking military professionals in government will depend upon the quality of the incumbents. The nation deserves military advisers who both seek and can speak with well-founded authority on a broad range of public policy issues. Such men and women will be available only if they are well-educated and trained, challenged by their jobs, and sense that their expertise is taken seriously in public policy decision making. They must receive from their civilian masters support for their professional needs commensurate with their acceptance of personal sacrifice in the interests of public service.

The status of civil-military relations in the latter 1970s bears a resemblance to the interwar period of the 1920s and '30s. Many contemporary challenges posed by reformers have a familiar ring, suggesting cycles in civil-military relations. The reformist programs of the 1920s resulted in small, poorly equipped, and ill-trained armed forces. The resolve of allies, the space of two oceans, and American will, ingenuity, and material resources permitted the time required for protracted war mobilization at the outset of World War II. But times have changed. Nuclear and conventional deterrence require well-equipped, highly trained, well-educated standing military forces in the decade ahead.

In the likely national security environment of the 1980s and beyond, the required expertise of the military profession will be advising on and participating in the management and application of military resources in deterrent, peacekeeping, and combat roles in the context of rapid technological, social, and political change. Future challenges to maintenance of that professional expertise will be several. How best can educated men and women be attracted to and retained in an all-volunteer force? Will trends in specialization and toward unionization fragment the military profession in ways inimical to mission accomplishment? Will military authority in national security decision making be commensurate with military operational responsibilities? Each of these issue areas has a bearing on the maintenance of the professional military expertise required in the national security interest of the 1980s and beyond.

Notes

1. See Morris Janowitz, *The Professional Soldier* (New York: The Free Press, 1960), pp. 5-7; Samuel P. Huntington, *The Soldier and the State* (New York: Random House, 1957), p. 16; and Morris Janowitz, "The Emergent Military," in Charles C. Moskos (ed.), *Public Opinion and the Military Establishment* (Beverly Hills, Calif.: Sage Publications, 1971), p. 258.
2. Sam C. Sarkesian, "Political Soldiers: Perspectives on Professionalism in the U.S. Military," *Midwest Journal of Political Science,* Vol. XVI, No. 2 (May 1972), pp. 241-242.
3. Amos A. Jordan and William J. Taylor, Jr., "The Military Man in Academia," *The Annals,* Vol. 406 (March 1976), pp. 130-132.
4. Charles C. Moskos, Jr., and Morris Janowitz, "Volunteer National Service: A Prerequisite for Federal Employment," draft manuscript of February 1977, p. 3.
5. See Lauri A. Broedling, "Industrial Democracy and the Future Management of the United States Armed Forces," in William J. Taylor, Jr., et al. (eds.), *Military Unions for the United States: Issues and Alternatives* (Beverly Hills, Calif.: Sage Publications, 1977).
6. David G. Bowers, "Work Related Attitudes of Military Personnel," in Nancy R. Goldman and David R. Segal (eds.), *The Social Psychology of Military Service* (Beverly Hills, Calif.: Sage Publications, 1976), pp. 91-99.
7. Alvin Toffler, *Future Shock* (New York: Random House, 1970), p. 149.
8. For a detailed discussion of the officer education system, see Amos A. Jordan and William J. Taylor, Jr., pp. 140-145, and Lawrence J. Korb (ed.), *The System for Educating Military Officers in the U.S.* (Pittsburgh: International Studies Association, 1976).
9. William J. Taylor, Jr., and Donald J. Bletz, "A Case for Officer Graduate Education," *Journal of Political and Military Sociology,* Vol. 2 (Fall 1974), p. 261.
10. See William J. Taylor, Jr., et al. (eds.); and Ezra S. Krendle and Bernard Samoff (eds.), *Unionizing the Armed Forces* (Philadelphia: University of Pennsylvania Press, 1977).
11. William J. Taylor, Jr., "Issues in Military Unionization," a paper presented to the Foreign Policy Research Institute Conference on Unionization of the U.S. Military, Philadelphia, Pennsylvania, April 22, 1977.
12. From Ronald M. Pavalko, *Sociology of Occupations and Professions* (Itasca, Ill.: Peacock Publishers, 1971), p. 26.
13. Bruce N. Gregory, "Union Representation in the Foreign Service," a paper presented at the Annual Conference of the International Studies Association, St. Louis, Missouri, March 16-20, 1977.
14. *Army Times,* April 11, 1977, p. R12.
15. See *The New York Times,* April 5, 1977, p. 1, and Albert D. Biderman, "Where Do They Go from Here? – Retired Military in America," *The Annals,* Vol. 406 (March 1973), p. 152.
16. See, for example, Senator William Proxmire, *Report from Wasteland* (New York: Praeger Publishers, 1970), chap. 7; and Albert D. Biderman, "Retired Soldiers Within and Without the Military-Industrial Complex," in Sam C. Sarkesian (ed.), *The Military*

Industrial Complex: A Reassessment (Beverly Hills, Calif.: Sage Publications, 1972), pp. 95-124.
17. See Biderman, pp. 152-161.
18. For a list of the others, see Ezra S. Krendle and Bernard Samoff.
19. Source: Department of Defense, OASD Comptroller, *Selected Manpower Statistics,* June 1976, p. 9.
20. *Ibid.,* p. 10
21. *Ibid.,* p. 30
22. Samuel P. Huntington, *The Common Defense* (New York: Columbia University Press, 1961), pp. 3-7.
23. Robert G. Gard, Jr., "The Future of the Military Profession," in *Adelphi Paper* No. 103 (London: The International Institute of Strategic Studies, 1973), p. 3.
24. See Vice Admiral Gerald E. Miller, USN (Ret.), in the *Proceedings* of the 28th Annual Student Conference on United States Affairs, November 17-20, 1976, West Point, New York, p. 58.
25. Vice Admiral Gerald E. Miller, USN (Ret.), "The Future Demands of Military Professionalism," a paper presented at the 1976 Regional Meeting of the Inter-University Seminar on Armed Forces and Society, Maxwell Air Force Base, Alabama, October 22-23, 1976, pp. 7-16.
26. For the best compilation of the various issues involved, see Bengt Abrahamsson, *Military Professionalization and Political Power* (Beverly Hills, Calif.: Sage Publications, 1972), pp. 71-79.
27. Raoul Alcala, "Education and Officer Attitudes," in Lawrence J. Korb, pp. 133-149.
28. See Mark N. Lowenthal, "Appointing Military Officers to 'Civilian' Positions," unpublished Congressional Research Service paper, February 7, 1977, pp. 1,2,5.
29. *Ibid.,* p. 6.

Selected References

The more recent classics on the military profession are Samuel P. Huntington's, *The Soldier and the State* (1957), Morris Janowitz's, *The Professional* Soldier (1960), and Bengt Abrahamsson's, *Military Professionalization and Political Power* (1972). Continuing analysis of the military profession and civil military relations is being done under the auspices of the Inter-University Seminar on Armed Forces and Society (IUS), chaired by Morris Janowitz and headquartered at the University of Chicago. The IUS journal, *Armed Forces and Society,* and IUS-sponsored Sage Research Progress Series on War, Revolution and Peacekeeping represent some of the best work in the field.

FOREIGN AFFAIRS OFFICIALS: PROFESSIONALS WITHOUT PROFESSIONS?

William I. Bacchus, *Consultant*

To a casual observer, the Foreign Service of the United States may appear to be among the best established governmental professions, with its high visibility and extensive traditions. This is a doubtful conclusion, since today serious questions exist about its ability to adapt to changing circumstances, the degree to which it is able to establish or retain exclusive functions, and therefore about its future role. Many of the same questions arise with respect to the much larger group of government officials who are not in the Foreign Service but who nevertheless devote their efforts to the conduct of foreign affairs.

Such uncertainty is not new. Diplomacy in the United States has existed as a non-political, career occupation only since the turn of the century. The modern Foreign Service did not come into being until the Rogers Act of 1924, which amalgamated the previously separate Diplomatic and Consular Services, and through stringent entry standards, provided the basis for the development of a self-consciously elite corps of generalists. By most accounts, the service was well equipped to carry out its limited responsibilities in the period until the beginning of World War II. Wartime is never auspicious for diplomats, and by 1945 the Foreign Service faced a pressing need to rebuild itself (attrition and suspension of recruitment had considerably reduced its size) and to find an appropriate place in the new world of postwar diplomacy. The chosen instrument of this renewal

---

The views expressed in this article are entirely the author's. They should in no way be seen as reflecting official Department of State policy, or the opinions of any current officials of the Department.

William I. Bacchus has most recently been a consultant to the Director General of the Foreign Service, U.S. Department of State, on questions of personnel system reform. Prior to that, he was associate research director of the Commission on the Organization of the Government for the Conduct of Foreign Policy. He has taught at the University of Virginia, and received his doctorate from Yale University.

was the Foreign Service Act of 1946, drafted primarily by members of the Service itself and under which (as amended) it still operates today.[1]

The architects of the Act did not foresee, however, the radical transformation of American foreign policy which would occur in the following decades, or the pressures such changes would bring on the Service. In the first two decades of the period, until the mid-'60s, there was a doubling of the number of countries with which the United States had formal diplomatic relations; the creation of new foreign intelligence, assistance, and information agencies; increased international interest and activity by virtually the whole government; and the proliferation both of overseas programs and of representatives of agencies other than the Department of State abroad. Overseas involvement and engagement, including numerous formal alliances and membership in an ever-increasing number of international organizations, became routine for the first time in our history outside of war.

The implications of all this for foreign affairs staffing did not go unnoticed, but proposed changes to meet new conditions either did not resolve the difficulties (such as the amalgamation of the Foreign Service and the State Department's home service as a result of the 1954 Wriston Report), or were never placed into effect (e.g., the "family of compatible Foreign Affairs Services" for the several foreign affairs agencies proposed by the Herter Committee in 1962).[2]

As time passed, problems increased as still other changes occurred. Most striking perhaps was the frequently noted expansion of the foreign affairs agenda into new functional areas of interdependence, particularly related to science and economics and bringing new participants and demands for new kinds of expertise. A relative decline in U.S. military, economic, and political predominance became noticeable, reducing the national margin for error. Policy making became a more complicated process, as the line of demarcation between foreign and domestic policy eroded and in some areas disappeared. Partially as a result, traditional acceptance of the premise that foreign policy "belongs" to the Executive Branch began seriously to be challenged by the Congress.[3] In response to these challenges, reports and studies proliferated, but reform has not kept pace with demands, largely because no agreement exists about what is needed.[4]

The fundamental point of all this is that there has been a major evolution in the nature of foreign policy, bringing with it great diffusion of responsibility and confusion about what a profession in foreign affairs is or should be: "If it was ever true that foreign affairs was a technical specialty, best managed by experts, it is true no longer."[5] What is equally true is that great ambiguity now exists about who should do what. Finding a profession under such circumstances is extremely difficult. To focus exclusively on the Foreign Service Officer (FSO) Corps is to ignore those who carry out the majority of official activity germane to foreign affairs; but to focus on this considerably larger group is to stretch standard definitions of a profession beyond recognition.

The Murphy Commission identified more than 20,000 civilian professional and executive level civilian government employees involved exclusively in international activities, and this excludes an even larger number, nominally unconcerned with foreign affairs, whose actions today may have significant impacts abroad. By contrast, the total number of FSOs is now about 3,500, as it has been for some years.[6] Even if administrative and support personnel and those charged with managing operating programs are excluded to leave a group most directly related to policy, the remaining 2,300 FSOs are far outnumbered by those civilian professional and executive level government employees employed outside the Department of State.

At least in Mosher's liberal usage of the term profession (a reasonably clearcut occupational field which ordinarily requires higher education and offers a lifetime career to its members)[7] the Foreign Service Officer corps qualifies, more because of institutional base and service orientation than exclusive function; the larger grouping of foreign affairs officials by almost any definition does not. More restrictive definitions, for example those including individual work autonomy or shared and specific education, would exclude even FSOs.[8]

The Jurisdictional Problem

The failure of the Foreign Service (unless explicit reference includes non-FSOs in the Foreign Service, the terms "FSO corps" and "Foreign Service" are used interchangeably hereafter) or of foreign affairs officials in general to be accepted as constituting a true profession begins with their inability to establish a monopoly over knowledge necessary for the conduct of foreign affairs, much less of the exclusive right to apply that knowledge. Unlike lawyers, doctors, military officers, or even economists, it has been impossible for them to sustain claims to be the sole practitioners of their trade. This has been compounded by the already-cited emergence of a whole new range of international policy issues. Diversity, the need for an increasingly wide range of technical and specialized competence, and the often conflicting bureaucratic interests of the many units of government with legitimate stakes in the international arena also act to impede development of the group cohesiveness — whether the result of common perspectives, skills, education, or experience — which marks most established professions.

It has been suggested that there are now both "old" and "new" foreign policy agendas, the former consisting of traditional bilateral issues between nations, and the latter of those new or newly important economic, scientific, technical, and resources problems of interdependence — including trade and investment, international monetary arrangements, food, energy, weather modification, oceans, environment, technology transfer, nuclear proliferation, and the like. Such problems are global in nature, and are increasingly dealt with through multilateral organizations. As a generalization, the right of the Department of State and of the Foreign Service to a leading role is much more accepted with respect to the first agenda than the second. But just as other foreign affairs officials encroach on the traditional domain of the Foreign Service, the former in turn find the rest of government contesting their right to exclusive control of the new global agenda, since every important problem in this area has major domestic implications.

In short, the boundary lines of activity which might define a full-fledged profession or professions in foreign affairs are indistinct, and likely to become more so.

Contrasting Approaches: Generalists and Specialists

Differences between the old and new foreign policy agendas tend to be mirrored by different approaches to dealing with them. In a way, this takes the form of the long, inconclusive, "generalists versus specialists" controversy about the appropriate nature of the FSO corps. The "either-or" form of this argument is now clearly dated.

Both mid-career generalists who can deal with a wide range of issues and carry out diverse policies skillfully abroad, and senior generalists able to integrate disparate policy strands are needed; and varying degrees of specialization are required within the total system. Division of labor may be both inevitable and necessary in the face of how much more needs to be known and done today, but it brings with it the critical problem of avoiding fragmentation. The distinctions drawn below between FSOs and foreign policy analysts are not absolute, but they do represent central tendencies of each group.

While there have been some recent steps toward equipping the FSO corps with greater specialist capability, especially in economics, the depth of specialization is still low, and the prevailing mode still emphasizes widely applicable diplomatic skills. Recruitment is designed to ferret out general background and aptitude, presence, and the ability to cope with stressful circumstances, with less concern for specific knowledge. FSO careers are built upon short assignments with varying functional requirements and rotation among a number of countries abroad, and quite different responsibilities in Washington. Primary emphasis is given to the career as a whole, with less to the expertise necessary for any single position. In the best examples, this produces broad-gauged individuals with diverse experiences who are fully equipped as senior officers to deal with many kinds of situations. Unfortunately, this is not always the result, and in any event a price is paid with respect to detailed knowledge about any one policy area, familiarity with Washington bureaucratic mores, and understanding of relationships between foreign policy and domestic political issues.

In contrast, most of those in the career foreign affairs community other than FSOs specialize in one area of related policy issues, or occasionally a country or geographic area. Whereas most FSOs enter at the bottom, recruitment for these others can be at any level, and is on the basis of qualifications, including both relevant academic training and job experience, for the responsibilities of specific positions. Each change of position is dependent upon having the required qualifications, and is generally made by selection among several qualified candidates. Service is likely to be in the same locale throughout the career (mostly Washington), and more often than not in the same agency or department. At the same time, there is some movement to and from those parts of the private sector concerned with the same range of policy issues. The result tends to be deep familiarity and expertise with respect to a relatively narrow set of related problems, but often at the price of inability to accommodate conflicting perspectives and a constricted view of broad national interests. The frame of reference is that of a functional specialty practiced in an international affairs context; in contrast, for most FSOs, that context or some geographically defined part of it is the paramount occupational interest.

Conducting the Public's Business: Ethos, Values, Methodology

These very different patterns of entrance and experience, as reinforced by the incentives each career experience provides, strongly conditions performance and tends to legitimate different operating styles and modes of problem solving. The FSO "sub-culture" (a term sometimes used only half facetiously by its members) is rooted in its overseas responsibilities. This involves the need to be conversant with the whole range of U.S. policy, particularly as it may affect the foreign government to which accredited, and to develop personal relationships and contextual knowledge which will facilitate accurate reporting of developments, including how that government will react in a wide variety of circumstances. A premium is thus placed upon experience (rather than academic training), "feel," and intuition as preferred elements of problem solving. Rigorous analysis ranks lower on the scale.

The Washington foreign affairs expert community also reflects its (very different) operating milieu. Formal training is likely to be valued more highly (although experience is by no means ignored), and the more technical and narrower nature of individual responsibilities combine to place a higher weight upon analysis and formal problem-solving approaches. At the same time, analysis may be influenced by the bureaucratic forum in which it is undertaken, as well as by engaged domestic political interests, and is likely to become one of the weapons to further agency or client group interests in the inter-agency policy fray.[9]

These stylistic differences underscore the obvious but frequently neglected fact that two very different forms of activity are involved. As Harold Nicolson argued, policy and negotiation should not be confused with each other, nor should these "two branches" of the subject be called by "the same ill-favoured name of 'Diplomacy.' " Foreign policy for him was for the executive to decide; in contrast, its execution was best "left to professionals of experience and discretion."[10]

The Foreign Service is oriented toward diplomacy in the second sense of execution. By training and by predilection its members are best equipped for negotiation and for carrying out national policy abroad, and not for the rough and tumble that characterizes the modern American foreign policy making process in Washington. Used to an environment at post in which a sense of unity is likely to prevail and to relatively smooth working relationships with representatives of other agencies at the mission, Washington is often a shock difficult for FSOs to absorb.

Under the best of circumstances, the Foreign Service provides important support and information for policy makers, a task likely to become even more important as it becomes increasingly necessary to be able to predict how other governments will react to contemplated U.S. actions.[11] This reporting falls more naturally into the categories of input to and feedback about the process, rather than being an integral part of that process itself. Success in these core activities of the Foreign Service requires a compromising style, and at times a passive, non-aggressive approach.[12]

In contrast, most of the Washington-based foreign affairs bureaucracy is more directly concerned with policy determination, even though its role may primarily be that of providing analysis, alternatives, and argumentation for more senior, politically appointed policy makers. Because these officials almost invariably represent specific agency and departmental viewpoints (usually along narrow functional lines and responsive to client groups and explicit congressional interests), the process of which they are a part is often featured by intense advocacy, aggressive behavior, and disinclination to compromise. While this policy bureaucracy is well attuned to the dynamics of the policy process, the domestic political implications of proposed policies, and facts and analysis, it is too often unknowledgeable and uncaring about overseas ramifications of what is done at home, and uninformed about the ease or difficulty of implementing a given policy abroad.[13]

This overseas-domestic dichotomy has been complicated for the Foreign Service at least since the Wriston program of the 1950s, which moved domestic employees of the State Department into the FSO corps, partly in order to open positions in Washington for what was virtually an expatriate Foreign Service, the better to "re-Americanize" them. Since that time, the large majority of the key career positions in State have been filled by FSOs, serving on tours of limited duration. While there have been a number of outstanding exceptions, FSOs for the most part have never been completely at ease with these responsibilities, especially those whose entire career has been in the Foreign Service.[14] Their non-activist style, limited job continuity, and lack of technical expertise have sometimes placed them, and therefore the Department of State, at a disadvantage in contending with members of other bureaucracies who have been dealing in depth with the same issues over an extended period.

A striking example of the orientation of FSOs comes from their self-chosen institutional affiliation. Rather than saying, "I work for the State Department," as others would mention Treasury or Commerce, their answer is most likely to be, "I'm an FSO." In short, the overseas career is still the primary focus of the Foreign Service; problems result from their need to participate in domestic policy making as well.

The two quite different kinds of foreign affairs occupations described ought not to be in conflict, for both are essential for successful national policy. The past tendency has been to downplay the differences, or to try to force both occupational groups into a common mold. With its demand for greater specialization — and therefore, paradoxically, the requirement for a higher order of integrative, generalist competence to mold the pieces together — the future requires a total process which accommodates and values the different contributions each group can bring to bear on increasingly complicated policy issues.

Career Preparation

The Janus-like nature of current FSO responsibilities causes uncertainty about skills and attributes needed for successful performance, which in turn raises questions about the most appropriate type of formal education and career experience as preparation for senior responsibilities. If, as argued above, duties in Washington are very different from those in the field, requiring quite different competences, the question arises of which "cluster" of skills should be emphasized in recruitment and career development.

Quite different answers have been given through the years. A decade ago, Harr found in his comprehensive survey that FSOs strongly endorsed management, negotiating, and reporting as the central functions of the diplomatic profession, with considerably less emphasis placed on policy development.[15]

William Macomber, who as Deputy Under Secretary of State for Management came to hold a broader view, emphasized not only the need for traditional diplomatic skills such as reporting, negotiating, and persuading, but also specifically the need to be able to analyze objectively and to develop sound and creative policy choices. These skills were needed by all officers, independent of speciality; in addition, substantive knowledge, in many cases of a specialized nature, was held to be essential.[16]

Still later, in 1976, a staff study conducted by several mid-rank FSOs for a professional development working group attempted to isolate qualities and skills needed by the "ideal" foreign affairs executive, based in part upon those of a group of senior officials generally agreed to have been successful and therefore good role models. The list emphasized management, operational skills, persuasiveness and negotiation, with less concern about expertise or analytic skills.[17]

What is striking about these and other self-analyses is the degree to which the generalist mentality persists, augmented by an increasing concern with program management (at a time when the need to operate large programs abroad is diminishing). Few of the qualities cited suggest that different kinds of senior positions may require individuals with different configurations of skills. Moreover, analytic, conceptual, and integrative skills presumably critical for policy development are also invariably down-rated or missing entirely. As long as such lists of qualities reflect what the service itself thinks it needs, it is not likely to recruit or develop individuals with specialized expertise, or who have the combative style needed to contend more successfully in the Washington arena.

That generalists are still preferred is reflected by the recruitment process. Broad formal education is clearly an asset in doing well on the FSO examination; technical training is less valuable. Even more telling than the continued preponderance of history and political science majors among new FSO classes is the lack of any system designed to put to use specialized expertise that new FSOs do bring with them. Experience gained on the job (sometimes augmented by service-conducted training) still counts for more than formal education.

Another problem is the bifurcation of the FSO career. The system recruits at the bottom, giving primary weight to those generalist qualities thought to be necessary a quarter-century later for service abroad as an Ambassador. However, many of the middle-level policy-related jobs through which FSOs pass in the intervening period are best filled by those with substantial specialized expertise. This is particularly true in the functional bureaus of State, such as those dealing with economics, environmental and scientific affairs, and political-military affairs.[18] When such expertise is lacking, the Department is unable to play an across-the-board role as integrater of policy because it is overwhelmed by the greater technical competence of the more functionally oriented units of government. State can never duplicate the amount or depth of expertise found elsewhere, but it needs enough to keep the policy process honest.

There is little incentive for FSOs to acquire such competence. Since they are evaluated as generalists for promotion to senior ranks, the best personal strategy is to be sufficiently specialized to survive in the middle ranks where promotion is on the basis of functional competition, without becoming overly narrow. This perception of self-interest leads to under-utilization of skills; e.g., it is seen as safer to be a more general economic/commercial officer than a more specialized financial economist, even when there may be a more critical need for the latter. Service in such specialized areas over the extended period necessary to develop professional-level expertise is not likely to establish the credentials required for promotion to senior ranks, nor even to provide the generalist skills required at that level.

Another problem exists at the most junior ranks, where highly talented individuals with generalist potential *and* in many cases specialized education are often dissatisfied because they are given little responsibility or opportunity to apply what they know best. A rank-in-person, total career oriented personnel system has a number of virtues, but is poorly suited for an environment the demands of which do not allow smooth progress from bottom to top. This is exacerbated for the Foreign Service by the very different overseas and domestic responsibilities, and by the need to gain greater technical expertise to deal effectively with new kinds of international issues.

The rest of the foreign affairs community is by no means fully equipped for evolving responsibilities, but in many respects its problems are less complex. Focusing almost exclusively on Washington needs and on a more limited functional spectrum, its many sub-elements can be less schizophrenic than the FSO system. Since hiring and promotion is on the basis of qualifications for specific positions, and there is easier access from outside at the middle as well as junior levels, it is possible to respond to changing needs with less difficulty than in a bottom-entry system. Furthermore, it is the organization rather than the profession which controls entry, making it easier to change standards to be more responsive to new circumstances. How effective the system is in providing needed experts depends upon how well it is administered, which varies considerably from agency to agency.

While a task-oriented system is superior at gaining specialized talent, it is less clear that it can produce broad-gauged policy generalists in the numbers or sub-categories needed. This is a governmentwide problem, not one limited to the foreign affairs area. To date solutions such as the broadening programs of the Federal Executive Institute have provided only a partial answer to the question of how best to change specialists into effective broad-gauged policy makers.

Responsiveness and Adaptation

The foreign affairs community faces major changes in the domestic and international environments in which its members practice their trades, especially with respect to specialization, policy integration, accommodation to the domestic scene, analytic capability, and self-perceptions.

Implications of the evolving, more technical international issue agenda for the competences which will be required are not yet clearly recognized. In the State Department, some FSOs gain specialized skills through multiple assignments dealing with one set of issues and accompanied by short-term training, but within the context of overall generalist career patterns. But no fundamental changes in recruitment practices seem likely, such as bringing any significant number of established professionals in economics or science into the service at mid-levels. Actions taken to date to meet new demands reflect a preference for minimizing impact on the existing structure and mores of the FSO culture. At the same time, some policy expertise is also acquired for the Department through non-FSO appointments. Specialists from the private sector or elsewhere in government are appointed in limited numbers both temporarily (for periods of five years or less) and permanently, using Foreign Service Reserve, Reserve Unlimited, and Civil Service authorities.

The concept underlying these two approaches taken together is that many or most FSOs might eventually be "generalist/specialists," while "deep specialists" would be employed in other categories.[19] While many doubt the efficacy of this strategy, it may be the best practical solution as long as FSOs must fill more generalist roles abroad at the same time the Department of State has an urgent need for greater functional competence at home. From the standpoint of the FSO corps, however, it may bring the risk of increasing irrelevance in Washington. It is conceivable that influence and responsibility will in the future flow more heavily to subject matter experts, both non-FSOs in State and officials and analysts in other agencies.

Whether or not the FSO corps is able to adapt sufficiently to retain an important portion of the Washington "action," a major problem will remain of meshing effectively the quite different overseas-generalist and headquarters-specialist policy perspectives. Policy synthesis will be at a premium, and it is unclear that either the FSO corps or the policy analyst/specialist group will be able routinely to provide sufficient individuals with the necessary integrative ability to excel at senior-level responsibilities.

The Foreign Service is also under increasing pressure of a different sort, to become more representative of American society. Specifically, its critics want it to include more women, minority group members, and individuals whose geographic and educational background will help make the composition of the FSO corps more nearly resemble that of the total population. The rationale is to insure that the American people as a whole are adequately represented abroad. There has been progress, but the service remains heavily white and male. A related drive has been to bring FSOs who have been serving abroad back into close touch with the American people, and not just the Washington community. Most recently, this has been legislatively mandated through the Pearson Amendment, requiring that a number of mid-career officers be assigned to tours of duty in state and local government positions each year.

The impact may be mostly symbolic, but such concerns as these about the FSO corps give strong evidence that it will be increasingly difficult for it to be elitist, on the basis either of achievement or social background.

The strongest suit of the Foreign Service should be the application of its foreign-related knowledge across a broad spectrum of issues. Even here, there is evidence change is needed. Recent critiques conclude that reporting from overseas needs to be more analytic than it now typically is, and much more attuned to U.S. domestic political realities and to the Washington policy context.[20] The Murphy Commission argued that the major future function of State — both embassy personnel abroad and the Washington establishment — will be foreign assessment, or "analysis of probable host country responses to emerging issues of concern to the U.S.," including not only factual information but also "predictions and proposals on specific issues." Its goal should be to explain why foreign governments act as they do and the most likely impact of proposed U.S. actions, and to present such information in a way that suggests "how U.S. initiatives can be designed or modified to have their desired effect."[21] In short, traditional reporting must become more analytic, pertinent, and timely — and thus more integrated into the policy-making process.

Adjustment also seems inevitable in the most sacrosanct of FSO functions abroad: representation and negotiation with foreign governments. It is sometimes argued that the era of bilateral, state-to-state relationships has passed, being replaced by multilateral diplomacy carried out in an ever increasing number of specialized and general purpose international organizations. But the rise of multilateralism and of the related technical issues of interdependence are more likely to place additional burdens on those who carry out bilateral relations. It will be increasingly necessary, with the decline in U.S. power advantage, to seek support for American positions on multilateral issues through individual persuasion of other nations, rather than expecting it to come naturally. FSOs will be critical to the success of such efforts. Moreover, since such issues are likely to be highly technical (law-of-the-sea, food production, resources, e.g.), sufficient specialized knowledge to insure effective negotiation will be needed; and of course, many of the more purely bilateral issues, for example landing rights for Concorde, will be more technical as well.

Given all these pressures, perhaps the most fundamental adaptation facing FSOs collectively will be perceptual, in bringing their self-assigned roles into greater congruence with existing realities. Recognition that the FSO corps does not have proprietary rights to the exclusive conduct of the nation's foreign affairs, or even increasingly to a primary place, is necessary if the Foreign Service is to serve well the more restricted but critical responsibility of bringing consistency to the totality of foreign policy. Other parts of the Washington policy community, by virtue of more restricted interests and parochialism, cannot be a surrogate for the Department of State and the Foreign Service in playing this role.

Public Servants or Employees?

In the face of such challenges, and of changes in American society, it is not surprising that today much of the Foreign Service is restive. Some members are hostile to any major adaptive efforts, while others are scathing in their contempt for the status quo. To the outside observer, it sometimes appears that almost everyone, FSO or not, considers him- or herself to be part of a beleaguered minority, contending with others who are seen as gaining a disproportionate share of the limited rewards the system can offer. In addition, some of the traditional attractions of service overseas have dissipated. The cost of living has increased everywhere, and the dollar declined in value. Allowances for hardship duty and other purposes are increasingly inadequate, the tax situation is becoming threatening, an increasing number of posts are undesirable places to live, more spouses are frustrated if they cannot pursue their own careers abroad, and a number of recent episodes have driven home the threats to personal safety which exist.

As a result, the morale and comradeship which hold the Foreign Service together have declined. A major change has occurred in perceptions of appropriate relationships between individuals and the leadership of the service and of the Department of State. Officers are more assertive about their careers, less willing to accept any assignment offered, and more inclined to enter into formal actions to obtain redress for personally disadvantageous management actions. For their part, managers lament the loss of discipline in the service. Contentiousness and mutual suspicion are increasingly the norm.

It is under these circumstances that the American Foreign Service Association has evolved in the past decade from a professional association into what is for all practical purposes an employee union, and one that is often aggressive. In 1973 it became the exclusive employee representative for Foreign Service employees of the State Department, AID, and USIA through National Labor Relations Board representation elections. Since that time, many issues which in earlier years would have been settled informally among colleagues have become subject to formal employee-management consultation and negotiation.

AFSA, however, has not yet succeeded in convincing many Foreign Service professionals, particularly those who are not FSOs, that it is able effectively to represent their interests. In 1976, the American Federation of Government Employees (AFGE), a more established government employee union, succeeded in displacing AFSA as exclusive representative for USIA employees, in a new election. Moreover, AFSA's internal politics have sometimes been worthy of the Borgias, with factionalism making it very difficult in some cases to arrive at a unified position, or to be effective in negotiations.

The trend toward organization of public employees seems well-established throughout the government, even while questions remain about the extent to which union membership is compatible with professional status. It is argued by some that AFSA ultimately may have to choose whether to revert to its earlier form as strictly a professional association, leaving employee representation to another organization, or alternatively to become a true union, because it cannot effectively do both.

Whatever the future mechanism of employee representation, a more formal and less accommodating relationship between the Foreign Service and its members seems almost inevitable. Careerism in its negative sense is a clear danger. New grievance procedures have been legislated, and there is little reluctance to use them. It seems possible that all this activity, which is highly focused upon individual concerns and bread-and-butter issues, rather than on the service ethic which has so long been characteristic of the Foreign Service, may undercut the image of the FSO corps as an elite professional group of public servants, reducing differences between them and other government employees in the public mind. Like the rest of the foreign affairs community, they may become more an occupational group than a profession.

Future Prospects

Perhaps the only future certainty is that there will continue to be a need for diplomats abroad and for policy analysts at home. Evolution in the institutional and professional means by which they are provided and in the career services of which they are a part may be inevitable.

One possibility, with the advantage of having the least impact on individuals except those at the top, is the Murphy Commission plan to establish a foreign affairs communitywide Executive Corps, somewhat similar to the 1971 proposal for a governmentwide Federal Executive Service.[22] Each of the existing personnel systems in the involved agencies would serve as feeders, with individuals being selected for the most senior positions on the basis of having the specific skills necessary for a given job. Ideally, such an arrangement would allow the Foreign Service Officer to focus for most of his or her career on skills most needed overseas, while the Washington-based counterpart remained a policy specialist. Individuals in each category who demonstrated the necessary bureaucratic skills and integrative talents could rise to the top on the basis of equitable competition.

Alternatively, it is conceivable that the Foreign Service as it exists today might disappear, being merged into the larger federal service and operated on rank-in-job principles. Another, less likely, plan, advocated within the Department of State as a result of a 1974 inspection of the personnel system, would retain the rank-in-person principle through the middle grades, switch to rank-in-job at the top, and recruit and evaluate all members below senior levels as specialists. Both of these approaches would encourage employment of individuals with specialist skills, but might have a negative impact on the development of broad-gauged diplomatic generalists, since each would impede assignment of individuals to a variety of different tasks during a career.

Whether the future brings adaptation of the current system, or adoption of some such alternative as described, a prior condition for the success of any approach is a clearer sense than now exists of the demands professionals in foreign affairs must meet, and of the roles they should play in making and carrying out national policy. Many of the usual criteria of a profession will never be present in foreign affairs occupations, so the focal point must be a combination of sense of mission and of stewardship for U.S. relations with the rest of the world. Diversity of function must be accompanied by unity of purpose. Anything less will guarantee that the national interests will not be well served in the challenging years ahead.

Notes

1. The most useful sources for the early years of the Foreign Service are Warren F. Ilchman, *Professional Diplomacy in the United States 1779-1939: A Study in Administrative History* (Chicago: University of Chicago Press, 1961); and William Barnes and John Heath Morgan, *The Foreign Service of the United States: Origins, Development, and Functions* (Washington, D.C.: Historical Office, Bureau of Public Affairs, Department of State, 1961). For the history of the Foreign Service Act of 1946, see Harold Stein, "The Foreign Service Act of 1946," in Stein (ed.) *Public Administration and Policy Development: A Case Book,* The Inter-University Case Program (New York: Harcourt, Brace and World, 1952), pp. 661-737.
2. The Wriston Report is published as *Toward A Stronger Foreign Service,* Report of the Secretary of State's Public Committee on Personnel, Department of State Publication 5458 (Washington, D.C.: U.S. Government Printing Office, 1954); that of the Herter Committee as *Personnel for the New Diplomacy,* Report of the Committee on Foreign Affairs Personnel (Washington, D.C.: Carnegie Endowment for International Peace, 1962). A fuller listing of postwar reform efforts can be found in William I. Bacchus, "Diplomacy for the 70's: An Afterview and Appraisal," *American Political Science Review,* Vol. LXVIII, No. 2 (1974), pp. 736-748, esp. n. 3, pp. 736-738.
3. The current interdependence literature is voluminous. For discussions that closely reflect the premises upon which this article has been written, see Peter L. Szanton, "The Future World Environment: Near-Term Problems for U.S. Foreign Policy," in "Foreign Policy for the Future," Appendix A to the *Report of the Commission on the Organization of the Government for the Conduct of Foreign Policy,* Appendix Volume I (Washington, D.C.: U.S. Government Printing Office, 1976), pp. 5-10; and Joseph S. Nye and Robert O. Keohane (eds.), "The Management of Global Issues," Appendix B to the Report of the Commission, Appendix Volume I, pp. 41-255. The Commission is hereafter referred to in the text as the "Murphy Commission," after its chairman.
4. Two of the most prominent later reform studies can be found in *Toward A Modern Diplomacy,* A Report to the American Foreign Service Association by its Committee on Career Principles (Washington, D.C.: American Foreign Service Association, 1968); and

Diplomacy for the 70's: A Program of Management Reform for the Department of State, Department of State Publication 8593, Department and Foreign Service Series, 1430 (Washington, D.C.: U.S. Government Printing Office, 1970).
5. Graham Allison and Peter Szanton, *Remaking Foreign Policy: The Organizational Connection* (New York: Basic Books, 1976), p. 123.
6. James W. Clark, "Foreign Affairs Personnel Management," in "Personnel for Foreign Affairs," Appendix P to the Report of the Murphy Commission, Appendix Volume 6, p. 222. This appendix is heavily devoted to the concerns discussed in this article.
7. Frederick C. Mosher, *Democracy and the Public Service* (New York: Oxford University Press, 1968), p. 106.
8. Cf., for such definitions, Talcott Parsons, "Professions," in *International Encyclopedia of the Social Sciences* (New York: Free Press, 1968), Volume XII, pp. 536-547; and Richard L. Schott, "Public Administration as a Profession: Problems and Prospects," *Public Administration Review,* Vol. XXXVI, No. 3 (May/June 1976), pp. 253-259.
9. Charles E. Lindblom, *The Policy-Making Process* (Englewood Cliffs, N.J.: Prentice-Hall, Inc., 1968), pp. 30-34 *et passim,* develops the idea of the relationship between analysis and the bureaucratic politics of policy making.
10. Harold Nicolson, *Diplomacy,* 3rd ed. (London: Oxford University Press, 1963), p. 3.
11. Allison and Szanton, p. 131; and the *Murphy Commission Report,* pp. 40-41 and 118-119.
12. For further treatment of this theme, see Chris Argyris, *Some Causes of Organizational Ineffectiveness Within the Department of State,* Center for International Systems Research, Occasional Paper, 2 (Washington, D.C.: U.S. Government Printing Office, 1967).
13. For the importance of implementation and the problems Washington has comprehending what is involved, cf. I.M. Destler, "National Security Advice to Presidents: Some Lessons from Thirty Years," *World Politics,* Vol. XXIX, No. 2 (1977), pp. 143-176.
14. Cf. William I. Bacchus, *Foreign Policy and the Bureaucratic Process* (Princeton: Princeton University Press, 1974), pp. 229-230, for discussion of the possibility that "non-typical" FSOs, i.e. those with career experiences outside normal career patterns, may be more likely to succeed in the Washington environment.
15. John Ensor Harr, *The Professional Diplomat* (Princeton: Princeton University Press, 1969), pp. 242-244.
16. William B. Macomber, *The Angel's Game: A Handbook of Modern Diplomacy* (New York: Stein and Day, 1975), pp. 39-58.
17. Professional Development Working Group, Department of State, *Final Report and Action Recommendations,* Tab 3, "Characteristics of the Senior Foreign Affairs Executive," unpublished, U.S. Department of State, 1976.
18. Cf. for a recent discussion of this problem, T. Keith Glennan, *Technology and Foreign Affairs,* A Report to Deputy Secretary of State Charles W. Robinson (Washington, D.C.: U.S. Government Printing Office, 1976), *passim.*
19. Professional Development Working Group, Department of State.
20. Henry A. Kissinger, "Reporting from the Field," Department Notice, U.S. Department of State, November 7, 1973; William D. Coplin, Michael K. O'Leary, Robert F. Rich, and associates, "Towards the Improvement of Foreign Service Field Reporting," Appendix E to Report of Murphy Commission, Appendix Volume II, pp. 207; Carol C. Laise, "From The Director General: Reporting – Cornerstone of the Profession," *Department of State News Letter,* No. 188 (1977).
21. Commission on the Organization of the Government for the Conduct of Foreign Policy, *Final Report* (Washington, D.C.: U.S. Government Printing Office, 1975), p. 118. See note 9.
22. *Ibid.,* pp. 183-188; cf. for a more comprehensive discussion, Hugh Heclo, *A Government of Strangers* (Washington, D.C.: The Brookings Institution, 1977), pp. 249-253.

Further Reading

In addition to items listed in the footnotes, the following will provide additional background on the future of the Foreign Service and of other foreign affairs officials in government: Graham T. Allison, *Essence of Decision* (Boston: Little, Brown, 1971); John Franklin Campbell, *The Foreign Affairs Fudge Factory* (New York: Basic Books, 1971); Francis E. Rourke, *Bureaucracy and Foreign Policy* (Baltimore: Johns Hopkins University Press, 1972); and Donald P. Warwick, et al., *A Theory of Public Bureaucracy: Politics, Personality and Organization in the State Department* (Cambridge, Mass.: Harvard University Press, 1975). For problems of reform and reorganization, see Frederick C. Mosher, "Some Observations About Foreign Service Reform: Famous First Words," *Public Administration Review,* Vol. XXIX, No. 6 (November/December 1969). In addition, those with a serious interest should consult monthly issues of the *Foreign Service Journal* and of the *Department of State News Letter.*

Educational Administration: An Ambiguous Profession

Edith K. Mosher, *University of Virginia*

One may draw ready parallels between educational administrators and other public managers in the larger aspects of their work. They all head up agencies or substantial subagencies that provide specialized and expert services; they operate with public funds and legal authority; they conform to the dictates of their own professional standards and ethics. But there is also much deeply engrained sentiment in public and professional circles that "schoolmen" are somehow different — a class apart from their peers. It is useful to explore the attributes which tend to explain and justify these views.

In the first place, almost all citizens have firsthand acquaintance (unless they have always lived in very populous communities) with several school administrators, in particular, the principals of the schools they or their children have attended. Because teachers typically rely on principals for assistance with problem children and situations, this acquaintance may have come about under tense and unpleasant conditions in which an erring student and his/her parents feel the full weight of official authority. More benign perceptions of the principal are those of the advocate in school district councils for the good of "our school," or as a friendly and supportive advisor to individual students and families. In any case, this largest category of school administrators is closer at hand than other public officials and much more likely to become emotionally identified or involved with their clienteles.

Another basis for differentiation is important in the relations of educational administrators with other public officials, and almost a source of envy to the latter. That is the relative independence and isolation of school personnel from other institutional involvements. This is in part because of the practice of segregating elementary and secondary school age children from the rest of society during their years of formal schooling. It stems mainly, however, from the development of a separate system for organizing and controlling schools that is sometimes referred to as "the fourth branch of government." Educators are also distinctive in having spent almost their entire lives under the socializing influence of this same institution. A 37-year-old person first appointed as a school superintendent has been "in school" for 31 years, as a child, as a college and graduate student, as a classroom teacher, and as a principal or supervisor. A reasonable parallel to an urban public school superintendent might be the Roman Catholic bishop who is trained in parochial schools and sent at an early age to the seminary.[1]

These significant aspects of educational administration grew out of the American context; they are not universal nor fully consonant with the development of the other public service professions. It is instructive at the outset, therefore, to examine the existing structure of educational administration and the historical roots of its claims to professionalism.

The Scope and Structure of School Management

In 1974 there were 16,300 local public school systems in the United States, just under 100,000 school board members, an elementary and secondary school enrollment of more than 45 million students, and annual expenditures of nearly $57 billion. These systems were administered by 13,000 full-time-equivalent superintendents, 23,000 assistant superintendents, 100,000 principals, and 38,000 supervisors of instruction.[2]

Nonpublic schools enrolled 5 million students and had 267,000 instructional staff members.[3] Assuming that the percentage of administrative personnel are comparable to that of public school systems, there were approximately 19,000 nonpublic school administrators. To this total of 193,000 local school administrators, public and nonpublic, should be added an estimated 8,000

Edith K. Mosher is associate professor in the School of Education, University of Virginia, where she teaches in the Department of Educational Administration and Supervision. She holds a doctoral degree in educational administration from the University of California at Berkeley, and previously was a personnel and administrative officer in several federal government agencies. She is co-author with Stephen K. Bailey of *ESEA: The Office of Education Administers a Law* and author of numerous articles in the fields of politics and economics of education.

persons with managerial or supervisory responsibilities in federal, state, and regional educational agencies.[4] The professional ranks also include an estimated 2,000 university-based academicians whose primary interest is teaching and research in educational administration.[5]

The scale of administrative operations at the local public school district level ranges from that in a relatively few large urban systems with tens of thousands of students to the still relatively numerous and mostly rural systems which enroll fewer than 300 students. In 1974 the majority of the 16,300 public systems in the country had fewer than 1,000 students, an average number of 5.4 schools in all districts, and an average of 500 students per school in daily attendance.[6] Thus the task of administering the typical school district appears to be of relatively modest scale; however, some districts provide a marked contrast. The 22 largest urban school districts, each enrolling more than 95,000 students in 1973, accounted for 11 per cent of the total public school enrollment in the country.[7] A little more than one per cent of all districts, those with enrollments of more than 25,000 students, account for 29 per cent of the total number of students. These are of course the locations in which educational administration displays well-developed bureaucratic complexity.[8]

Who Are the School Administrators?

Two surveys published in the early 1970s[9] provide the following data concerning the "typical" American school superintendent: a 48-year-old white male who became a classroom teacher at age 24, a principal or supervisor at 30, and a superintendent at 36. He was more than twice as likely to have begun his career in secondary rather than in elementary teaching, and the chances are almost eight in ten that he once coached some sport. He has not held a post-college noneducational position. His highest academic degree is a master's in education, obtained by part-time study at one of the less prestigious colleges and universities. The smaller the school district enrollment, the more likely the possibility that the superintendent was reared in a rural or small town community; overall, 86 per cent reported such origins. In comparison with the general population, and even with other professions, school superintendents have stable marriages, are active members of Protestant churches, and are identified as Republicans.

The basic recruitment pool for school administrators — classroom teachers — is two-thirds female, but women are far less likely to serve as administrators; 86 per cent of assistant principals and principals, 93 per cent of assistant and deputy superintendents, and 99.9 per cent of superintendents are male. Their salaries are comparable to, and in many communities exceed, those of local and state peer professionals. In 1977, the mean salary for superintendents in districts enrolling 25,000 or more students was $42,069, and for all superintendents was $33,233. The mean salaries for elementary school principals was $20,800, and for high school principals, $24,225. Assistant principals in the two categories were paid on the average, $17,561 and $20,714, respectively. The mean salary for classroom teachers was $13,119.[10] The large incremental increase for administrative positions is in part attributable to the duration of such employment for a full year rather than the school year of nine months.

In his study of the succession patterns among educational administrators, Carlson distinguishes between the "place-bound" and "career-bound" superintendent. The former places a high value on long-time residence in a specific community, has a known history in the organization's informal structure, and is likely to carry over to the position a tendency to conform to expectations and wishes of his subordinates. The career-bound superintendent, on the other hand, lacks commitment to the specific community in which he is employed, is not well acquainted with its social history, and seeks to further his career ambitions by more or less frequent changes of locale. National surveys indicate that two out of three superintendents might be classed as "career-bound," rather than "place-bound." The greatest proportion of the former are found among superintendents in districts enrolling fewer than 10,000 students, but uneven distribution of the two types is found in particular regions, types of districts, and at various periods of time.

In spite of this evidence concerning career aspirations, superintendents, as of 1970, were not especially mobile professionals. Those reporting two or more incumbencies held each position 5½ to 6 years and tended to move to districts of about the same size within the same state.[11] Carlson characterizes the superintendency as a profession for which barriers to entry in the way of class origin, formal education, or exceptionally high intelligence seems to be few. Its holding power is not especially strong, since before reaching retirement many superintendents abandon the profession.[12]

One avenue of mobility for educational administrators is to college and university departments in this field. The profile of the professor of educational administration shows very similar personal characteristics to that of a superintendent, except for the greater tendency of the former to be identified with the Democratic Party and to be a graduate of a more prestigious university. Half of the academicians report that they previously held five or six positions in education, presumably coming up the same administrative ladders as do the practitioners. Their teaching is confined to fledgling or experienced practitioners, and they tend to have more extensive field contacts than do other professors. They also appear to have little time for, or inclination toward, research.[13] Campbell and Newell comment on the "alarming homogeneity" and the ivory-tower views of the professorship. They note with some dismay the complacency which their informants showed about a number of frequently cited problems in the field, and wonder "how the study and training arm of the profession can be so pleased with itself while the practice arm of the profession is in such difficulty."[14]

Superintendents and Composite Roles

Until about 1890, most American schools were managed entirely by boards of local citizens, who built facilities, hired teachers, chose books, and, in many cases, examined the pupils. The duration of schooling was brief — the average child remained in school for five years — and the tasks of the school were relatively straightforward. As communities and schools grew in size, school boards often divided themselves into subcommittees to handle the specialized administrative tasks of what gradually became large-scale enterprises. Their mode of operation was probably not any better or any worse than that of other locally elected political officials of the period.

When they found they needed help in overseeing the daily operations of the schools, they began to appoint superintendents to supervise the teachers and the pupils. However, they generally retained authority for all the key management decisions, and most of the early superintendents were primarily clerks or factotums.[15] They were just doing what the board members felt themselves capable of doing if they just had the time! Only in a few cities were a few outstanding men able to work actively with their boards and exercise personal leadership.[16]

Several converging developments of the late 1800s brought what has been called "the first revolution" in the management of public education. Among these were the growth of the cities, the development of corporate forms of industrial management, and, within the intellectual community, an evangelical faith in scientific rationality.

Concurrently, the public perception of education as a means of upward mobility in an increasingly technical society brought demands that the schools expand their offerings in quantity and quality. The corrupt and inefficient school boards of the cities came under attack from a loosely allied coalition of citizen activists, university professors, and concerned superintendents.[17] They agreed with the "public-regarding" philosophy of the Progressive reform movement which, in due course, brought wide adoption of the council-manager form of city government.

To achieve similar goals of impartial and competent educational administration, the school reformers sought legislative changes which would make the schools more independent of City Hall, would retain the school board as representatives of the public but reduce its size, and would elevate the superintendency to a position of executive leadership.

These initiatives, so reflective of the corporate image of organization, spread very rapidly. By 1920 the widely accepted pattern of overhead school management had become boards of five to nine members, elected at large on a nonpartisan basis with independent taxing and expenditure authority. Boards appointed a superintendent to act as an executive director of the school system. In many cities, he headed a sizable bureaucracy: central office management and education specialists, school site principals, their teaching staffs, clerks, and custodial workers. Agencies outside the school systems had entered the scene, such as state educational agencies with credential requirements, teachers colleges providing better trained entrants to the field, and the federal government with the first grants-in-aid for vocational education.

Predictably, changes of this character gave birth to ideas of "evolutionary professionalism" in educational administration. The view was most emphatically expressed by Elwood Cubberley in his

1916 publication, *Public School Administration,* a book which became the source of revealed wisdom for a generation of educators. Cubberley depicted educational administration as coming of age in the 20th century, following a period in which many gifted amateurs and pioneers had struggled to create the conditions under which expert executives would one day rule the schools according to an emerging science of education, free of the kinds of politics that had crippled superintendents in the past. Thus, he wrote, the field of education was rapidly changing from an intuitive trade, or one based on common sense, into a specialized profession whose principles and factual base were rapidly being discovered. Few contested Cubberley's basic assumptions about the bridging of theory and practice or his faith in professionalism.[18]

In the light of actual school practices, however, this vision of professionalism was deceptively optimistic and idealized. A recent study of the writings and speeches of urban superintendents between 1880 and 1950 indicates that their conceptualizations of the position were more complex and ambiguous. They tended to see that it comprised three inter-related roles: (1) teacher-scholar, (2) chief administrator, and (3) negotiator-statesman. Over the 70-year period, the teacher-scholar role, which had first dominated, gradually become less important until, by 1950, the role of chief administrator was assigned equal status. Similarly, the role of negotiator-statesman, which was much less prominent than the others, was gradually given greater weight.[19]

The evidence is that the three combined roles still place disparate and conflicting demands on the managers of school systems, and that the effort to fulfill them has had some revealing effects on their performance and on educational governance. The effort also shapes the perceptions of those outside educational systems: politicians, other professional groups, higher education faculties, parents, and students.

The Role of Teacher-Scholar

The role of teacher-scholar was fairly well understood by all concerned in the "pre-scientific" period. The claims of educators to new expertise could be based on the adoption in school systems of such products and processes of scientific research as survey methods and psychological tests, by the growth of undergraduate and graduate professional training, and by a greatly expanded interchange of information about pedagogical and managerial problems and strategies among organized professional sub-groups. The role undergirds the continued requirement that to speak with authority even school superintendents must first serve as teachers and principals. The result was a system for personnel recruitment and advancement that was virtually closed to non-educators.

This concept of the administrator role was implicit in the development of professional associations, such as the National Education Association and its state and local affiliates. Their membership included all educational "professionals" — from teacher to superintendent — and, not surprisingly, association leaders were recruited from the latter group.

Public regard for expertise and licensing procedures may account for some of the credence given to the claims of educators concerning their professional status, but in the leading universities, research and scholarship in departments and colleges of education has almost never obtained recognition comparable to that in the academic disciplines or some of the other professional schools.

The Role of Chief Administrator

Perhaps the most visible evidence of the change in educational administration between 1900 and 1920 was the assumption by local school superintendents of the role of general manager, an organizational transformation which had wide support in prevailing mores that valued economy and efficiency in provision of public services, especially at a time when school populations expanded rapidly at both elementary and secondary levels. Superintendents in effect joined a movement which was sweeping other public and private organizations, and they could and did borrow the rhetoric and procedures of business and industry. They talked of "differentiation of plant," "cost accounting," and "stockholders" (citizens).[20] They attempted to demonstrate to their school boards and their communities that programs and operations were benefiting from standardization, centralization, and the attainment of specific, quantified objectives.

Hierarchy in the schools relied heavily on the dominance of men in the outside society — the male boss symbolized authority.[21] Thus the acceptance of organizational discipline was doubtless enhanced by the prevalence of women in the teaching force. Superintendents who were successful in the executive's role mingled as equals with business leaders in their communities, and their social status and salaries rose accordingly.

Thoughtful academicians in the universities were skeptical of the new "cult of efficiency," recognizing that children in the schools could not be equated with the identical components of a factory assembly line and that claims about a scientific basis for organizing the teaching-learning process were shaky at best. More visible and effective challenges to the complete dominance of scientific management practices arose, however, because the schools were inescapably public institutions, responsive ultimately to popular will and occasionally to interference by school board members and other lay influences. One eminent educational historian sees the willingness of school superintendents to embrace and promote their managerial role as a shield against their vulnerability to outside political pressures.[22] Others dispute this single-cause explanation, but agree that superintendents actually performed another largely unacknowledged and contradictory role.

The Role of Negotiator-Statesman

Evidence in support of the vulnerability "hypothesis" is abundant in the persistent support for local prerogatives in educational policy making, the diversity of school systems, and the uneven spread of professionalism in various sections of the country. Even when the transfer of powers to the superintendents was well advanced, they continued to be employed on short-term contracts and could not relax their vigilance in building support for their activities. The eminent New York City superintendent, William Maxwell, had this view of the situation: "The superintendent should be not merely a schoolmaster but a statesman who has a definite policy and who knows how to take advantage of time and opportunity to secure results."[23]

No matter how much the carrying out of this prescription might constitute political activity, as currently defined, educational administrators shied away from acknowledging involvement in politics. A strong public reaction to the earlier ward-heeler style of partisan school politics reinforced their urgings that education of children be regarded almost as a sacred rather than a secular responsibility, which should therefore be set apart from the rough and tumble of partisan conflicts. Instead it could be entrusted to expert and ethical experts ("statesmen") who would protect the public interest. The part-time, nonpartisan school boards who embodied the reformist view of lay representation in educational management were, in the main, quite willing to assume a passive role and delegate policy planning and execution to their superintendents.[24] In this instance, the concepts of apoliticality and professional expertness served political ends. As Cuban comments, "This is neither the first nor the last time that fervent ideals and occupational self-interest marched to the same tune."[25]

Whatever the difficulties superintendents may have had in balancing divergent roles, the policy making system generated by the "first revolution" in educational administration stayed firmly in place for the generation between 1920 and 1950. Educational policy and programming were initiated by professionals, legitimated rather than scrutinized by lay boards, prodded rather than motivated by state level authorities, ignored by the national government, and remained largely impervious to popular disruptions.

As might be expected when a political institution grows dramatically in size, raises taxes, acquires property, and touches sensitive areas of individual lives and fortunes, outside influences were not entirely dormant. When opposition did sporadically occur, the educational administrators developed considerable skill in devising routines for building organizational unity and defusing conflict. In fact, this type of folk wisdom — accepted practices for maintaining professional dominance — was elevated into ethical principles which were incorporated into the education and on-the-job socialization of educational administrators.[26]

A Profession in Turbulence

During the 1950s educators busied themselves with recovery from the retrenchments of the '30s and '40s and with expanding the school systems to accommodate the "baby boom" that followed World War II and the Korean War. Almost before they became aware of it, a "second revolution" in educational administration was upon them. It is still in progress. Its beginning is often said to be the 1954 U.S. Supreme Court decision ordering the end of the de jure school desegregation, but no single event set it off. Schools were just one of the American institutions shaken for two decades by the profound social and political changes stemming from their confrontations with the reality of pluralism. Challenges to traditional values have brought the demise of the "melting pot" myth and a quickening of the struggle for equality by various minority groups. They demanded not just "equality of opportunity," but equality of benefits and adequate representation at policy levels as well.

The schools, particularly those in the cities, have been an epicenter of turbulence, perhaps in part because education had long been the acknowledged path to upward mobility and the key facilitator of the "Americanizing" concept. The schools were indicted for failing to meet the needs of disadvantaged minorities and, in fact, for falling short in the services provided to the middle class which had so long predominated in the membership of school boards and the profession. No aspect of entrenched practice escaped attack — governance, finance, student and employee personnel practice, curriculum, relations with the community and with other governmental agencies.[27]

The validity both of the accusations and of the efficacy of the many proposed and attempted solutions for the shortcomings of the schools remains controversial and continues to generate a flood of journalistic and scholarly writing, acrimonious public debate, and personal malaise among parents and students. We can only inquire here: "How is the second revolution affecting educational administrators?" It is perhaps most expeditious to reexamine the composite role conceptions that were previously discussed, focusing on a few of the contemporary developments that have brought the most obvious alterations in school management.

Erosion of the Claims to Expertise

During the early '50s a "Theory Movement" was sparked by a few university departments, with foundation support, which attempted to bring to the study and practice of educational administration the theories, findings, and methods of the social sciences. A somewhat similar movement was underway in public administration.[28] Twenty years later, the results in developing conceptual frameworks and a body of research-based findings to undergird professional claims of expertise are generally conceded to be disappointing, if not quite non-existent.[29] The field of educational research did expand markedly under the stimulation of federal governmental initiative, but funding for administrative research held low priority. A National Institute of Education was established in 1972, on the model of the National Institutes of Health, and its subsequent precarious history is indicative of the chasm which still gapes between the disparate words of scientific and educational problem solving.

Never a high priority in the training of educational administrators, scholarly qualifications have been recently competitive with those of sex and race, as university departments and school systems have attempted to respond to mandates that more blacks and women be employed. Further, the schools are under pressure to educate effectively clienteles which were not previously part of the traditional child populations: those less than five years of age, those with physical, mental, and emotional handicaps, and those from non-English speaking families. Even the most loyal supporters of public education cannot assume that the professionals have adequate or exclusive expertise to meet these new challenges.

Perhaps the most frontal assault on the administrators' role as teacher-scholar has come from another quarter. Classroom teachers, once so subservient to administrators, have begun in many places to contest their claims to expertise in curriculum and instructional matters, to insist on a greater role in educational programming, to form their own associations — in short, to preempt the "teacher-scholar" cachet. The mass of persons employed in education no longer unquestioningly accepts the definition of professionalism which they once shared with the principals and superintendents.

Weakening of the Superintendency

The major expression of teacher militancy is in the rapid growth of unions and collective bargaining. The superintendent is still the executive officer of the school board; but, where unionism is strong, he represents neither the local spokesman for the teaching and nonteaching staffs nor the chief representative of the school board. Goldhammer, long a student of the superintendency, describes the change as follows:

> In 1974, his authority was curtailed by new exigencies and commitments. Rather than developing recommendations for policies within the school district, he had to interpret social policy established by other agencies to which the school district had, to some extent, to conform. His ability to exercise authority and control was strictly circumscribed within the federal guidelines established for the operations of various programs within the schools; (by) the decisions of courts on cases involving his

own or other school districts .... and (by) contracts which were negotiated with various groups of employees or patrons .... the superintendent was no longer an independent executive, exercising the authority of his position on the basis of his professional judgment, training, experience, and wisdom.[30]

Goldhammer points out that subordinate members of the administrative team in large districts can no longer be generalists like the superintendent. They need specialized managerial expertise in business, legal, personnel, or data processing operations. If the current interest in greater decentralization of management to individual school sites escalates, then the role of principals is expected to become more autonomous. With the polarization of administrative and teaching staffs that accompanies collective bargaining, a loosening of tight hierarchical controls by the superintendents and principals is clearly predictable.

A New Politics of Education

The confrontation politics of the 1960s and 1970s brought demonstrations and civil disorder to the schoolhouse door; vandalism and arson have wreaked unprecedented destruction within the walls. An administrative negotiating style that relies largely on invoking lofty principles, building consensus through friendly intermediaries, and studiously avoiding overt partisanship is no longer effective in the more populous school districts. Administrators are spending more time on union negotiations and in carrying out procedures to protect their operations from litigation charging violation of due process. They are beginning to acknowledge the basically political aspects of their management responsibilities, especially when it comes to competing for resources with the other public services.

The hazards of the coming period of retrenchment will make mere survival a test of leadership skill. The moves of state and local agencies to regulate localities cannot be ignored. Thus it is not surprising to find the educational administrators supporting lobbyists in the state capitals and in Washington, cultivating the acquaintance of legislators and their staffs, and joining in drafting protests to the bureaucrats. A new "politics of education" is in the making from the local community to the White House level.[31]

What About the Future?

There is little question that the profession of educational administration — if it is or ever has been a profession — is hard-pressed, anxious, and defensive. Personal qualifications and role conceptions that practitioners could once meld into socially acceptable performance of agreed-on functions are out of phase in today's confusing, problematical world. Both administrators and professors have been slow to come to terms with these perplexities, but scattered efforts among professional leadership groups are now underway, seeking to design and implement activities responsive to contemporary demands. For example, the University Council for Educational Administration, a consortium of 47 leading universities offering doctoral degrees in the field, now has under consideration the recent report of a high-level independent commission which appraised the extensive activities and services of the organization and pointed out the need for significant and vigorous future programming.

Among several activities which the Commission recommended to receive high priority were:

Investigation through studies and seminars of ways of improving the making of education policy and relating it to other public policies;

Reappraisal of the basic purposes and objectives of education in the light of the transformations that are taking place in American society and the complex worldwide interactions among peoples, cultures, economies and governments;

Examination of efforts to supplement school experiences with educative experiences provided by other agencies;

Evaluation of measures to promote cultural pluralism and integration.[31]

If these recommendations were to be widely accepted and implemented, even in part, they would stimulate a reexamination and updating of educational purposes, increase the collaboration between the schools and other public and private agencies, and broaden the base of educational services to varied clienteles. Perhaps most cogent to the theme of this symposium is the probability that the now widely prevalent exclusionist forms of educational policy making, dominated by professionals, would be supplemented by policies and procedures that relate education more effectively to the other public services.

Notes

1. David B. Tyack and Robert Cummings, "Leadership in American Public Schools Before 1954," in Lavern L. Cunningham, Walter G. Hack, and Raphael O. Nystrand (eds.), *Educational Administration: The*

Developing Decades (Berkeley, Calif.: McCutchen Publishing Corp., 1977), p. 58.
2. Geraldine J. Scott and Peter M. Dunn, *Statistics of School Systems 1973-74,* National Center for Educational Statistics, Education Division, U.S. Department of Health, Education and Welfare, NCES 76-152 (Washington, D.C.: U.S. Government Printing Office, 1976), Tables 1, 4, and 10.
3. *Ibid.,* Table 51.
4. *Ibid.,* Tables 2 and 3.
5. Roald F. Campbell and L. Jackson Newell, *A Study of Professors of Educational Administration* (Columbus, Ohio: University Council for Educational Administration, 1973), pp. 11-13.
6. Scott and Dunn, Tables 6 and 9.
7. National Center for Educational Statistics, Education Division, U.S. Department of Health, Education and Welfare, NCES 75-412 (Washington, D.C.: U.S. Government Printing Office, 1975), Table 34.
8. *Ibid.,* Table 44.
9. Stephen J. Knezevich, *The American School Superintendent* (Washington, D.C.: American Association of School Administrators, 1971), pp. 11-13; and Richard O. Carlson, *School Superintendents: Careers and Performance* (Columbus, Ohio: Charles E. Merrill Publishing Company, 1972), pp. 26-35.
10. *Salaries Paid Professional Personnel in Public Schools, 1976-77,* Part II of National Survey of Salaries and Wages in Public Schools (Arlington, Va.: Educational Research Service, Inc., 1977), Table 1.
11. Carlson, pp. 41-47.
12. Knezevich, p. 12 and Tables 10, 19.
13. Carlson, pp. 35-37.
14. Campbell and Newell, p. 141.
15. Tyack and Cummings, p. 51.
16. Larry Cuban, *Urban School Chiefs Under Fire* (Chicago: University of Chicago Press, 1976), p. 112.
17. *Ibid.,* p. 118.
18. Tyack, pp. 48-49.
19. Cuban, pp. 121-126.
20. Tyack, p. 54.
21. *Ibid.,* p. 56.
22. Raymond E. Callahan, *Education and the Cult of Efficiency* (Chicago: The University of Chicago Press, 1962).
23. Cuban, p. 119.
24. The relationships of superintendents and school boards are among the most widely studied aspects of educational administration. A recent collection of research analyses on various aspects of school board operations is to be found in Peter J. Cistone (ed.), *Understanding School Boards,* (Lexington, Mass.: D.C. Heath and Company, 1976).
25. *Ibid.,* p. 120.
26. *Ibid.,* p. 136.
27. Bernard C. Watson, "Issues Confronting Educational Administrators," in Cunningham, Hack, and Nystrand, pp. 67-73.
28. James W. Fesler "Public Administration and the Social Sciences: 1946 to 1960," in Frederick C. Mosher (ed.), *American Public Administration: Past, Present, Future* (University, Ala.: University of Alabama Press, 1975), p. 97.
29. See the assays by Andrew W. Halpin and Andrew E. Hayes, "The Broken Ikon, or, Whatever Happened to Theory?" and W.W. Charters, Jr., "The Future (and a Bit of the Past) of Research and Theory," in Cunningham, Hack, and Nystrand.
30. Keith Goldhammer, "Roles of the American School Superintendent, 1954-1974," *ibid.,* p. 157.
31. Politics of education has also emerged during the past decade as a relatively new field of disciplined inquiry, involving both educators and political scientists as collaborators. Two recent books are indicative of the breadth and quality of this development: Jay D. Scribner (ed.), *The Politics of Education,* The Seventy-sixth Yearbook of the National Society for the Study of Education (Chicago: The University of Chicago Press, 1977); Edith K. Mosher and Jennings L. Wagoner, Jr. (eds.), *The Changing Politics of Education: Prospects for the 1980's* (Berkeley, Calif.: McCutchen Publishing Corporation, in Press).
32. "UCEA Commission on Planning and Evaluation, Conclusions/Recommendations," *UCEA Review,* Vol. XVIII, No. 3 (May 1977), p. 8.

THE CITY MANAGER: PROFESSIONAL HELPING HAND, OR POLITICAL HIRED HAND?

Richard J. Stillman, II, *California State College, Bakersfield*

Nearly 100 million Americans reside in cities served by city managers or chief administrative officers (CAOs). Today, 2,655 city managers and CAOs are appointed by city councils as full-time administrators of their community governments. In a typical council-manager plan city, a small council made up five, seven, or nine representatives, generally elected on a nonpartisan, at-large basis, serves as the chief policy-making body of the city principally through its legal powers of approving city ordinances, personnel policies and budgetary appropriations.[1] The council appoints a chief executive officer, a city manager, or CAO who generally serves without tenure "at the council's pleasure."

A complex working relationship evolves between the elected legislative policy makers on council and the appointed chief administrator. Under the manager plan, the mayor generally performs part-time ceremonial functions, with the manager assuming full-time, day-to-day responsibilities over all or most line functions of local government. CAOs normally have fewer direct line departments of the city to supervise by comparison to managers, though both managers and CAOs exercise vital and powerful roles through budget preparation and personnel recruitment, as well as through formal and informal advisory activities with council.[2]

The "professional" nature of managers' work in terms of their on-the-job activities, skills, experience, training, and career is legally prescribed by most council-manager city charters, as well as promulgated as official doctrine by the International City Management Association (ICMA), the professional association of city managers and CAOs. For instance, the typical council-manager charter that outlines the manager's job reads: "As chief administrative officer, the city manager provides professional counsel to the city council.... His work is performed with professional independence...." The introduction to the ICMA's Code of Ethics for managers also emphasizes that one of their primary purposes is: "...to strengthen the quality of urban government through professional management."[3]

However, political scientists over the last two decades, drawing on sophisticated community power studies and decision-making analyses, have evolved another view of managers and CAOs strikingly different from that of traditionally autonomous professionals subject to an independent code of ethics, peer group review, and their own standards of expertise. Rather, a manager is viewed from this perspective as one of the chief actors in community politics, responsive to local interests and decision makers and, in turn, influencing the general course of city affairs.

In the words of Norton Long, managers are in reality "politicians for hire," or as Karl Bosworth put it more concisely, simply "politicians" who derive their considerable influence within city hall and the community at large from their control over budget preparation, personnel appointments, and formal as well as informal council advisory functions.[4] For this "realist" school of political scientists, the very term "professional" simply disguises one of the best politicians in town, and, as they view it, "professional" is both a meaningless and deceptive term that fails to describe a manager's "real" activities and functions.

This article will attempt to sort out the two prominent but seemingly contradictory views of

---

The author wishes to thank the following individuals who kindly took the time to review and comment on this article: Professor Ronald O. Loveridge, University of California, Riverside; David Arnold, director of publications, International City Management Association; David Bauer, chief administrative officer, New Haven, Connecticut; James Buell, assistant city manager, Bakersfield, California; and Marjorie Sauer, assistant to the academic vice president, California State College. Vice President Phillip Wilder and Dean Richard Wallace at Cal State Bakersfield generously provided research and travel funding for the author's work.

Richard J. Stillman II is a professor of public administration at California State College, Bakersfield, and is the author of the book, *The Rise of the City Manager* (1974), as well as several articles: "The Modern City Manager," "The Revival of Literature in the Field of City Management," and "Richard Childs and Louis Brownlow: Two Saints of City Management Reconsidered." The author has also served as an assistant to two city managers.

managers/CAOs — that of "professional helping hands" versus "political hired hands" — by beginning with a brief look at their unique triad of historic values which did much to create their contemporary occupational identity confusion.

The Business Corporation, Neutral Expertise, and Pragmatic Reform

Unlike other public officials, city managers were originally conceived as the centerpiece of a normative reform theory or "model" for restructuring and redirecting the very purposes of local government. Thus, the manager's occupation was at its very inception deeply enmeshed within a peculiar frame of political values that was the handiwork, not of a seasoned public official nor profound political thinker, but of a relatively obscure New York City businessman, 28-year-old Richard S. Childs, who pursued a part-time hobby of municipal reform. Shortly after graduating from Yale College, Childs in 1904 with another prominent Progressive of that day, Woodrow Wilson, set out to rid cities of boss rule by promoting the "short ballot" idea, which sought to improve and rationalize voting processes through shortened ballots. He later was attracted for similar reasons to "the commission plan," first popularized in Galveston, Texas, but in 1909 his eye fell accidentally on an experiment in Staunton, Virginia, that had recently hired "a manager" as chief full-time administrator.[5] From his one-room New York City short ballot office, Childs soon produced a steady stream of anonymous articles and stories praising the virtues of city manager government as superior to the commission plan (giving the mistaken impression that the manager plan was already in widespread operation). Childs wielded a powerful pen that made him a virtuoso at publicizing manager government. News editorials and after-dinner speakers soon were repeating his catch-phrases that became stock-in-trade programs of the Progressive municipal reformers. By 1918, 100 cities, one as large as Dayton, Ohio, had adopted "the manager plan." Ironically, while all this occurred, the man who claimed to be "the plan's inventor" remained so inconspicuous that no one had ever heard of him at the first meeting of city managers (I doubt few managers today have ever heard of Richard Childs).

To Childs' credit, however, he recognized early that to mobilize support for the idea it "must be condensed to a catch-phrase first, even if such a reduction means lopping off many of its vital ramifications and making it false in many of its natural applications." Childs had an undeniable knack at simplification and promotion, yet as a Progressive reformer, Childs also had a genuine and vital concern about the need for better local government by means of widening popular participation in community affairs through structural change. The manager plan was his prime vehicle of structural reform that, as Don Price rightly observed,[6] rested on the manipulation symbols then dominant (and still I would venture to argue popular today) in American culture — the business corporation, neutral expertise, and pragmatic reform.

These three fundamental values behind the plan I would argue operate simultaneously on three levels: at the first level in engendering popular support and public acceptance for the plan and hence creating the very occupational role a manager performs in a community; at a second level in influencing the particular and unique formal structure within which a manager's job is performed; and on a third level in giving rise to the persistent and fundamental value problems associated with this line of work. Table 1 illustrates the "interrelatedness" among the three fundamental values of the plan and the three levels of "impact" upon the city management occupation:

While much of Table 1 is self-explanatory, I would argue that the enduring and critical value problems of city managers depicted under Level Three stem frequently from the difference between the popular expectations of the plan (Level One) and the practicalities of governance that managers encounter in making the plan work (Level Two). The business model, for instance, which sells well to voters by establishing a council-manager government on the basis of a business corporation and which sharply separates policy from administration, is in practice a terribly difficult, if not an impossible dichotomy to achieve on a daily working basis, because, as numerous political scientists have noted,[7] so much policy "slips and slops" into administration that the distinction between the two becomes both fuzzy and blurred.

Similarly, the second value of neutral expertise implicit in a manager's official title may warm the hearts of voters because of its apolitical symbolic appeal, but neutrality on the practical level of running cities is extraordinarily hard to achieve in pluralistic communities where a five-man council

TABLE 1

Triad of Values Implicit in "Plan"	Means for Impact	Level One: Symbolic and Popular Appeal of "Plan's" Values to Voters	Level Two: Structural "Impact" of "Plan's" Values on City Management Practitioners Today	Level Three: Critical Operational Issues Posed for Managers by Values of the "Plan"
Corporate Value	Formal model for city government enacted by law in council-manager charters.	Pattern of local government modelled on business corporation denoting central values of economy/efficiency	Provides a formal bureaucratic hierarchy for local government with a sharp differentiation between policy-making role of council and administrative authority of manager.	Clear-cut idealized dichotomy between politics and administrative poses perpetual and complex practical problems of relations between manager and council in matters of governance, policy formulation, and cooperative direction.
Neutral Expertise	City charter that establishes a professional city manager's post	Word "manager" denotes energetic, nonpolitical leadership.	Centralizes decisional authority and responsibility in *one* individual who takes a "communitywide approach" to solving city problems.	Complex problems associated with finding the "public interest," or "community good" in order to apply neutral expertise in achieving a pluralistic community's desired goals.
Pragmatic Reform	Immediate demands for improvements and changes in local government by city council and community when "plan" is adopted.	The council-manager plan denotes a reform measure designed to generate specific changes in government as well as general civic progress.	Council-manager government serves to respond to specific community needs by reforming community government structure and providing improved and "effective" municipal services.	Reformers have frequently oversold the plan by promising the manager can do the impossible, like lower taxes, etc.

may indeed have five different opinions about any issue it faces. Also, the value of pragmatic reform may sell the plan well, but sometimes at a price, in that managers are expected to achieve the humanly impossible under the plan, such as reducing taxes in an inflationary economy.

In short, the persistent disparity between the ideals implicit in the plan – ideals that, of course, make the very existence of a city management occupation possible – and the human practicalities of day-to-day operational problems of urban governance force managers to assume perpetually a sort of schizophrenic double identity – "a professional identity," one defined by law in city charters and given popular credence from the general public's support of "the plan" – and a "political identity" that requires them to exercise a great deal of savvy of an astute politician in terms of "fitting" the ideals of the plan into a real world. No other public official is forced to operate within a legacy of this sort of a triad of values that causes persistent tensions and identity crises in terms of his/her own self-image.

The Shape of City Management Today: Its Contemporary Values and Social Trends

What is the shape of the city management field today? In what directions is it evolving? While I do not pretend to offer up a list of all changes that are occurring within city management (the diversity of the field makes a comprehensive listing impossible), among the eight most noteworthy major trends over the last two decades that influence the direction of this line of work as well as the individual roles of managers are the following:

1. A continued popularity and growth of managers/CAOs and a rise in the multiplicity of their responsibilities but with a concomitant "dispersion" of their authority.

Since World War II, an average of 65 cities annually have adopted council-manager government. War and depression have slowed the growth of the plan, but the relative prosperity of the 1960s and 1970s with demands of growing city/suburban populations for better municipal services and new federal money from revenue sharing has helped to spur the growth rate of city management. Furthermore, with the broader ICMA criteria for general management recognition established in 1969, a record 159 communities were recognized as approved council-manager cities in 1973, and 110 were approved in 1975. The statistical growth of the plan of course leads to increased occupational opportunities for city management practitioners. As indeed recent surveys have shown, managers themselves remain relatively optimistic about the future expansion of their field.[8]

As the plan itself has grown, so too have managerial responsibilities widened. New demands for their expertise applied to new areas like environmental protection, affirmative action, pollution control, and energy conservation have contributed to significantly expanding their roles, activities, and interests. Managers, like front line soldiers on the battlefield, are frequently the first public officials to face the assault of new issues and innovations affecting government, and thus are frequently the first to learn how "to cope" with the new problems.

Along with rising responsibilities, managers have faced in recent years a concomitant "dispersal of authority," due on one side from the rapidly increased "intrusion" over the last decade by federal/state authorities into what once was the manager's pretty much exclusive "turf." The intergovernmental layer cake that turned into a marble cake has meant the dispersal of the once clear lines of authority of managers over their own internal administrative functions. Federal and state oversight and interest in city government has risen, thanks largely to its generous fiscal support which usually has strings attached.

The challenge to managerial authority comes equally from below as well. Public employee unions' growing demands at the bargaining table for better pay and working conditions make unions now equal or almost equal partners with managers in setting administrative priorities and policies for communities. Similarly, new minority participation in local government further has served to widen the circle of citizenry in the community decision-making processes, and further serves in "fuzzing" the manager's traditional authority. As one manager who recently resigned his post in one small community told the newspapers on his departure:

> I have a philosophy that local government doesn't have as much effect on city government as regional and state policies. Most of the policies the city implements don't originate locally ... and 95 percent of the revenue the city receives, including where it is obtained and how it can be spent, is controlled by the state and federal government. Local government is an ebbing entity ... that is becoming increasingly diverse and complicated.[9]

2. In response to the growing cross-pressures

on managers from "above" and "below," the traditional core values of their occupation have also been significantly broadened from an emphasis on technique-oriented engineering efficiency to more general public management based upon recent social science knowledge.

One of the best barometers of the widening concerns and values of city management is found by an examination of the most widely used educational publication of the ICMA's Municipal Management Series (commonly referred to as the Green Book Series, which first appeared in 1934). These green books for 40 years have attempted to outline "the best" practices of the field of local government administration, covering such subjects as police administration, planning, fire protection, community health, and public works. The "flagship" of the green books has traditionally been *The Technique of Municipal Management.* In its last edition in 1958 its expressed purpose was "to define the job of management in municipal administration and to suggest techniques and practices which will help municipal officials." This book, as its title suggested, was something of a how-to-do-it manual for city managers, and its chapters enumerated many of the best techniques for efficient internal management of local administration, including sections on: "Techniques of Directions," "Programming Municipal Services," "Administrative Planning and Research," and "Administrative Measurement."

The 1974 edition of this book, edited by James M. Banovetz of Northern Illinois University, was retitled *Managing the Modern City,* and adopts a much broader perspective of the subject for training practitioners. Drawing on the last two decades of organization theory, decison making, and human relations research, the new edition attempts to relate modern social science research to the practical world of municipal affairs. In contrast to the 1958 edition, representative chapters cover such topics as: "The City: Forces of Change," "Environment and Role of the Administrator," "Decision Making," "Leadership Styles and Strategies," "Administrative Communication," and "Administrative Analysis." New emphasis is placed on computer technologies and intergovernmental relations, as well as PPBS. Clearly in the years that transpired between this book's 1958 and 1974 revisions, the vertical and horizontal dimensions of city management values and interests were considerably broadened and extended.

3. Despite the growth of the city management field and its ever-widening concerns, city managers remain a fairly small, homogeneous occupational group with a strong small town-suburban orientation.

City managers as a social group from their very beginnings have shown consistent homogeneous social patterns: white, male, in their early 40s, middle-class, protestant. Their incomes have grown over the years (currently averaging $19,962 per year) and their remuneration compares favorably with other professionals today — the average lawyer now earns $22,000 and a school superintendent $20,000.[10] But blacks, women, young, or religious minorities are found only in token numbers in the city management field. The heavily suburban, small-town setting in which most manager plans function is one of the chief causes for the small numbers of minorities by comparison to other professional groups.[11]

4. Managers increasingly are better trained with less engineering-oriented education, combining both an "administrative generalist" and "specialist" background.

Managers have always been a well-educated group of men. Even in 1934, Ridley and Nolting reported 64 per cent of them held baccalaureate degrees; in 1975 an ICMA survey showed 76 per cent having bachelors degrees, and 48 per cent of these had masters degrees.[12] An even higher percentage of their assistants (86 per cent) today have baccalaureate degrees. In recent years there has been a noticeable shift, however, away from engineering as the preferred preparation for city management. In 1934, 77 per cent of managers held bachelor degrees in engineering, but today that figure is only 18 per cent, with 34 per cent of modern managers majoring in political science or government and 78 per cent of those who hold masters degrees obtaining them in the field of public administration. Today only 3 per cent of managers' advanced degrees are in engineering.

A generalist management background in public administration seems now to be the preferred training for the field and also may be an indication for the reduced demands on the part of city councils for technicians as opposed to administrative generalists. Most managers now cite the more administrative generalist educational areas as being the most useful job preparation for city management, particularly the fields of budgeting and finance, administration and organization theory, public relations, and personnel. Also, informal specialization in narrow skill categories of solid waste removal, collective bargaining, or grantsmanship is found among many managers. Increasingly, a generalist administrative education coupled with "skill specialties learned on-the-job" seems to be the most common training background for city management. No doubt, the advanced degree gives the practitioner a professional image while the on-the-job training gives the pragmatic skills for coping with daily hazards of occupational survival.

5. *While there is still no prescribed professional career pattern in city management, informal common career patterns have developed that seem to prefer the "in-and-outer" administrative generalist.*

Statistics show career patterns informally have developed in the city management field. Most managers take their first jobs in the field in their late 20s or early 30s, frequently after working as an assistant city manager or with a consulting firm in city management. Their average local government service is 13 years, while their average tenure in a single city is five years. More than a third of the managers today were alerted to the field by college or graduate training, and another third by a job after school.

Generally, most seem to "drift" into the field from many jobs, but primarily most have been experienced administrators prior to becoming city managers: 29 per cent had some previous experience in government service, 47 per cent had prior business administration experience, and 16 per cent had some engineering background before taking their first job in the field. Unlike most careers, breadth of experience in different types of challenging administrative jobs in public and private agencies is encouraged, even preferred, and so city management remains one of the few "open fields" that a person can enter comparatively late in life without having been specifically trained. Indeed, many do take up city management as a second career after service in the military or private industry.

6. *Managers see themselves as "career professionals," though not all are "careerists."*

Surveys of managers emphasize that the chief perception they hold of themselves and their community roles places them squarely in the "professional category." While only 23 per cent of managers view themselves as in an established profession like law or medicine, 75 per cent see themselves as in a new professional field, akin to diplomacy or school superintendency. Less than two per cent claim that their line of work is not professional at all. Moreover, they reflect an optimism about the future of their careers, with more than half believing that there will be increasing numbers of cities adopting city management form of government.[13]

However, recent surveys of managers also find that not all managers can be classed as "careerists" in their field. Only one-quarter of the managers spend most of their working careers as city managers. Better than one-half of the managers are more accurately classed as administrative generalists or "in-and-outers" moving into and out of city management from and to a wide variety of jobs in both business and government. A quarter of the managers must be categorized as "local appointees" or "hometown boys" who took the job because it was easily available to them. Local appointees by definition have no aspirations beyond the local horizons. The high percentage of in-and-outers and local appointees within city management is perhaps ultimately due to the political hazards, as Paul Ylvisaker aptly described: "A manager's job tenure is only secure until the next council meeting."

7. *The professional association of city managers, the International City Management Association (ICMA), has significantly broadened its outlook and scope of activities in recent years, but nonetheless, remains a weak voluntary association with little or no influence over the entrance, promotion, training standards, and ethical performance of individual city managers.*

In the late 1960s, the ICMA undertook several important reforms which were healthy as a whole for the urban management field: it moved its national headquarters to Washington, D.C., staffed its ranks with new leaders, enlarged its research and training programs, adopted a new code of ethics, and changed its name from "manager" to "management" association in order to include administrative professionals in the many related management fields of local government.[14] Yet, in spite of its intense new look of the last decade, the ICMA, unlike the American Bar Association or American Medical Association, exercises no control over the entrance or promotion into the field of city management. And while the ICMA has a code of ethics and publishes the popular Green Book Series, and *Public Management,* it enforces neither ethical nor educational standards for city managers.

The ICMA can recommend and indeed does actively encourage such standards, but the hiring and firing of managers remains squarely with independent local city councils across the nation. The limited extent to which managers are aware of any peer group influence in their field was demonstrated by a recent survey that asked managers to rank the top three city manager practitioners — few could even name one person.[15]

8. *Increasingly city managers seem to take an activist view of their community policy roles, but three variables – city size, politics, self-definition of leadership roles – largely seem to determine the extent and nature of a manager's policy activity.*

While Richard Childs and other early founders of the manager plan stressed "a neutral expert role" for the city manager, a number of community power studies written by political scientists over the last two decades seem to agree that the city managers today are not merely inconspicuous public administrators, but rather their empirical analyses conclude that managers play very influential roles in determining public politics within their respective communities.[16]

After a careful analysis of several council-manager cities in Florida, Gladys Kammerer and her associates found "no managers ... who were not involved in making, shaping, or vetoing policy proposals." A similar study, conducted in North Carolina by B. James Kweder, pointed out that "... in many cities the city manager clearly emerges as a person who has the greatest influence on what is happening at every stage of the policy-making process." Aaron Wildavsky's *Leadership in a Small Town*, which examined decision making in Oberlin, Ohio, revealed that the city manager was frequently the central figure in determining the important outcome of community policy issues. Oliver P. Williams and Charles R. Adrian made similar observations in two out of the four Michigan cities they studied: "the city manager was the key leadership figure and policy innovator." Even surveys of managers themselves show a remarkable shift away from a view of themselves as neutral experts and toward a proactive policy involvement.[17]

While contemporary political scientists and surveys of managers' own views on their policy roles have concluded that managers are no longer merely neutral administrators, the extent and scope of a manager's policy-making role seems to be also very much influenced by three key variables. The first, as would be expected, city size, is an important factor determining a manager's policy involvement. Large city managers, because of the urban diversity and sizes of their city resources, are more inclined to be involved with broader, more abstract policy matters such as shaping the city budget, advising city councils, negotiating with unions, dealing with inter- and intra-governmental matters — policy issues akin to those of large corporation executives.

On the other hand, small town managers whose role involves more technical matters like parking, snow removal, sewer repair, and the like are involved more frequently with the mundane technical side of administration. Limited staff assistance and fewer resources force small town managers to solve on their own many diverse technical as well as non-technical problems of communities. Like small businessmen, small city managers must not only make up their financial accounts, but also stock the store themselves.

The political environment of the community also decisively shapes the policy role that managers play in their communities. Edward C. Banfield and James Q. Wilson classed manager cities in five categories ranging from small homogeneous, "faction-free" cities to large, highly factionalized communities.[18] Those cities they found with a high degree of political conflict force managers frequently into roles of "negotiators" and "conflict resolvers," while the more homogeneous communities or those with the large stable majorities provide managers with greater consensus on policy matters and, therefore, give managers a freer hand in finding effective and efficient techniques for implementing agreed-upon goals.

As John Bollens and John Ries have pointed out,[19] managers tend to fare better in those homogeneous, growing communities as opposed to stable or declining cities with considerable political conflict. The former group of cities demand technical competence to cope with their growth, which is the premium stock-in-trade skill of managers, while the latter type of city, one enmeshed in continuous political combat, requires an able politician more versed in the arts of negotiation and compromise rather than efficient administration.

Ronald Loveridge, in his excellent role analysis of San Francisco Bay area city managers, emphasized a third important determinant influencing policy involvement among city managers: i.e., self-definition of their own leadership role. Professor Loveridge's analysis found four classes of managers in terms of how they perceived themselves as "activists" in their policy roles in communities:[20]

A. *Political Leaders* who take the broadest view of their policy role and see themselves as idea men and change agents in communities. These managers espouse a political readiness to act as plaintiffs for good government and the public interest.

B. *Political Executives.* This group of managers believes they should be policy innovators and leaders yet they are less willing to stick their necks out in pushing councilmen toward major policy decisions. They take a more pragmatic and less moralistic view of their political roles as managers.

C. *Administrative Directors* are convinced that managers should actively participate in the policy process but, nevertheless, they articulate a reluctance to be a novel administrator or open community leader. They tend to be preoccupied with the art of the possible, stressing the constraints and the problems, the council's authority as opposed to the manager's expertise.

D. *Administrative Technicians* define their policy roles within the narrowest context with a focus on administrative or housekeeping functions. They see themselves as staff advisors who are clearly subordinate to city councils and rather than proposing or instituting changes, they view themselves as curators of the established goals.

Professor Loveridge's fourfold classification of the self-perceptions of management leadership roles influences very directly the breadth or narrowness of the managers' goals, strategies, and results which they expect to achieve in community government. Loveridge argues the "political leader-type" frequently has the best contemporary education in public administration and exhibits great willingness to introduce new ideas for making broad city improvement projects by openly soliciting or "playing politics" with council members for their votes on various issues. At the other extreme, Professor Loveridge points up that "administrative technicians" have very often limited formal managerial training and are more inclined to view their own roles in communities as strictly subserviant to the city council's wishes. While city size is not found to be correlated with "type of managerial style," Professor Loveridge believes there may be a certain self-selection process that occurs, with cities seeking out managers and managers seeking out cities most compatible to their own particular favored style of public management.

Taking Stock of the Occupation

What can be said about city manager professionalism from the standpoint of the foregoing summary of current statistical and social trends in city management? Can managers be classed as "professionals" or not? What are attributes that favor as well as prevent ranking city management as a professional career? Table 2 shows them to have a foot on both sides of the fence.

Table 2 should emphasize clearly that city managers are different from other public professionals. They have developed into a clear-cut occupational field as administrative generalists in city management — but they are a Janus-faced occupation that looks simultaneously in the directions of "professionalism" with its peer group-defined norms of expertise and behavior as well as being very much in politics with primary orientation toward and demands for community responsiveness and accountability.

Managers cannot totally embrace either role of professional or politician. If managers became neutral experts without reference to the political facts of life, they would jeopardize their own survival, but if they became politicians without responsible knowledge or expertise in urban affairs, they jeopardize their credibility and worth to the public they serve. In short, managers cautiously and continuously tread a middle ground between the two poles of politics and expertise.

The Future of the City Manager: As An Envoy of the Potomac?

What does the future hold for the city management field? If the past 70 years of unabated growth of the "manager phenomenon" is any guide to the future, the prominence and influence of city managers, individually and collectively, in the context of American community life will no doubt continue, even expand. The technological and social complexities of modern urban life increasingly require their specialized administrative talents in coping with the myriad of insistent problems like energy, pollution, crime, minority recruitment, urban planning, and mass transit. Moreover, as the local public sector is pressed urgently by citizen and federal government alike to deal with these kinds of problems, city managers and their counterparts — CAOs, county managers, town managers, city administrators — with their central and full-time responsibilities on the local scene for planning, budgeting, personnel selection, and advice to council will remain the indispensable link between the conceptualization and achievement of community goals.

TABLE 2

Attributes Favoring Professional Status	Attributes Favoring Non-Professional or Political Status
General influence on American life Significant and growing in terms of numbers of managers/CAOs with increasing job responsibilities	"Dispersing authority" due to increased participation of federal/state action in local government and new minority/union participation
Ethos and outlook Outlook characteristically of an administrative generalist	Exercise of administrative/leadership skills highly dependent upon and subject to shifting political nature of community life, causing the bulk of managers to be "in-and-outers"
Informal social background of managers Homogeneous/middle class occupation with professional level salary	Social make-up of city management, especially influenced by parochial small town, suburban political pressures
General educational preparation Survey shows increasing college/graduate educational preparation	No required degree or certification to obtain employment
Core skills necessary on the job Informally favors administrative generalist background with preference for skills of budgeting, personnel, and management, as well as newer specialties like energy conservation or federal grantsmanship (which depends on needs of individual communities)	No skills specified by law for employment
Career patterns An informal route of career advancement developing for many managers through assistant managerships, consulting work, business or related government careers	None legally or formally specified
Lifetime occupation Possibility for all managers	The bulk of managers are "in-and-outers" — moving across a broad range of comparable administrative type jobs
Self-perception of occupation Most managers see themselves akin to public professional groups like diplomats or school superintendents	Less than one quarter of managers believe that they are "an established profession" like law or medicine
Peer-group influence of professional association—the ICMA The ICMA informally promotes professional and ethical codes of conduct through training programs, meetings, and publications	No formal control by the professional elite or professional association relative to entrance, work standards, promotions in profession, nor does ICMA attempt to enforce ethical code of behavior on the practitioner. Employment of manager remains subject to local council's decision.
Degree of professional autonomy in relation to politics and community affairs Classic theory of the manager plan as well as most manager charters view managers as neutral experts in municipal affairs	Reality of management role deeply affected by nature and distribution of community politics. Extent and scope of manager involvement in policy leadership is influenced by (1) community size, (2) degree of political conflict, and (3) self-definition of leadership styles.
Conflict or Possible Competition with Other Professional Groups In theory managers are viewed as the chief professional administrator *in charge of* various professional services	In reality possibilities exist for wide array of conflict with community professional as well as minority and union groups.

At the same time, strong countervailing pressures in the opposite directions, away from the extended application of professional expertise, are at work in the city management field. Growing demands for widespread citizen participation, minority employment, and union involvement — in short, widening political representation — are constant pressures on city managers and urban government as a whole. Managers are now and will remain at the delicate fulcrum point where these fierce twin cross-pressures for both narrow expertise and wider citizen representation meet and are balanced.

Yet, on the horizon is the ominous and rapidly growing intergovernmental intrusion "from above" with which most managers (like most local public officials) must contend. Greater federal and state presence on the local scene unquestionably will mean an ever-increasing dispersal of the manager's real authority over internal community functions. Many managers already spend a third or more of their time on intergovernmental matters, and this percentage seems to be growing every year.

Our cultural mythology of "home rule" to the contrary, American city managers may indeed play at the present time a role more akin to the French Prefect in responsiveness to the national capitol's dictates and demands than we or even they care to imagine. Today Washington's "unseen hand" is as invisible and omnipresent as ever was Adam Smith's.

The hard fact is, so long as local government continues to ebb as an entity in the national structure of governance, for better or worse, we may expect managers in service more as envoys of the Potomac than of Peoria. And no doubt in response to this shifting locus of authority, the traditional twin images of the manager as "a professional helping hand" and "political hired hand" will have to be recast to fit the new political realities of this line of work. Certainly these future changes will demand a reappraisal of traditional managerial functions, educational preparation, career orientation, professional associations, and the like, though the old political mythology and verities of managers' roles changes slowly, if at all.

Notes

1. It is important to emphasize at the outset the distinction between the "manager plan," which is essentially a theory of local government, and the "city manager," which is a recognized and established public service occupation. This article focuses principally on the latter subject though, of course, the "plan" and "occupation" are closely related.

2. In recent years the distinction between CAOs and managers in terms of their functions and authority has grown increasingly "fuzzy," and since the ICMA includes CAOs (along with "kindred spirits" like town managers, city business managers, etc.) now in their membership, this article also will lump them together within the city management field. For a separate discussion of CAOs, read Edwin O. Stene, "Historical Commentary," in *Public Management* (June 1973), p. 6; Charles R. Adrian, "Recent Concepts in Large City Management," in Edward C. Banfield (ed.), *Urban Government* (New York: Free Press, 1969); and James B. Hogan, *The Chief Administrative Officer* (Tucson: University of Arizona Press, 1976).

3. My unproven observation is that four very real pressures are constantly upon managers moving them in the direction of increased professionalism in terms of their work substance and attitudes: (1) greater numbers of higher educational institutions throughout the nation, specifically schools of public administration and public affairs, are turning out increasing numbers of students with professional administrative skills and outlook; (2) an increasing competition for a limited number of openings in the city management field helps to insure a high quality "crop" of managers (particularly true in the tight white collar labor market today); (3) well-trained and upwardly mobile managerial staffs found in most middle-sized and large cities constantly press both expertise and professionalism upon managers; and (4) city managers' regional associations, perhaps even more than the national ICMA, serve informally as "professional informational exchanges" and a very important avenue for many managers in terms of keeping their professional expertise current.

Readers will note throughout my essay that I back off from trying to define the actual substance of city management professionalism for in my view it leads into a hopeless semantic bog that is represented by the essay of Robert Kline and Paul Blanchard, "Professionalism and the City Manager: Examination of Unanswered Questions," *Midwest Review of Public Administration* (July 1973), pp. 163-175.

4. Norton Long, "Politicians for Hire?" *Public Administration Review*, Vol. 25 (June 1965), p. 119; Karl A. Bosworth, "The City Manager is a Politician," *Public Administration Review*, Vol. 18 (Summer 1958), pp. 216-222; and for both a lively and more contemporary essay following this line of reasoning written by a city manager, read: William V. Donaldson, "Continuing Education for City Managers," *Public Administration Review*, Vol. 33 (November/December 1973), pp. 504-508. For an excellent insight into the role of city managers in the budgetary process, refer to Arnold J. Meltsner, *The Politics of City Revenue* (Berkeley: University of California Press, 1971), pp. 51-60.

5. For the unusual story of the development of the

council-manager plan, read John Porter East, *Council-Manager Government: The Political Thought of Its Founder, Richard Childs* (Chapel Hill: University of North Carolina Press, 1965); and Richard J. Stillman 2nd, *The Rise of the City Manager, A Public Professional in Local Government* (Albuquerque: University of New Mexico Press, 1974).

6. Don Price, "The Promotion of the City Manager Plan," *Public Opinion Quarterly* (Winter 1941), pp. 570-571. There is considerable controversy in the historic literature over Childs' actual role in the development of the manager plan. Price terms Childs' role as "a manipulator of symbols"; Herbert Emmerich saw it as "an inventor of the plan"; but Childs liked to describe himself as the "minister" who performed the marriage between the commission and manager plans. My own view is that Richard Childs is best understood from the historic perspective as a child of the American Progressive Era and its reformist spirit.

7. There is an immense literature on this subject. Perhaps one of the best and most thoughtful analyses of this issue is found in Clarence E. Ridley, *The Role of the City Manager in Policy Formulation* (Chicago: International City Manager's Association, 1958). For more current views of this subject, read Arnold J. Meltsner; Timothy A. Almy, "City Managers, Public Avoidance, and Revenue Sharing," *Public Administration Review*, Vol. 33, No. 1 (January/February 1977), pp. 19-27; and Robert P. Boynton and Deil S. Wright, "Mayor-Manager Relationships in Large Council-Manager Cities: A reinterpretation," *Public Administration Review*, Vol. 31, No. 1 (January/February 1971), pp. 28-35.

8. See Stillman, p. 73. For the high degree of general satisfaction with this field by its practitioners even among those who leave city management altogether, read Fremont J. Lyden and Ernest G. Miller, "Why City Managers Leave the Profession: A Longitudinal Study in the Pacific Northwest," *Public Administration Review*, Vol. 36, No. 2 (March/April 1976), pp. 175-181.

9. Sali and Walt Damon-Ruty, "Former Taft City Manager Tells Viewpoints," *The Bakersfield Californian* (March 10, 1977), p. 33. I realize that this issue of the dispersal of authority of city managers and of all public professionals in general is an important subject that deserves considerably more attention than I have given it. Certainly the subject deserves book-length treatment rather than a few paragraphs. In my view one of the best books to date to treat this subject in relationship to cities as a whole is Norton Long, *The Unwalled City: Reconstituting the Urban Community* (New York: Basic Books, 1971).

10. Survey data drawn from the following sources: Laurie S. Frankel and Carol A. Pigeon, *Municipal Managers and Chief Administrative Officers, A Statistical Profile, Urban Data Service Reports*, Vol. 7, No. 2. (Washington, D.C.: International City Management Association, February 1975); Richard J. Stillman, chap. 4; *Directory of Recognized Local Governments, 1977* (Washington, D.C.: ICMA, 1977); *The Directory of Assistants* (Washington, D.C.: ICMA, 1977); and Robert Huntley and Robert MacDonald, "Urban Managers: Organizational Preferences, Managerial Styles and Social Policy Roles," *Municipal Yearbook* (Washington, D.C.: ICMA, 1975), pp. 149-159.

11. No large city over 500,000 (except Cleveland) has ever adopted the manager plan, and Cleveland threw it out after two years. Several manager plan communities, though, adopted it prior to growing over 500,000. Most large cities like New York, San Francisco, and New Orleans have opted instead for vesting administrative authority in a CAO or deputy mayor. Perhaps large-city municipal problems are less administrative and more political, so voters prefer to have a strong mayor "on top" and an administrator "on tap" rather than the reverse under manager government. The classic debate over the application of the manager plan to large cities appeared in the pages of the *Public Administration Review* between Wallace S. Sayre, "The General Manager Idea for Large Cities," Vol. 14 (Autumn 1954), pp. 253-258 and John E. Bebout, "Management for Large Cities," Vol. 15 (Summer 1955), pp. 188-195.

12. Clarence Ridley and Orin Nolting, *The City Manager Profession* (Chicago: University of Chicago Press, 1934). Also for good early statistics on city managers, see Joseph Cohen, "The City Manager as a Profession," *The National Municipal Review* (July 1924), pp. 391-411. Certainly the most significant determinant of managerial selection are the attitudes and preferences of city councilmen. For one of the best discussions of this subject, read Efraim Torogovnik, *Determinants in Managerial Selection* (Washington, D.C.: ICMA, 1969). In the Torogovnik study public administration ranked first as the preferred background of managers by councilmen, with business administration and engineering second and third respectively.

13. Here I can be criticized for sidestepping the whole issue of what constitutes city manager professionalism, but as I pointed out in footnote 3, in my view one enters a hopeless semantic bog when one attempts to define this term. The important point I feel is that most managers believe themselves to be professionals, even though the substance of their professionalism has never been adequately defined.

14. For an extended account of the significant changes that have occurred within the ICMA during the last decade, read Stillman, chap. 3. I must also emphasize that I do not want to leave the impression from this essay that the ICMA is totally impotent with regard to enforcement of professional standards; indeed, from time to time it does expel members for the most flagrant violations of its professional code of conduct. For a recent case of expulsion, see *ICMA Newsletter* (Feb. 28, 1977), p. 1. Nevertheless, I feel my point still stands that ultimate authority for enforcement of professional standards rests not with the ICMA but local city councils.

15. Stillman, p. 74.

16. For the rather complex evolution of thinking on this subject over the last 70 years, refer to Stillman, *ibid.*, chaps. 1-3. I should qualify this point somewhat by

pointing out that while "the early founders" like Childs did stress a neutral role for managers, the early managers hardly approached their work in a neutral manner. Indeed, not handicapped by federal or state guidelines and mandates as are modern city managers, early managers probably exercised considerably more control over internal city matters and were not hesitant to exercise very broad policy initiatives over many areas of city activities, see particularly the early chapters of Leonard White, *The City Manager* (Chicago: University of Chicago Press, 1926). Today perhaps the real change is that the managers' own view of their policy roles (as reflected by the ICMA's Code of Conduct) better reflects their actual community policy involvement. The paradox today may be that this pro active ideology may vastly overestimate their real power and authority over community affairs, given their general "dispersal of authority."

17. The results of the Stillman survey of city managers, pp. 73-74, contrasts sharply on this subject by comparison with the 1934 Ridley and Nolting survey.
18. Edward C. Banfield and James Q. Wilson, *City Politics* (New York: Vintage, 1963), pp. 168-186.
19. John C. Bollens and John C. Ries, *The City Manager Profession: Myths and Realities* (Chicago: Public Administration Service, 1969). More recently, the Bollens-Ries thinking has been refined further by Cortus T. Koehler in "Policy and Legislative Oversight in Council-Manager Cities," *Public Administration Review*, Vol. 33, No. 5 (September/October 1973), pp. 433-441. Koehler divides councilmanic policy oversight into three types: "average," "blind faith," and "politician," and depending on the composition of these type councilmen in the makeup of any council, the degree of managerial autonomy over policy issues is thus determined.
20. Ronald O. Loveridge, *City Managers in Legislative Politics* (Indianapolis: The Bobbs-Merril Co., 1971). Unquestionably the Loveridge book is one of the best on city managers to appear in recent years. Timothy A. Almy, "Local-Cosmopolitanism and U.S. City Managers," *Urban Affairs Quarterly* (March 1975), pp. 243-272, is an interesting and useful essay that builds further upon Loveridge's typology by utilizing Gouldner and Merton's localism-cosmopolitanism concepts. Professor Almy demonstrates empirically how the local vs. cosmopolitan backgrounds of managers significantly shape their policy roles.

Further Reading

The two outstanding classics on the city manager and the city manager plan, which are still useful in terms of providing historical perspectives on the development of the city management field, are Leonard White's *The City Manager* (1926) and Harold Stone, Don Price, and Catherine Stone, *City Manager Government in the United States* (1940). Two interesting early statistical surveys of managers are found in Joseph Cohen's "The City Manager as a Profession," *The National Municipal Review* (July 1924); and Clarence Ridley and Orin Nolting, *The City Manager Profession* (1934). For the best current surveys on contemporary city managers, read Ronald O. Loveridge, *City Managers and Legislative Politics* (1971): John Bollens and John Ries, *The City Manager Profession: Myths and Realities* (1969); and Richard Stillman, *The Rise of the City Manager: A Public Professional in Local Government* (1974). John Porter East's *Council Manager Government: The Political Thought of Its Founder, Richard Childs* (1965) is the most authoritative and thorough analysis to date of Child's thought, ideas, and involvement with the development of the manager plan.

URBAN PLANNERS: DOCTORS OR MIDWIVES?

William C. Baer, *University of Southern California*

While urban and regional planners have reason to be euphoric these days, they also find themselves in a state of malaise. The contradiction arises from the conflicting demands which have beset planners since their origin — conflicts which are emblematic of those confronting society at large.

The euphoria stems from local, state, and federal governments at last bringing to the fore the very issues planners have been urging upon them for years. Not only have land-use planning issues been placed at the head of the public agenda, but courts have increasingly upheld the planners' recommendations. For instance, exuberant growth philosophies of Chambers of Commerce are now giving way to planned growth concepts consonant with the needs and resources of the community as systematically inventoried and programmed by planners. The legality of this planned growth has been upheld recently in Petaluma, California, and Ramapo, New York.

State governments are strengthening planning efforts by requiring that zoning conform to the general plan; that housing, transportation, and open space matters be adequately dealt with; and that areas of critical interest such as coastal, lake, and mountain areas come under the purview of special planning commissions. The federal government now requires Environmental Impact Statements to accompany proposed government developments, and Congress has been seriously debating the merits of national land-use legislation. Planners have been advocating all of these changes for years.

Why, then, is the profession in a state of malaise? For several reasons. Where once planners believed they performed the above activities in the public interest, they now are not sure what that interest is. Their efforts on behalf of the many have frequently done good for only a few. Their professional stance stresses science and progress, while their plans often reveal a romantic nostalgia for yesteryear. Their practice emphasizes rational decisions, while decision makers frequently use the act of planning as a cover to disguise choices made on quite different bases.

Listing these contradictions might at first appear to be yet another castigation of the field. It is not. Nor is it an apologia for planners. These contradictions are really specific manifestations of some of the basic conflicts embodied in our society at large; conservative versus liberal, humanist versus technocrat, public versus private, elitist versus mass, and utopian dreams of fair shares to all versus the practical politics of who is to get what, when, and how. The planning profession merely has the unenviable task of crystalizing these conflicts in the context of planning and society, and in the course of articulating its own role.

We will return to these conflicts and contradictions in the course of reviewing the field's evolution, describing its current circumstance, and suggesting some likely courses for future development.

Evolution of the Planning Field

There are two quite different strains in the field's intellectual development. These have combined, diverged, and rejoined in various permutations over the years, accounting for some of the contradictions described above.

Two sources have stimulated the city planning movement and have shaped its development. The one, an offspring of the German Rationalization and the scientific management movements, cast city planning in the role of the city engineer who sought to improve efficiency in the city's physical plant. The other, an offspring of the earlier social reform movements, cast it in the role of the social

---

The author wishes to thank Francine Rabinovitz for the many ways in which she has helped him on this article, and to express his appreciation to his other colleagues in the school, especially Mel Branch and Lowdon Wingo, who have reviewed earlier drafts. This is not to say they necessarily agree with all that has been said here, but they have helped the author to state more clearly his own views.

William C. Baer is an assistant professor and assistant director of the School of Urban and Regional Planning at the University of Southern California. He has worked as both a planner and an administrative assistant in local government and has graduate degrees in both urban planning and political science. His areas of interest include planning implementation and housing and community development.

reformer who sought to improve the lot of people living in cities.[1]

These two sources were manifest in the people who converged on city planning from quite different backgrounds. The design professions — architecture, engineering, and landscape architecture — sought to improve the lot of people through manipulating the physical environment by the design and location of urban facilities (the layout of streets, subdivisions, water and sewer lines, and buildings). People with public health, recreation, and housing backgrounds brought to planning a consuming desire to transform the conditions of the urban poor so that they too would take on the values and qualities of the American middle class. Thus, the hubris of the architect as "Master Builder" merged with the technical competence of the engineer as "problem solver," and both invoked the purposive rationale of the social reformer to combine in an ideology of city planning which, in Webber's words, was "out to perfect history."[2]

In the 1920s the architect, engineer, and landscape architect dominated the field. They stressed aesthetics and efficiency in locating parks, designing civic centers, and rationalizing land-use and protecting property values through zoning. The social reformers interested in housing, public health, and ameliorating poverty had at best a modest influence in these early days.[3]

The 1930s saw the two strains continue, now manifested along governmental lines. While local planners continued with zoning, land-use, and general plans, those interested in housing and health looked to the federal government to inject these considerations into local planning efforts.[4] The federal public housing program of 1937 was the result of their efforts. Its formula of federal funds to local governments for social planning programs set the pattern for most grant-in-aid programs through the early 1970s.

Following the Second World War, the Housing Act of 1949 and its many subsequent amendments (including the 701 program of 1954 which provided federal funding for local general plans) became the principal vehicle for using federal funds to achieve local goals and for relating social aims to physical plans.

Cause-effect linkages have long lags in urban affairs. Even before the results of the early experiments from urban renewal in the 1950s were in, new planning experiments were undertaken in the 1960s culminating in the Model Cities program. This growth in federally sponsored social programs along with the growth in planning schools was indicative of how urban planning's intellectual leadership had shifted from the local to the federal level and from practitioners to academics. Planning's Master Builder tradition of the architects was transformed into the Master Model Builder of economists. "Problem solvers" as engineers in planning were superseded by problem solvers skilled in operations research. Social reformers articulated theories of "social planning" and sometimes adopted the legal model, becoming "advocate planners" who pled the case of special interests (the poor) instead of the public interest. Community participation in planning decisions for neighborhoods was embraced by much of the profession at this time.

Meanwhle, the traditional city planning focus on physical planning and land use was very much down-graded in the new federal programs and in the planning schools. Broader intellectual/ professional outlooks were stressed, along with an emphasis on sophisticated analytic techniques.

By the 1970s, however, urban planning's age was beginning to tell. The social programs of the War on Poverty days were not very successful. Furthermore, the profession was having to confront its own backwash of earlier years. Ideas once championed by planners alone — separation of land uses through zoning, new towns, mass transit, minimum housing and development standards, revitalization of urban cores — were now being advocated by much of the public. In the meantime, planners were coming to realize that considerations of equity, the incidence of costs and benefits, difficulties in implementation, and the immense costs of these undertakings seriously offset the supposed benefits.

The difficulties and frustrations planners had encountered were cause for a search for better theory and knowledge.[5] In all of this there was retreat from economic efficiency toward the psychological aspects of planning and the quality of life as the guiding rationale.

But if the problems of achieving social reform were reason for malaise, there was reason for euphoria as well. The public's interest in the environment provided planners with a rationale for intervention that had decidedly more political appeal than did social reform. Federal and state requirements for environmental impact analyses of proposed public and private actions gave planners new authority in forcing politicians to consider the wider ramifications of narrowly conceived developments. New legal and financial mechanisms were enacted to preserve open space, as were special planning processes for environmentally critical areas which preempted certain developmental decisions that had long been the perogative of local control. Surprisingly, in all of this change it is land-use planning, hitherto academically discredited, which has emerged as critical.

Thus the profession seems to have come full circle. The evolution in the field has resulted in the practice of the 1970s resembling that of the 1920s. Land use is once again in the fore of professional involvement, while social programs have receded. Local government is the prime source of program innovation, while the federal government's role has diminished (although not financially). Practitioners have once again taken the initiative in establishing new directions for the field.

Still, there are differences today from the 1920s. The most important lies in the legal side of the practice, and in the legislated authority of plans. In the 1920s, local plans were devised, admired, and shelved: to be used only as background for community decisions. Today, communities may be sued to force new development to conform to the local general plan or to comply with considerations in environmental impact reports. Planners in turn must be far more rigorous and systematic in their preparation of these plans and reports so that their recommendations can withstand legal challenge and cross-examination. Furthermore, both state and federal legislation now spell out in some detail the required components of the required plans. Thus the law and the legislatures are shaping professional practice today — making it more routinized and bureaucratic — in ways planners had neither urged nor anticipated.

Current State of the Profession

Some numbers are in order. Kaufman[6] estimates there are 11,750 government planning bodies in the United States, one-quarter of them with professional staffs, providing employment for some 16,000 planners. A national survey of the American Society of Planning Officials (ASPO) and a tally of the 1976 roster of the American Institute of Planners (AIP) suggests the proportion of planners working in the private and public sectors.[7] As shown in Table 1, more than half work in the public sector, and of these, most work for local government. About one-quarter of the planners work for the private sector. The ASPO survey also revealed that overall, women comprised about eight per cent of the profession.

TABLE 1
ESTIMATED DISTRIBUTION OF PLANNERS
BETWEEN PUBLIC AND PRIVATE SECTORS

	ASPO Survey	AIP Roster
Public Sector	64%	54%
Local government (city, county, and special agencies)	37%	30%
Regional or metropolitan planning agencies or COGs	15	13
State	8	7
Federal	4	4
Private Sector	23	30
Private consultants	20	27
Other (development companies, business: private or voluntary)	3	3
Other	13	16
	100%	100%

Source: Derived from Corby, pp. 20-21, Table 2, and *AIP News,* Vol. 11, No. 6 (October 1976), p. 5.

The field has grown substantially in the last 25 years. In 1956, for cities between 500,000 and one million, the average planning staff size was 11 and the budget $100,000; by 1973, the figures were 35 and $640,000. The two professional associations — AIP (members must pass a professional examination) and ASPO (composed of professionals, planning commissioners, and lay people) — have grown tenfold in the last 20 years, with membership currently exceeding 10,000 and 11,000 respectively (about 54 per cent of the membership is overlapping).[8] Their ranks will continue to grow as more than 1,400 students with masters degrees in planning and 70 PhDs graduate every year from 73 colleges and universities across the United States.[9]

What do these practitioners do, and what is it those students hope to do? At a high level of abstraction, planners have exceedingly ambitious goals which reflect the merger of the two intellectual strains described earlier. Planners may attempt "deliberative social change" or hope to encourage "social learning" or seek to correct adverse "externalities." In these views, planning is a comprehensive process, seeking to understand society in all its awesome complexity and then prescribing for its betterment. At the level of practice, these ambitions and efforts find expression in a variety of tasks and organizations which reflect the evolution of the field. A good summary of the public sector is provided by Godshalk:

At the local level, the traditional planning agencies (city planning departments) still exist, but in addition, there are planning organizations for human resources, for neighborhood and community economic development, for functional areas such as transportation and health. There are regional organizations for A-95 review of local grant proposals, for water resources and waste management planning, and for review of environmental impact statements. There are special purpose agencies concerned with certain geographic areas, such as Appalachia or the Coastal Zone. At the state level, there are policy planning units connected with the governors' offices, development corporations and in-house planning groups in budget offices and functional agencies dealing with transportation, health, education, criminal justice and the like. At the federal level, there has been a similar growth in the number and type of planning organizations.[10]

In the private sector, planners work for planning consultant firms and in firms oriented towards the more established professions of architecture, engineering, and landscape-architecture, while links are being established with law firms dealing in land-use and environmental law. As private practitioners, planners either do specialized work for public agencies, or work on residential, commercial, or industrial developments in the United States or overseas, particularly in the developing nations.

Of late planning has moved closer to public administration, providing still another type of employment. Planning's success in effectuating change is now seen to be not only dependent upon planning skills, but also upon implementation and management.[11] Conceptually, this recognition was part of the movement toward planning, programming and budgeting systems. Although the term PPBS has now fallen into disfavor by some, the underlying concepts of linking goals, plans, and resources are still applicable and practiced at all levels of government by planners in conjunction with administrators.

Local governments are linking planning and management now through reorganizations of city departments. Traditionally, urban planning was undertaken in separate planning departments whose functions were largely the preparation of reports, plans, and zoning ordinances. This separation meant that other departments saw to the financing of the plan and its implementation, or enforced the zoning ordinance, or interpreted the planners' stipulations for zoning variances or special use permits. Consequently, the goals, biases, and requirements of other departments frequently intruded or conflicted with the planners' intent.

To better integrate the planning stage with the implementation stage, local governments have been merging planning departments with building inspection, engineering, urban renewal, and housing into departments of community development headed by planners or public administrators. Nationally, such cities as Baltimore, Indianapolis, and Los Angeles have reorganized in this fashion, as have regional governments such as Minneapolis-St. Paul. A recent survey of California revealed that more than 40 cities had this new administrative structure, and that planning and administration were the most important skills for staffing these departments.[12]

The growth in the planning field over the last 20 years has been vigorous, exceeding even the marked overall growth in state and local governments.[13] Despite its vigor, this growth has been erratic, leading to some difficulties, at least in the short run. The political system, while attempting to integrate planning at all levels of government, has had to mediate and temporize between conflicting elements in society which either demand even more planning or protest that there is already too much. Thus planning functions are established at one level of government, without establishment of an appropriate counterpart at the others; regional planning efforts may be mandated, requiring coordination with innumerable jurisdictions in the area, yet many of these lack the staffs or funds to do the necessary planning for the coordination. Like the urban sprawl and leap-frog development that planners contend with, the growth in planning institutions has been itself unplanned and unsystematic.

These problems have caused private sector uncertainty as to public intentions and have resulted in an increase in development costs to cover the waiting time for development approvals. Much of this uncertainty should abate with time. Just as the urban complex works for all its seeming inadequacies, so also is this planning system working and becoming more robust as experience is gained and the institutional interstices are filled in.

Is Planning a Profession?

The growth in the planning field has slackened of late, reflecting a slowing of our national economy and the financial stringencies of the public sector. The tightening job market has intensified interest among planners in licensing or certification and among planning schools in accreditation or professional recognition.

Despite the presence of architects, landscape architects, and engineers in the field since its earliest days, each of which is a licensed profession, planners have had no licensing requirements until recently (and only in certain states).[14] Virtually anyone can call himself/herself a planner, and of those who do, probably most would be recognized as planners by others who go under the same appellation.[15] As a consequence, the field is still relatively open.

Planning in America has always been eclectic in adopting technique and norms, and catholic in accepting new trends and styles. By contrast, in England although the intellectual evolution of the field developed along somewhat similar lines, entry into the Royal Town Planning Institute (RTPI) was more restricted and entry into governmental service was largely limited to corporate members of the RTPI. The requirement that only a "Chartered Town Planner" was eligible for civil service planning jobs in England is without counterpart in the United States, but the very "chartering" of planners in England has apparently confined the profession to the early architect/engineering emphasis with adverse implications for the profession's future.[16]

Recently, Catanese[17] has advocated a kind of chartering for American planners which would be similar to the certification received by accountants (CPAs). This certification would be administered by a board composed of planners and related professionals. It would be uniform across the nation (not dependent upon the licensing procedures of 50 different states) and would be wide enough ranging in scope to avoid the RTPI problem.

This in turn raises issues of academic program accreditation. Currently, the American Institute of Planners has a process for "recognizing" approved planning programs, but the requirements are minimal. Planning faculty are currently participating in regional and national meetings to debate which of four possibilities should be selected to improve the accreditation process from an academic point of view, yet keep it creditable with registration or certification efforts by the practitioners.[18]

Planners as Professionals and Midwives

The anxiety and inferiority felt by planners won't simply go away, however, by requirements for licensing or certification. Their malaise goes deeper than that. It stems from difficulties within their own theories and belief systems, and from society's own ambivalent views of planning.

Planning has always had a strong strain of utopianism and reform. People are attracted to the field because they are dissatisfied with the status quo. They wish to change our living conditions and make them better. Why else plan? In the early days planning was seen as a comparatively easy task: Design a plan to cure urban ills and follow the plan the way an architect follows the blueprint. Planners have since learned they do not possess the theory, knowledge, skills, and competencies to carry out such a procedure, nor do they possess the political power or the public support and confidence to engage in such a process. Planning is considerably more complex than first supposed, requiring a multiplicity of actors, many of whom are not planners.

Current planning theory has retreated from the "Master Planner" view to a more exploratory, experimental approach. Planners are now more willing to accept their limitations, incorporating "feedback loops" and citizen participation in their planning procedures to allow for re-evaluation of means and ends, to allow for serendipity, and to allow for other points of view. Despite these changes, planners still see themselves as appropriately being major decision makers in their own right, or as close advisors to decision-makers. For instance, the feedback loops are to be monitored by planners who decide the significance of the information, while community participation means to planners only a sharing of control, not relinquishing it.

Such views are stimulating to planners, but they are not always realistic. In practice planners often fall short of even their more modest ambitions. Democratic societies rarely accord planners those positions and powers planners desire, nor do these societies even accede to the wisdom implied: planning is too important to be left to the planners. Instead, society's true ambivalence is revealed. Planning departments are established, planners are hired, they are told to plan, but they are never left alone to do so. Many other people engage in the process. For instance, most local governments require planners to serve three bosses — the chief executive officer and the city council, plus the planning commission. The latter is a lay board (usually appointed by the mayor, often dominated by realtors and developers) acting as the initial review body before making planning recommendations to the city council which ultimately decides their merit. Planners often find themselves caught between the city council's and the planning commission's conflicting wishes, not to mention the chief executive officer's agenda.

Thus outside observers note that planners are not usually movers and shakers as their literature suggests; they are more often facilitators so that others can move and shake. Political scientists, like Altshuler[19] and Rabinovitz,[20] and sociologists like the Needlemans[21] suggest that planners usually play a middleman role. They may pose agendas for others to react to; they may interpret urban problems in a technical light for decision makers to ponder; they may mobilize latent community resources to engage in community issues; they may act as brokers between competing interest groups to facilitate a solution; and they may function as actors, salesmen, con-men, or even charismatic leaders in their efforts to mediate between neighborhood groups and city hall. But planners rarely make things happen; they usually only facilitate. While seeing themselves as the main gears in the urban machinery, other observers see them as the lubricants, alleviating the squeaks and lessening the friction of urban processes, but rarely acting as important cogs themselves.

Planners therefore face still another contradiction. They fancy themselves as appropriately possessing the power and authority of the traditional professions, such as law or medicine, yet society frequently consigns them the power and authority of quite a different profession — the midwife.

The profession of midwifery is a model not to be disdained by planners: the profession is far older than planning, it is often licensed, and with proper minimal training and exercising of care, the midwife is far more cost-effective than elaborate hospitals with overskilled doctors and anesthesiologists in attendance. Planners must recognize that their role as midwives is a necessary and appropriate part of their practice, of considerable value to society and offering opportunities to themselves as professionals.

Nonetheless, the orientation with midwife as the model shifts the planner from doer to helper, from general to aide-de-camp. In practice planning is not usually an immediate and direct cause/effect, stimulus/response, problem/solution kind of practice. Rather, its results are more often long-term and indirect, and cause/effect-*inducing,* or stimulus/response-*evoking,* or problem/solution *suggesting.* In a complex world with multiple actors, planning rarely could be anything else.

The rationale for planners as midwives is more fundamental than the above would indicate. Socrates used the art of intellectual midwifery *(maieutics)*[22] to bring into full consciousness conceptions previously latent in people's minds. By asking a careful order of questions, he attempted to destroy prejudices, remedy false (although often fashionable) beliefs, and reveal the incorrectness of answers delivered in ignorance. If Socrates was himself unsure precisely where the truth lay, he nevertheless helped others come closer to it by his art of maieutics.

Planners can practice the art of maieutics as well. The history of planning thought is filled with well-intentioned theory which has proved less than correct. But planners can learn from their mistakes. Where once planners believed they knew the public interest, they now admit to knowing only how difficult it is to know. Where once planners placed a blind faith in the rationality of planning, they now are more aware of the immense demands on knowledge and resources that simple obedience to rational method engenders. Where once planners believed that technique and technology could solve urban ills, they now know that planning is value-laden and political, beset by the moral and social issues those characteristics embody. Where once planners believed that a carefully formulated plan would proceed inexorably as formulated, they now know that plan implementation reopens settled issues and introduces new ones, thereby continuing the planning process.

This kind of knowledge — knowing what is not known, what cannot be prematurely decided — can be of immense benefit to society. Planners can help structure societal inquiry by posing sophisticated questions and cautioning against simplistic answers. In addition, planners can induce the public and politicians to formulate their latent concepts of society and show their connections with reality.

In the process planners can address themselves to another contradiction as well. Dyckman[23] has correctly pointed out that planning theory has never successfully come to grips with political theories of the state. With this absence, planning too frequently finds itself used as a tool of the state — planning as functional rationality — without confronting the substantive issues of what is and should be the function and purpose of the state in the first place. Yet this latter question is very much part of planning's historical traditions of uptopianism and reform. In its intellectual and theoretical aspect, Dyckman suggests that planning can serve to critically monitor the state as a way of improving it. In its *professional* aspect, planning can use its maieutic abilities to facilitate — not create — the perpetual birth of an evolving society which is seeking answers to the same issues.

This account of maieutics in planning practice is not a prescription; planners are already behaving in this fashion, although not yet using the term or invoking the rationales. Nor does the art of maieutics imply radical departure from present training or planning school curricula — only a shift in the emphasis. Planners have traditionally stressed technical abilities and quantitative methods as crucial ingredients to their skills. But recent surveys of planners reveal that language and interaction skills (skills in oral and written communication) are the most important to practitioners.[24] And these are the very skills most needed in their role as facilitator.

In summary, the substance of planning issues and the procedures of planning practice have assumed increasing importance in society. The planner's authority that might have been granted in these matters, however, has not been forthcoming. The contradiction is part of the ambivalence that society feels about planning in general — the need for it in the abstract, but the reluctance to leave it solely to experts when concrete decisions will be made which fundamentally effect different interest groups. As planning becomes more important, the profession must expect its role to become more modest — but no less essential. When professional expectations are made more congruent with society's, planners may even find that their malaise has lessened, that they are in fact accomplishing what society expected of them all along.

Notes

1. Melvin M. Webber, "Planning in an Environment of Change: Part II, Permissive Planning," in *The Town Planning Review*, Vol. 39, No. 4 (January 1969), p. 279.
2. *Ibid.*, p. 281.
3. Robert A. Walker, *The Planning Function in Urban Government*, 2nd ed., (Chicago: University of Chicago Press, 1950), pp. 35-36.
4. Mel Scott, *American City Planning* (Berkeley: University of California Press, 1969).
5. John Friedman and Barclay Hudson, "Knowledge and Action: A Guide to Planning Theory," *Journal of the American Institute of Planners*, Vol. 40, No. 1 (January 1974), pp. 2-16; and Martin H. Krieger, "Some New Directions for Planning Theories," *Journal of the American Institute of Planners*, Vol. 40, No. 3 (May 1974), pp. 156-163.
6. Jerome L. Kaufman, "Contemporary Planning Practice: State of the Art," in David R. Godschalk (ed.), *Planning in America: Learning from Turbulence* (Washington, D.C.: The American Institute of Planners, 1974), pp. 111-137.
7. Linda L. Corby, "What Kind of Planner Reads Planning," *Planning*, Vol. 40, No. 5 (June 1974), pp. 20-22; and *AIP News*, Vol. II, No. 6 (October 1976) p. 5.
8. Kaufman.
9. Michael P. Brooks (ed.), *Guide to Graduate Education in Urban and Regional Planning* (Chicago: American Society of Planning Officials, 1976), 1976 edition.
10. David R. Godschalk, "Learning From Turbulence," in Godschalk, p. 4.
11. Lawrence E. Susskind, "The Future of the Planning Profession," in Godschalk, pp. 138-160, esp. p. 158.
12. William C. Baer, Lionel Hodge, and Gail M. Lewis, *A Survey of Departments of Community Development in California*, School of Urban and Regional Planning, University of Southern California, June 1976, mimeo, 18 pp.
13. Kaufman, p. 114, reports that AIP membership and multi-county planning agencies increased tenfold from 1953-54 to 1973-74, although much of this increase was due to federal support for planning. In contrast, Sunley states that the increase in local and state spending overall between 1955 to 1974 was only sixfold. Emil M. Sunley, Jr., "State and Local Governments," in Henry Owen and Charles L. Schultze (eds.), *Setting National Priorities* (Washington, D.C.: The Brookings Institution, 1976), pp. 371-409.
14. Michigan and New Jersey both now license planners.
15. Full members of the American Institute of Planners may use the professional designation AIP after their names, and over the years the AIP has applied increasingly stringent tests for full membership

(although the examination is not yet equivalent in rigor to the typical licensing examinations for more traditional professions).
16. Brian McLoughlin, "The Future of the Planning Profession," in Peter Cowan (ed.), *The Future of Planning* (Beverly Hills, Calif.: Sage Publications, 1973), pp. 69-72.
17. Anthony J. Catanese, "Planners Need Seal of Approval," *Practicing Planner*, Vol. 6, No. 4 (September 1976), pp. 8-10.
18. The choice is between the American Institute of Planners, as the accrediting body, or selecting: (1) a national, voluntary, non-profit, non-governmental Council on Post-Secondary Accreditation (COPA); (2) the Commissioner of Education, Office of Education, U.S. Department of Health, Education, and Welfare; or (3) the Association of Collegiate Schools of Planning.
19. Alan Altshuler, *The City Planning Process* (Ithaca, N.Y.: Cornell University Press, 1965).
20. Francine F. Rabinovitz, *City Politics and Planning* (New York: Atherton Press, 1969).
21. Martin L. Needleman and Carolyn Needleman, *Guerrillas in Bureaucracy* (New York: John Wiley & Sons, 1974).
22. Webster's defines maieutics as follows: "of or relating to the dialectic method practiced by Socrates in order to elicit and clarify the ideas of others."
23. John W. Dyckman, "Three Crises of American Planning," paper prepared for the Conference on "Planning: Challenge and Response," Center for Urban Policy Research, Rutgers University, September 8-9, 1976.
24. See Donald A. Schon, Nancy Sheldon Cramer, Paul Osterman, and Charles Perry, "Planners in Transition: A Report of a Survey of Alumni of M.I.T.'s Department of Urban Studies, 1960-71," *Journal of the American Institute of Planners*, Vol. 42, No. 2 (April 1976), pp. 193-202; and Edward M. Bergman, George C. Hemmens, Susan A. Lieberman, and Robert M. Moroney, *The Practitioners Viewpoint: An Exploration of Social Policy Planning Practice and Education*, Part 2: The Findings (Chapel Hill: Department of City and Regional Planning, University of North Carolina, March 1976).

Further Reading

The best single source for further reading is David R. Godschalk (ed.), *Planning in America: Learning From Turbulence* (Washington, D.C.: The American Institute of Planners, 1974), and an earlier equivalent: Ernest Erber (ed.), *Urban Planning in Transition* (New York: Grossman Publishers, 1970). The Schon et al. article (see footnote 24) provides an excellent description and analysis of the job skills used by planners; the book by Scott (see footnote 4) provides a complete (but not analytic) history of the profession; those thinking of pursuing a graduate degree in planning should review the program and curriculum descriptions found in Brooks (see footnote 9).

THE PROFESSIONALIZATION OF POLICE: EFFORTS AND OBSTACLES

Richard A. Staufenberger, *Police Foundation*

During the past 40 years there have been many efforts directed toward defining an agenda for police improvement. These include the Wickersham Commission (1931), President's Commission on Law Enforcement and Administration of Justice (1967), and the National Advisory Commission on Standards and Goals for the Police (1973). For the most part, these reports, rather than meeting a classical definition of professionalism, deal with upgrading the American police in operational terms. Indeed the answer to the question of how well the American police conform to the traditional criteria of a profession seems much less relevant, and much more difficult to answer with specificity, than detailing the efforts and obstacles in recent years in the drive to upgrade the police.

Consequently, for the most part, this article will be concerned with selected indicators of police improvement. Nevertheless, many of the indicators reviewed have a close relationship to the traditional criteria of a profession.

Selected Indicators of Police Improvement

Policing in America encompasses approximately 500,000 persons scattered throughout some

---

Richard A. Staufenberger has been an assistant director of the Police Foundation since 1973. He holds a doctorate in political science from the University of Maryland and is co-editor of the text *Police Personnel Administration*. Mr. Staufenberger has taught at the University of Maryland, Howard University, and the University of Nebraska. He has also been associate director of the National Civil Service League; assistant to the dean, College of Business and Public Administration, University of Maryland; and assistant registrar of the University of Maryland.

17,500 public agencies. Many of these agencies are relatively large (for example, the New York City police department has nearly 30,000 members); yet, the median department in cities of more than 10,000 people has only 39 members.[1]

In fact, of the 17,500 departments, 280 account for more than 60 per cent of the total law enforcement personnel. Observers suggest that the dispersal and relatively small size of most police agencies affect such things as salaries, training, career development, and, consequently, professionalism. Whether this is a fair observation, or whether these observers are confusing organization efficiency with professionalism, is debatable. However, the wide variations in policing throughout thousands of departments make it difficult to give an account of the state of the art of policing.

For every generalization about some aspect of the occupation, one does not have to look far to find an exception. This is so, even supposing that the following observations are based on valid generalizations rather than on anomalous situations. With that caveat, what follows is an overview of three general characteristics of American policing that are indicators of both increasing professionalism and police improvement; no area presents a totally positive picture. The list is not intended to be all inclusive; it is selective.

Organizational Arrangements

In the view of a number of police scholars, nothing serves to stymie professionalization more than the highly organized military rank structure that is an essential feature of most police agencies. The rank structure affects virtually every aspect of policing, including some aspects important to professionalism. The structure: (1) admits few civilians to policy-making positions in police agencies; (2) discourages lateral entry into the departments; and (3) severely restricts discretion and initiative in the basic police officer.

Unfortunately, while progress on other fronts gives cause for optimism, progress in altering the rank structure has been minimal. Even though a number of departments report that lateral entry is a possibility below the rank of chief, in practice such lateral transfers are extremely rare; in contrast, the British system of policing places a premium on mobility as a key ingredient in leadership development. Further, the lack of pension portability, the relatively few promotional opportunities afforded by the rank structure, and a general resistance to change have combined to cause the police to resist attempts to promote lateral entry.

Also, the rank structure provides little recognition for the importance of the role of the basic police officer. The President's Crime Commission suggested a decade ago that police departments consider a three-tiered system of police officers.[2] Such a system would be designed to provide recognition to the basic police officer function, a system of career advancement within that basic function, and lateral entry. As of 1977 such a system has not been adopted in most police agencies. It is not unusual for a basic police officer to reach maximum salary within a few years of joining a department. The choice then becomes remaining in a dead-end position or competing for the relatively few available first-level supervisory positions, usually at the rank of sergeant. Interestingly, the military, from which the police borrowed its basic structure, introduced a system of job specialization that provided for more career choices 20 years before it was considered by the police.[3]

Community Orientation

Though progress on changing the rank structure has been minimal, a trend in one aspect of the police organization has been significant. Not very long ago it was common to define a professional police department in terms of highly centralized control, strict discipline, and stringent selection procedures. Such departments often were found on the West Coast, and the Los Angeles Police Department was usually cited as a model.[4] The attribute of such a police system that gave it strength, highly centralized control, also became its greatest liability in some respects. Fostered by visions of efficiency, the centralized control with its mobile, motorized department produced patrol officers who were stripped of some discretion and who were faceless to the community. With the urban riots of the 1960s many police leaders reached the conclusion that efficiency had been achieved at the expense of effectiveness. Initial attempts to reestablish community ties were aimed almost solely at the minority community and often involved additions to the existing organizational structure. Community relations offices and store front police offices were not uncommon.

By the early 1970s, however, significant numbers of police agencies began to introduce more radical organizational changes which placed greater discretion in the hands of the patrol officer, in order to reestablish the police-community relationship. Under the name of team policing, the basic car plan and community-oriented policing themes have emerged. These include making officers responsible for a particular section of the jurisdiction rather than being mobile throughout the complete territory.

Another theme is the decentralization of control over many of the basic police functions. In Cincinnati, for example, there are five districts, each with three sector teams, each team acting to some extent like a mini-police department. This organization expands the role of police officers, often to include more responsibility for investigations, and reduces the need for centralized specialist units. Some departments have even reinstituted foot patrols as a crime control method which also brings the police in close contact with community problems.

The upgrading of the role of the basic police officer, the attempt to increase police discretion, and the goal of establishing closer community ties all should affect police professionalization.

Professional Organizations

There are a number of professional organizations that claim to speak for some segment of policing. However, it should be stressed again that none of these organizations has the same role within the occupation as the American Bar Association or American Medical Association have in their professions. The police do not have a national association that enforces or even attempts to establish national standards.

Of the organizations prominent on the national scene, clearly the best known and most prestigious is the International Association of Chiefs of Police (IACP). Founded in 1893, the IACP has a staff of about 100 people and a membership of approximately 10,500. As its name indicates, the organization is primarily an association of chiefs of police or heads of law enforcement agencies. Thus, the IACP is not an association representative of the basic police officer. This raises the immediate question of who in policing most closely meets the criteria of a profession. Students of professionalism argue convincingly that policing is a hierarchically organized occupation in which the professional skills are held by the people at the lowest level.[5] If that is accepted, the role of the IACP as a professional police association is somewhat in doubt.

In response to the need for a professional association to represent police officers, the American Academy for Professional Law Enforcement (AAPLE) was created in 1974. The new national organization, which resulted from the merger of two local organizations, was established to serve the needs of the college-educated police officer. It has a current membership of 1,400 and is growing at the rate of 10 per cent each year. Because it has been in existence only three years, it is much too early to determine the effect of AAPLE on police professionalism. It clearly does not possess the prestige of the IACP, but it does have a much broader base from which to draw its membership. It may be worthwhile to note that much of the early work of the organization centered on the development of ethical standards in a much more specific form than the IACP's code of conduct.

Although it is not a professional membership organization, there is little doubt that the FBI, as a national institution, has played an important part in the efforts to upgrade the police. For many years, under the leadership of J. Edgar Hoover, the FBI was criticized by many local police leaders who felt that, at best, it did little for the cause of upgrading the police and, at worst, actually set up obstacles to local police improvement. The climate has dramatically improved under Clarence Kelley. There is a new feeling of cooperation between the FBI and local police agencies. One manifestation of this cooperation is the increased training and educational opportunities provided to local police by the FBI through its National Academy.

Labor Organizations

While certainly the so-called professional associations have, and will continue to have, a profound effect on the movement toward police professionalism, a convincing argument can be made that their effect will be completely overshadowed by the burgeoning police union movement. This movement is still in its infancy, but its growth and impact are being felt on all aspects of police policy. Ten years ago there was no mention of police unions in the index of the President's Crime Commission report on the police. Now it is hard to find a police executive who would not put police unions high on the list of issues confronting American policing. Five years ago most police chiefs refused to recognize police unions formally.

Today it is difficult to find a chief who does not realize that the unions must be recognized and that they must be reckoned with in any major decision.

The rapid growth of the police union movement and its fragmentation are its two prime characteristics. In 1972 one national association, the International Conference of Police Associations (ICPA), reported about 150,000 members; by 1977 it claimed more than 200,000. The growth rates of some of the smaller unions have been even more impressive. The growth and potential membership of unions has caused a good deal of action at the national level. Organizations representing the police range from the traditional, such as the Fraternal Order of Police, the ICPA, and the International Brotherhood of Police Officers, to the American Federation of State, County and Municipal Employees, and the Teamsters. Competiton for membership, as in other public sector union movements, has tended to push the entire movement toward more militant stands.

With some confidence it can be said that the union movement will have a significant effect on upgrading the police. Whether that effect will be negative or positive is much more difficult to predict. One local police union may support a change, while another local will go to court to fight a similar change. On such issues as peer review of a police officer's actions, freedom from external review, and higher salaries, the union response is fairly predictable.[6] Somewhat less predictable is the union stance on lateral entry, or higher education as a requirement for entry and promotion. Some evidence exists, however, that union opposition can be expected, at least in respect to the former.[7]

Research

Writing in 1973, one police scholar made the observation "that during the previous decade the American police had received more research attention than during the previous 150 years of their existence."[8] Spurred by massive outlays of federal money, the pace has accelerated since 1973. Currently it is difficult to cite an aspect of policing that has not received some attention from the researchers. Research at some level has been directed toward: (1) police equipment, such as vests, shoes, computers, and automobiles; (2) personnel issues, such as selection tests, the effectiveness of women on patrol, and whether tall persons are more effective than shorter persons; (3) police tactics, such as preventive patrol, field interrogation, and response time; (4) productivity, such as the value of separating service-related functions from crime control functions, the relative effectiveness of one and two-person patrol units, and computer-aided patrol allocation; and (5) organizational issues, such as decentralization and specialization.[9]

For all of the criticisms directed toward the Law Enforcement Assistance Administration (LEAA), brought on probably in large part by the naive and inflammatory rhetoric of its sponsors that it would greatly reduce crime, the massive outlays of money (averaging approximately $800 million per year for the past five years) are the most direct cause for much of the research activity. Some of the LEAA money was earmarked specifically for research; critics contend it was too little and often addressed the wrong issues. In addition to the direct research support, the availability of large sums of money has drawn into the field great numbers of social scientists who have displayed a keen instinct for tailoring their research to the federal priorities. For example, organizations that had previously done work for the military, in the private sector, or in the "war on poverty," were quick to redirect their interests when criminal justice improvement funds became available. On the positive side then, much more is known about American policing than was known a decade ago. There have, however, been a number of basic problems with this research activity.

There exists, for example, the problem of codifying, recording, and coordinating the research. Only a very small portion of the research finds its way into the literature.[10] A related problem has been the pressure at the federal level to spend rather than to undertake systematic research. As a result, little energy has been devoted to such exercises as determining what overall police questions need answers, what questions or parts of questions there are currently answers for, and what questions remain. During the past six years efforts have been heavily directed toward changing the means of policing with little thought given to the desirable ends.

Another research dilemma is related to the somewhat insular characteristic of policing. Much, if not most, of the police research has not been formulated and conducted by the police themselves, but by outsiders. The police as an occupation and local police agencies have not seriously attempted to construct an internal program of research and study.[11] One logical explanation for this is that even given the rising educational level of most police, there still does not exist within the policing a sufficient level of research and methodological skills.

Given the lack of appropriate proprietorship for the research and the suspicion with which the police have often viewed academics, a substantial number of the police lack confidence in and consequently repudiate research results. In a speech last year, for example, the president of the IACP stated, "Quite frankly, I am concerned about reliability of much of the trash that comes to us in the name of research." He also denounced the "so-called law enforcement experts" who have undertaken "unscientific" work and cautioned against "uncritically accepting research findings made by aircraft and washing machine manufacturers."[12]

While most responsible researchers agree that the police must participate in defining research needs and also agree that much of the research conducted has been of sub-standard quality, they attribute the negative reactions more directly to the research results. Police research is still in its primitive stage and, as a consequence, it often has the effect of challenging the wisdom and effectiveness of police practices that have been in operation for years. As would be true with any occupation, for the police to accept research findings that directly challenge their conventional wisdom has been difficult. Finally, police geographic dispersal and the accompanying variety of police styles have sometimes caused police executives to question the relevance of research conducted in one city to their particular jurisdiction.

Some indicators are cause for optimism in the research area. Organizations that underwrite research are beginning to recognize the need for developing a systematic research agenda and to determine the interrelationships of research findings to date. A group of police executives, 39 at the latest count, recently formed the Police Executive Research Forum. The purposes of the Forum include research, experimentation, and an open exchange of ideas for the development of a professional body of knowledge. To some extent the Forum was a reaction to the negative attitude to research in parts of the police community. Its founders clearly believe research is an essential step in upgrading the police community and are therefore determined to assume a leadership role in supporting research.

As more and more police get advanced degrees and as the academic community concerned with criminal justice administration begins to stabilize, the potential for police-initiated research is increased. The Law Enforcement Education Program has, for example, supported criminal justice professors who have themselves undertaken research and has provided police officers with understanding of and interest in research.

Education

Even if there have been difficulties establishing a systematic body of knowledge for policing, virtually all of the studies about improving the police call for the upgrading of personnel through better education, training, and selection procedures. During the past five years, for the most part in response to equal employment legislation and litigation, police selection procedures have been the subject of much review and some change. In the same period the eligible pool from which the police select has also changed. Blacks, Chicanos, and women are now more prominent in most urban police departments. The most dramatic example of a change in police selection procedures has involved women. Before 1970 it was relatively rare in this country to observe women officers on patrol. Now major departments that do not have women on patrol are relatively uncommon, as well as risking potential litigation.

Perhaps, however, in recognition of the fact that personnel selection is much more an art than a science, the reformers concerned with upgrading police personnel have emphasized education. As long ago as 1931, the Wickersham Commission called for the police to use more highly educated personnel.[13] In 1967 the President's Crime Commission expressed the belief that police services could not be improved without higher educational requirements, and thus the Commission called for police officers to have two- and four-year degrees.[14] More recently, the National Advisory Commission on Criminal Justice Standards and Goals recommended a phased-in educational requirement so that by 1982 all police officers will be required to have a four-year degree.[15]

Given the almost total agreement in the police upgrading literature, combined with the importance of higher education in order for an occupation to become a profession, it is interesting to note the trends.[16] One obvious question to be asked is, how far have the police come in requiring a college degree as a prerequisite for entry into the occupation? In 1967 the Crime Commission reported that one agency, Multnomah County, Oregon, required a four-year degree for its police officers. In 1976 a survey by the International City Management Association showed that of 1,574 jurisdictions responding, only two required a college degree of their police officers.[17]

The figure must be disheartening to the people who use it as an indicator of progress along the road to professionalism and upgrading. In fact, there are some indicators that the police actually have lost ground in this one area since 1972.[18] The reasons for the lack of progress are many. One is the difficulty in changing local civil service requirements, an argument of particular significance, considering equal employment legislation and litigation since 1972. Virtually any requirement for entry has been the subject of some litigation. Given the success rate of such challenges, local personnel administrators are wary of adding new selection requirements that would further restrict the eligible pool, particularly requirements whose statistical relationships to actual performance are difficult to establish.

Some police administrators themselves have been reluctant to push for additional entry requirements. This reticence could result from a belief that, given the current role of police officers, it is unwise and unnecessary to recruit overqualified personnel. Such administrators argue that because policing includes so many mundane tasks, increasing the educational level of officers will only lead to frustration, lower morale, and higher turnover.[19]

Unions have also received some criticism for their general reluctance to embrace plans that alter selection and promotion procedures, although the picture here is somewhat mixed.

In dramatic contrast to the formal educational requirement as a license to practice is the rising educational level of the police. There are more police entering the service with a degree, and thousands of officers pursuing and receiving degrees during their employment. For example, in 1968 the Dallas Police Department had 11 officers with a college degree. A report in 1975 indicated that 625 officers now hold a bachelor's degree, 21 have master's degrees, and an additional 450 are pursuing degrees of higher education.[20] Another example of this trend is found in data compiled by the Florida Police Standards and Training Commission. In 1968, it was reported that six per cent of the local police officers had some college training. By 1975, 23 per cent of the officers held a two- or four-year degree. Indeed, the Commission reported 44 police officers with doctorates.[21] Although no claim is made that these figures represent an exact sample of officers nationwide, they are probably indicative of a national trend.

The largest share of the credit for the trend is generally given to the Law Enforcement Assistance Administration. Even though the LEAA has been the subject of much criticism regarding its overall spending policies, there seems little doubt of the significance of its impact on higher education for police officers. Under the Law Enforcement Education Program (LEEP) the agency has appropriated more than $220 million for tuition subsidies for criminal justice personnel since 1969. The program is currently funded at roughtly $40 million annually. In 1974 alone it was estimated that 64,000 police officers attended college under the program.

A related development in the area of higher education for police officers has been the increase in the number of police agencies which, while not requiring a degree for entry, have offered some type of incentive for the officers to pursue degrees. In 1970 responses to one survey indicated that 22.7 per cent of the responding police departments provided higher entry salaries for applicants who have education beyond high school, and 54.9 per cent reported educational incentives generally.[22]

Coupled with the large number of police officers seeking and holding degrees has been an astonishing increase in the number of college and university programs devoted to the study of criminal justice and police administration. In 1966-67, before the LEEP program, it was reported that the number of colleges offering police-related programs was 184.[23] By 1974 a report of schools participating in the LEEP program put the number at 1,030.[24] Much of the growth of these programs can be attributed to the demand for courses caused by the recipients of LEEP money. However, it is also probably true that once these departments are established, because most have to be self-sufficient, they encourage additional police officers to enroll in the program.

The growth of both numbers of police in higher education and institutions with criminal justice and police curricula has not been without problems. Included in questions currently being asked regarding higher education for police officers is one about its quality. Critics have charged that the educational level of faculty in these programs is below that of the traditional disciplines, that most programs lack a strong research component, and that too many of the courses are overly technical in nature, tending to duplicate what officers should be learning in the training academy.

The Academy of Criminal Justice Sciences, the organization for the teachers in the criminal justice field, with about 790 members, has recognized some of the issues and has begun to take steps to insure the quality of the programs. ACJS is now in the process of seeking accreditation authority from the national Council on Post-Secondary Accreditation, a step that, if approved, will bring criminal justice education, in a formal sense, closer to the education of the traditional professions.

Another response to the issue was the creation by the Police Foundation in June 1976 of an independent commission, the National Advisory Commission on Higher Education for Police Officers, to look into the myriad issues surrounding higher education for police officers. The Commission is currently in the process of sorting through the various issues, and it anticipates releasing a series of reports beginning in late 1977.

Paralleling the progress in higher education has been a tightening of police standards in training. Ten years ago it was not unusual for training standards to vary markedly among jurisdictions. In fact, it was not uncommon to find agencies that required little, if any, formal training. Now most states have begun to establish some training standards for their local police. In 1959 California established a Commission on Peace Officer Standards and Training. Currently, 45 states have followed California's lead and have created similar training councils. The average number of hours of training a police officer is required to have by the state training councils is 300. However, many states suggest or require more, while some obviously settle for less. About two-thirds of the state training councils have standards on selection, as well as training; at least two, Florida and Michigan, have initiated a pre-service training requirement for certification as a police officers. A national organization, the National Association of State Directors of Law Enforcement Training, was created in 1970 to coordinate the work of the councils and to continue the push for more rigid training and selection standards.

Unfortunately, most of the upgrading activity in training has been at the entry level. Few departments have made a concerted effort to provide in-service training to their personnel. Most departments seem to assume that whatever an officer cannot learn on the street is probably not worthwhile and that the skills that make a good street officer will also make a good supervisor. Thus, many police officers move into supervisory and executive positions with an apparent lack of skills to perform those jobs.

Part of the problem is undoubtedly resources. It is difficult for any single department, given the median size, to launch a quality program of executive training. At times various observers have called for an American national police college modeled after the National Police College in Great Britain at Bramshill, established in 1948. The closest parallel in this country to Bramshill is the FBI National Academy at Quantico, an impressive physical structure which lacks many of the essential ingredients that have made Bramshill an international model for police leadership development.

Conclusion

The progress the police have made during the past decade has to be encouraging even to the most severe critics. Selection procedures are more job related, training and conduct standards have been tightened, and higher education for police officers is much more the rule than the exception. Research on a scale never before seen is currently being conducted on almost every aspect of policing. Within the last several years at least two new professional organizations have been established for the purpose of upgrading the police.

Nevertheless, negative attributes such as closed promotional systems, the lack of mobility among officers, limited career opportunities, and an unhealthy pessimism regarding research and change all continue to plague those concerned with upgrading the police. Police unions, currently a mixed blessing in terms of police improvement, will assuredly play an increasingly important role.

On balance, taking into consideration the progress of the past several years, one has to be cautiously optimistic regarding the future of American policing.

Notes

1. International City Management Association, *Urban Data Service Report: Personnel Practices in the Municipal Police Departments: 1976* (Washington, D.C.: ICMA, December 1976), p. 1.
2. President's Commission on Law Enforcement and Administration of Justice, *The Challenge of Crime in a Free Society:* (Washington, D.C.: U.S. Government Printing Office, 1967), p. 108.
3. Carl F. Lutz and James P. Morgan, "Jobs and Rank," in O. Glenn Stahl and Richard A. Staufenberger (eds.), *Police Personnel Administration* (North Scituate, Mass.: Duxbury Press, 1974), p. 23.
4. For a full discussion, see James Q. Wilson, *Varieties of Police Behavior* (Cambridge, Mass.: Harvard University Press, 1968); and Harold F. Wilde, "The Process of Change in a Police Bureaucracy," Ph.D. dissertation, Harvard University, 1972, pp. 17-49.
5. George L. Kelling and Robert B. Kliesmet, "Resistance of the Professionalization of the Police," *The Police Chief,* Vol. XXXVIII, No. 5 (May 1971), pp. 30-39; and Maureen Cain, "Police Professionalism: Its Meaning and Consequences," *Anglo-American Law Review,* Vol. I, No. 2 (April 1, 1972), p. 217.
6. Salaries, incidentally, have moved along well in the past four years; in the period January 1971 to January 1975 entry salaries increased 30 per cent from $7,400 to $9,559. See International City Management Association, *Municipal Yearbook* (Washington, D.C.: ICMA, 1976), p. 101. Given the municipal budget squeeze, something not mentioned in this article but which will undoubtedly affect police upgrading, most observers are not optimistic regarding future increases.
7. Hervey A. Juris and Peter Feuille, *Police Unionism: Power and Impact in Police Sector Bargaining* (Lexington, Mass.: D.C. Heath & Co., 1973), pp. 103-118.
8. Egon Bittner, "Remarks," *The Police Year Book 1973* (Gaithersburg, Md.: International Association of Chiefs of Police, 1973), p. 116.
9. Agencies supporting the research cited include the Law Enforcement Assistance Administration, the Police Foundation, the National Science Foundation, and the National Institutes of Mental Health.
10. Of ten journals found dealing with police and criminal justice issues examined for this article, four have been started during the past six years.
11. Bittner, p. 118.
12. Richard C. Clement, president of the International Association of Chiefs of Police, "Upgrading Leadership," speech at the Police Foundation Executive Forum on Upgrading the Police, April 12-14, 1976.
13. National Commission on Law Observance and Enforcement, "Report on the Police" (Washington, D.C.: U.S. Government Printing Office, 1931), p. 56.
14. President's Commission on Law Enforcement and Administration of Justice.
15. National Advisory Commission on Criminal Justice Standards and Goals, 'Police" (Washington, D.C.: U.S. Government Printing Office, 1973), p. 369.
16. It is interesting to note that those persons advancing the idea of a college education for the police officer do so with little hard evidence to indicate that higher educated officers perform better. Given the current push, the federal government requiring the validation of all selection requirements, coupled with the massive outlays of federal money for education of police officers, it would seem that a scientific study comparing education to performance is a necessity.
17. International City Management Association, p. 4.
18. Terry Eisenberg, Deborah Ann Kent, and Charles R. Wall, *Police Personnel Practices in State and Local Governments* (Washington, D.C.: International Association of Chiefs of Police and the Police Foundation, 1976), p. 19.
19. Jerry V. Wilson, *Police Report: A View of Law Enforcement* (Boston, Mass.: Little, Brown, & Company, 1975), p. 175.
20. Dallas Police Department, "Pros – in the Fullest Sense," *The Dallas Police News,* Vol. XXI, No. 23 (November 7, 1975), p. 1.
21. Larry Sherman and Richard Staufenberger, "Higher Education for Police Officers: An Overview" (Washington, D.C.: an unpublished paper for the Police Foundation, 1976), pp. 5-6.
22. International City Management Association, pp. 5, 11.
23. Richard W. Kobetz, *Law Enforcement and Criminal Justice Education Directory,* 1975-1976 (Gaithersburg, Md.: International Association of Chiefs of Police, 1976), p. 3.
24. Comptroller General of the United States, *Report to the Congress, Problems in Administering Programs to Improve Law Enforcement Education* (Washington, D.C.: General Accounting Office, June 11, 1975), p. 2.

PART II

Introduction

This is the second of two symposia dealing with different professions in government. The first, which was published in the November/December 1977 issue of PAR concerned professions employed exclusively or primarily by government agencies: military, foreign service, educational administration, city management, city planning, and police. The essays which follow deal with professions employed in both the public and private sectors, including law, economics, accounting, engineering, sciences, and mental health. This symposium is closed by a general essay on "Professions in Public Service" by one of the editors, Frederick C. Mosher.

We deeply regret that the author of one of these articles, Ellsworth H. Morse, Jr., died suddenly on November 29, 1977. Mr. Morse was assistant comptroller general of the United States and had been a distinguished professional leader of the General Accounting Office for 31 years. His article on the accounting profession for this symposium had been submitted and accepted well before his untimely death and is here included intact.

Frederick C. Mosher, *University of Virginia*
and U.S. General Accounting Office
and Richard J. Stillman II,
California State College, Bakersfield

Lawyers in Government—
"The Most Serviceable Instruments of Authority"

Laurin A. Wollan, Jr., *Florida State University*

. . . a monarch will always be able to convert legal practitioners into the most serviceable instruments of his authority. There is a far greater affinity between this class of persons and the executive power than there is between them and the people. . . . (Alexis de Toqueville)

Lawyers in government are part of an established but troubled profession. It troubles are, for the most part, centered about those points that have made it a profession, and suggest a decline, or "deprofessionalization," the implications of which may interest the emerging as well as the established professions. The influence of lawyers in government, however, is likely to remain high, and might even increase, despite the call for "delawyering." But the nature, extent, and effect of that influence pose interesting and perhaps important questions, three of which will be addressed here: the limitations for policy-making of the phenomenon of "thinking like a lawyer," the importance in public administration of the ethical dimension of legal practice, and the implications of all of the foregoing for

---

This article was written with assistance from the staff of the American Bar Foundation on some statistical aspects and from numerous friends and acquaintances who provided insights into lawyers and their profession. The views herein, unless otherwise indicated, are the writer's and not necessarily representative of any persons, government agencies, or bar associations with which he has been associated. Peter J. Fannon, Elaine R. Johansen, Ann Marie Karl, Winsor Schmidt, and George Waas provided valuable comments on ' manuscript.

Laurin A. Wollan, Jr., is associate professor in the School of Criminology at Florida State University. He has J.D. (Chicago) and M.A.P.A. (Illinois) degrees and membership in the Illinois Bar. He has worked for governments at federal, state, county, and municipal levels in both the executive and legislative branches, and has been active in county, state and American Bar Associations. Recently he was an attorney-adviser in the Office of Policy and Planning of the United States Department of Justice.

legal education and the passage of the young lawyer into the bureaucracy.

The Number of Lawyers

There are estimated to be some 445,000 lawyers in the United States today. The most recent compilation of figures, the *1971 Lawyers Statistical Report,* shows for 1970 a total of 355,242. Thus, the number of lawyers per capita is increasing, especially the number of young lawyers, for there is now more than one law student for every four lawyers in the country, promising a total of some 600,000 lawyers by 1985—with only 500,000 jobs for them in the field of law.[1]

The number of lawyers in government has gone from 27,381 (or 13.4 per cent of all lawyers) in 1951 to 46,152 (or 14.3 per cent of all lawyers) in 1970, 1,498 of whom were women. By comparison with the increasing proportion of lawyers in government, the percentage—although not the number—of lawyers in private practice has declined, going from 176,995 (86.8 per cent) in 1951 to 236,085 (72.7 per cent) in 1970.[2]

The Influence of Lawyers

It is remarkable that there are so few lawyers in government, relative to the influence they are thought to have. According to the Civil Service Commission, right now there are but 3,357 "general attorneys" in the Department of Justice itself, a mere tenth of its personnel. The Commission's *Federal Career Directory* reports that there are 10,000 lawyers in the federal service in the executive branch, 150,000 engineers, 20,000 accountants and auditors, 10,000 physicians, 8,000 chemists and 6,000 physicists (suggesting that the aggregate of scientists is considerably higher), 4,800 foresters, 3,500 librarians and as many mathematicians, 2,000 psychologists and as many statisticians, and 1,500 architects, to name a few.[3] The engineers, accountants, doctors, and scientists, whose numbers equal or exceed those of lawyers, appear to have less influence than lawyers. Such assertions, however, must be qualified because measures of the influence of lawyers are elusive, largely intuitive, mainly anecdotal, and badly in need of scholarly attention.[4] But on such bases (*e.g.,* grousing about who has the "last word"), one can say that lawyers are the most influential of the professions—although a very good case can be made at the "macro" level of influence for the 4,000 economists. In few agencies does the architect or accountant, for instance, have the last word on many matters.

One institutional factor indicates the probable influence of lawyers: they are unique among the professionals in government because of their official presence, as lawyers, in virtually every agency, as a kind of "final filter" for major proposals and transactions. Few agencies have a military attache or a medical officer or a chaplain or environmentalist with that function and the omnipresent budget and information officers do not make much policy, but most agencies have a chief counsel or general counsel. In addition, where agencies do not have full-time lawyers in staff positions, most of them, right down to the mosquito-abatement districts, retain or hire lawyers for service on an occasional basis for major transactions and decisions. Moreover, many agencies with a legal staff, even if sizeable, will do what well-staffed business corporations do for major matters, that is, hire outside counsel, or "borrow" them from other agencies in the case of government, to beef up the total legal capacity of the organization.[5]

The work done by lawyers in government touches the full range of legal matters from abatement, adoption, and antitrust to zoning, with the nature of the work corresponding to practice in the private sector—advising, securing, negotiating, and advocating.[6] And much of it has to do with policy. Esther Lucile Brown, in her book, *Lawyers, Law Schools and the Public Service,* is persuasive in saying that the activities of government lawyers, even those seemingly remote from policy, have an impact on it nonetheless, whether it be through reviewing, interpreting, counseling, drafting, or litigating. "By pressing the right cases in the right order," she says of litigation, "both administratively before itself and afterward in the courts, an agency may establish its authority in obvious matters and lead from them to the less obvious in marking out the limits of its power."[7] The "house counsel" of an agency, like his business counterpart, ordinarily is involved regularly and deeply in policy-making and in much of its implementation. As in many corporations, top managers "drop in" for informal consultation and advice. How far these formal and informal aspects of the legal function influence the substance of policy is not easily discerned—and should be systematically studied, for there is a serious question of whether legal advice can and should be separated from policy advice. But it is safe to say that no other profession penetrates so far into the realm of the other professions. Even the professions clearly dominating their agencies (*e.g.,* foresters in the Forest Service, geologists in the Geological Survey) will share some degree of their policy-making authority with their lawyers. This owes in part to the lack of clear conceptual distinctions between legal and policy aspects of government activity and to the fuzziness of the distinction in practice between legal and policy advice. The deference to lawyers is no doubt due in large part to the combination of the legalistic nature of public administration and the lawyer's expertise in the rules, remedies, and procedures which are the stuff of administration. It is reinforced by the deference shown the agencies by the courts, that is, by the agency-lawyers' "brothers" on the bench. The effect is that a significant portion of policy has come to be the unquestioned prerogative of lawyers. How much innovation has been forsaken is an important but virtually unanswerable question.

The issue of the nature of the influence of lawyers on policy is posed sharply by the effect of the training and experience of government lawyers who lose their formal identity as lawyers in moving from the ranks of lawyers into executive positions. As Brown put it:

Such law-trained administrators and hundreds of others in less exalted posts have been lost to the legal fraternity only by count.

The professional training that they have had and their former experience as attorneys inevitably determine, to no small degree, the efficiency and social outlook that they will bring to the administrative post.[8]

Such lawyers are engaged in policy-making at its highest level, which puts directly the questions of what is distinctive about the thinking of lawyers and what is its impact on the shape and content of policy. But it is well to consider first whether it is likely that there will be more or fewer lawyers in government as time goes on, hence more or less of whatever influence it is that lawyers have on policy.

De-lawyering and Re-Lawyering

President Carter announced early in his administration that the agencies should cut back the number of their lawyers, or "delawyer," as it is now called. The premise is that lawyers, with nothing better to do, as he must have presumed of many of them, will generate superfluous regulations and other mischief. The evidence of this includes the growth of the *Code of Federal Regulations,* which has gone from 54,105 pages in 1970 to 72,200 pages in 1975.[9] And there may be truth in this: by analogy, some of the unnecessary surgery in this country owes to the overabundance of surgeons. But the force of the argument today is not its timeless quality ("let's kill all the lawyers," says Shakespeare's Dick the Butcher in the time of Henry VI, a half-millenium ago), but rather its coincidence with, or inspiration by, the proposals for deregulation of some areas of government activity and aggregation or decentralization of others, proposals which are taken quite seriously in the seats of government.

The implications for government lawyers are not entirely clear, but it is certainly premature to believe that there would be much less work for them under such proposals—at least not in the short run. For instance, taking some of the President's ideas,[10] under an executive order forcing detailed review of proposed regulations, the role of lawyers would seem to be hardly less than it is now. Public identification of regulation-writers, to make them more accountable, would not reduce regulation-writing so much as it would make it more time-consuming as heretofore-anonymous draftsmen would take ever so much more care; hence, without a reduction in the number or length of regulations (which is unlikely, even with the move to simplify "legalese"), there would have to be even more lawyers because the existing number would be less productive. Personal review of regulations at the Cabinet level would mean, in practice, yet another layer of lawyers, these attached personally to secretaries and under-secretaries. Reorganization, merger, retrenchment, and other strategies will, of course, make for much more lawyer-work, at least in transition, and there is nothing a lawyer loves like a corporate reorganization or lengthy liquidation, which is the private-sector analogue of what will happen under such governmental developments. Thus, any precipitous cutback in lawyers will sooner or later have to be made up—and then some, in all likelihood—by "relawyering" the agencies to facilitate such developments.

"Thinking Like a Lawyer"

Whatever it is that lawyers do, they do in a special way—or so we have long believed. Frederick C. Mosher described the phenomenon generally:

Each profession brings to an organization its own particularized view of the world and of the agency's role and mission in it. The perspective and motivation of each professional are shaped at least to some extent by the lens provided him by his professional education, by his prior professional experience, and by his professional colleagues.[11]

This raises interesting questions: do things divide for the economist into micro and macro, for the soldier into advance and retreat (or officers and enlisted men), for the doctor into health and pathology, for the bookkeeper into debits and credits—with half of reality toward the window?

In the case of lawyers, their characteristics have been observed at least since Plato had Socrates saying," . . . the lawyer is always in a hurry; there is the water of the clepsydra [water clock] driving him on. . . ." More recently Edmund Burke said that the study of law "renders men acute, inquisitive, dextrous, prompt in attack, ready in defense, full of resources. . . ." Later de Toqueville noted that those who study law "derive from this occupation certain habits of order, a taste for formalities, and a kind of instinctive regard for the regular connection of ideas. . . ." In our day Russel Baker has said: "The lawyer's nature is to make things more complicated. If you think it's simple, he will show you it's complex. Admit it's complex, and he will smile and show you it's incomprehensible."

The strengths of the legal mind are fairly well known. Judge Henry Friendly put it nicely: "The ability to come into an unfamiliar area, quickly to grasp the essentials, then to organize a solution, and finally to translate all this to others.[12] To get a bit closer to this phenomenon, the writer surveyed non-lawyer acquaintances with experience in or about government and with its lawyers. Some were quite outspoken: a chemist, after years in the bureaucracy, charged that lawyers think they can manage anything but cannot. Less bluntly, an industrial engineer with years of policy-level experience in both business and government said, "Lawyers think first in words and arguments and mainly linearly. If they think in multi-dimensions, they do so one item at a time, rather than in matrix." A sociologist observed a talent for the serial rather than the holistic. It suggests the comment made some years ago by Thomas Reed Powell: "If you think that you can think about a thing inextricably attached to something else without thinking of the thing which it is attached to, then you have a legal mind."[13] If that is indeed a quality of lawyers, it would seem to disable them from thinking effectively in the ecological mode of policy-making today. Personal observation of the policy-making process indicates that lawyers find quite uncongenial the sort of thinking that would array a multiplicity of measures interconnectedly against interrelated aspects of a complex of difficulties.

To a journalist, the essence of "thinking like a lawyer"

was deductive reasoning, by which the lawyer avoids observations that threaten him or his client and emphasizes instead what is supportive, even at the cost of acknowledging reality. Businessmen, by contrast, are more comfortable with the inductive approach and informal relationships secured by a handshake rather than an elaborate contract. Similarly, an economist contrasted unfavorably the lawyer's emphasis on incentives.

Another scientist observed that the lawyer, arguing as he typically does, from constitutions, statutes, and cases, is tradition-bound, so "the key is to find one's way through the maze without causing it to show a tilt." A biologist emphasized the lawyer's detail-mindedness, and a philosopher added to this the lawyer's concern for the interpretation of words, noting that lawyers are often hesitant to take a stand—a circumspection that is both good and bad in policy-making. This, combined with precedent-mindedness, would seem to handicap lawyers especially in the broad, future-oriented thinking which appears in more and more of policy-making today. Personal observation indicates that lawyers have little use for "visionary" thinking of any kind. All of these characteristics of "thinking like a lawyer" may be serious limitations to be overcome somehow by lawyers themselves and by those they serve or at least recognized as limitations.[14]

The Ethical Dimension

Much of the strength and weakness of the lawyer goes back to his fateful first year in law school. That year may be successful in one of its traditional objectives, which Karl Llewellyn stated this way in his classic lectures to law students, *The Bramble Bush*:

> It aims, in the old phrase, to get you to "thinking like a lawyer." The hardest job of the first year is to lop off your common sense, to knock your ethics into temporary anesthesia. Your view of social policy, your sense of justice—to knock these out of you along with woozy thinking, along with ideas all fuzzed along their edges. You are to acquire ability to think precisely, to analyze coldly, to work within a body of materials that is given, to see, and see only, and manipulate, the machinery of the law. It is not easy thus to turn human being into lawyers.[15]

"Neither," he added, "is it safe. For a mere legal machine is a social danger."[15a] Some would say the law schools have succeeded all too well in producing legal machines with deadened ethical sensibilities, capable of dealing superbly with the *how* of something, but not with the *why* or *whether*—especially not in ethical terms.[16] This may reflect the law schools' failure in the second phase of Llewellyn's program: ". . . as rapidly as we may, we shall cut under all attributes of *homo*, though the *sapiens* we shall then duly endeavor to develop and thus regain the *homo*."

If the ethical sensibilities of the lawyer remain dull, it is cause for some concern because the management of governmental organizations, like its corporate counterpart, commonly looks to lawyers, in the absence of governmental or corporate chaplains, for counsel on ethical matters as well as "purely legal" matters. But the former are often subsumed in the latter, so the ethical question becomes implicit and the lawyer's approval is taken to signify moral as well as legal approval. The lawyer, ironically, separates the two, if he recognizes the former, and eschews advice on the ethical matter, giving none in the typical case when he is not asked for it. Thus the "green light" from the lawyer means two different things, something legal to him, but something legal-and-ethical to his client.

There have been proposals recently, calculated to protect government lawyers from corruption from outside (e.g., prohibiting undocumented contacts with outside lawyers or lobbyists, prohibiting employment by regulated industries for a period of time), as if the problem were really external—as some of it is.[17] But there is little to protect the government lawyer from himself, from his ethical insensibility, or to bolster his instincts with principled defenses against corruption.

There would seem to be little need for such internal strength, however, given the legal profession's impressive body of ethical precept, interpretation, and application—formerly its Canons of Professional Ethics, now its Code of Professional Responsibility, and the thousands of decisions elaborating them, including the supplementary material developed by the Federal Bar Association for government lawyers.[18] But all of this eludes most law students and lawyers, as if it were truly esoteric stuff, like Chinese law.[19] Thus, questions of ethics rarely arise in practice, not because they are not there—they are there in profusion—but because they are unperceived: too many lawyers do not recognize an ethical dilemma even when they are on its very horns. One wonders, for instance, how many Illinois lawyers have known of the ethical obligation of a government lawyer to protest or resign when compensated without rendering substantial service.[20]

There has been a renewal of interest in ethics since Watergate. But despite some additional attention in law schools and on bar examinations, nothing has been done to put ethics on the same footing as the instruction, the "bread and butter" courses—torts, contracts, taxation, estates, civil procedure, and the like, that makes technicians of lawyers. It is, of course, not fair to single out lawyers for rebuke, when ethical weakness marks other professions as well, including public administration itself.[21] But lawyers invite rebuke, not so much because they are looked to for moral leadership, but because they hold themselves out, by virtue of their canons or standards, as ethically discriminating, if not virtuous. What would be both fair and constructive would be the determination of the nature, circumstances, and extent of ethical impropriety by lawyers in government.

Implications for Legal Education

Two-thirds of Brown's book deals with implications for legal education; much of this article could, too. Wistful longing for a legal education along the policy-oriented lines proposed by Professors Lasswell and McDougal a generation ago will not do; it is as unrealistic now as it was then, because most of the education of most of the lawyers must be oriented toward private practice, rather than public practice, let alone policy-making.[22] The law schools are training priests, as it were, not bishops. But more can be done so that when "the young men come to Washington," they will be somewhat better prepared for government service, especially in its policy-making aspects, than they were when Frankfurter wrote the article of that title[23] in the 1930's or now—ready, in other words, for the bishopric as well as the parish.

U.S. Supreme Court Justice Felix Frankfurter pointed to the important qualities of young lawyers: "disinterested enthusiasm, freedom from imprisoning dogmatism, capacity for fresh insight, unflagging industry, ardor for difficulties—these are the qualities that in the main youthful years must supply." Young lawyers have those qualities today, although perhaps with more (maybe less) freedom from ideological tilt than Frankfurter observed. Those qualities make young lawyers a great asset to any employer. But Frankfurter went on to claim, "Much of the work of government makes very little demand on that political sense and shrewdness in negotiation which age and experience alone can give. Scientists and lawyers in government work need little of such skill."[24]

That no longer seems to be so, whether because our sense of politics is more acute or politics is more pervasive, for today lawyers and even scientists in government need "political sense and shrewdness" for effective participation in administration and especially in policy-making process. Moreover, the work of lawyers in policy-making demands as well the converse of Frankfurter's pragmatism: today it demands familiarity with the philosophical aspects, the purposes of policies and programs—with much less to go around, certainly with less money to throw at problems, it takes a sharp sense of the *why* of what government does, for a sense of urgency will no longer do (and policy-making, it can be expected, will be more and more pitched, if not resolved, at the level of principles). As a technician, the young lawyer may, quite unknowingly, be handicapped in both the pragmatic and philosophical aspects of government work: as technician he is likely to be wedded to the ways of his profession, on the one hand, and insensitive to their purposes, on the other hand—and in either case unable, or able only with great and unnecessary difficulty, to grapple with purposeful innovation. The young lawyer could be better prepared by law school for both the pragmatic and the philosophical side of the politics of policy and its administration.

Law School Changes

There are some modest steps the law schools can take to ready their students for the policy-making and administrative functions, without going nearly so far as the grand reconceptualization proposed by Lasswell and McDougal. A handful of optional courses along with a few chapters of the casebooks, rather than a few paragraphs, highlighting the policy aspects of law and government would do well. Internships, speakers, "consulting" projects, and so on, would help make the student (and his teachers) more conversant with the workings of the policy-making process in and about government. Jurisprudence and ethics could be made more pointed and perhaps more attractive, particularly in the clinical mode, by aiming them at the governmental responsibilities of the lawyer. A fuller conception of law practice itself, which would take into account its public as well as its private aspects (and many lawyers in private practice have litigating and lobbying responsibilities with public-policy consequences) might broaden coverage of the bar examinations, which in turn would shift somewhat the curriculum of the law schools, especially in the "local" law schools, many of whose alumni make their way into public office and other policy-making positions. Such changes, slight though they are, might not only help prepare lawyers for these activities in government but also offset some of the trends treated in the next section, which may be causing a decline in the profession.[25]

The Prospect of Deprofessionalization

If the law is troubled along its ethical dimension, it is more troubled, although less obviously, along other dimensions that make it a profession. From its high position it would seem that it can only go down—and might well be doing so. If and as it does, since it is a prototype, the emerging professions should note well these difficulties, for they suggest that emergence as a profession holds less promise now than it has seemed to in the past. Specifically, the emerging professions may be slowed in their rise to levels once reached by the established professions, and the heights once gained by the established professions, if no longer held, may therefore be all the further from the reach of the emerging professions. Also, the "professional state" discerned by Mosher may turn out to be, if no less dominated by the professions, dominated as time goes on by groups less "professional" than once seemed likely to emerge, and therefore with diminished potential for those anticipated consequences deriving from professionalism. Moreover, if the authority and independence of lawyers in government have derived from those qualities of the profession generally, then any decline of the profession augurs ill for the members of the profession within the government—and, by implication, likewise for the members of other professions, established as well as emerging.

There is no definition of profession which all would accept. But there are certain elements on which most would agree. In addition to the ethical element, there are at least two others, the *vocational* (in the sense of "calling") and the *learned*, which combine with the ethical to give the profession *authority* over its "turf" and its members, first in admission and then in discipline, and *independence*, not only from community, and especially political intervention, but also in the relationship of professional to client (or patient or parishioner). Along these dimensions, the law is being challenged and appears to be losing some ground as a profession. This, however, is of interest in the field of public administration mainly in its effects rather than its causes; so the causes (the subject of a more intensive study the writer is now beginning) will be sketched in this section with the conclusion given over to speculation on one major consequence.

The ideal professional is "called" to his vocation, undergoes the sacrifice of prolonged education, hangs out his shingle, and holds himself out to the public, as a practitioner, unselfishly in his service to the community rather than to his own or any special interest. The gap between this ideal and the reality seems to be widening rather than narrowing: motivation today is more obviously financial gain rather than service,[26] resistance to *pro bono publico* work increases as enthusiasm for it declines,[27] the posture of non-solicitation of clients (or "business" as lawyers tellingly put it) is bending—some would say stooping—to permit advertising, like any other commercial enterprise. The business aspects of practice suggest a reconception of the profession, as William J. Fuchs pointed out, on the basis of a survey of lawyers themselves: ". . . the law firm of the future will look more and more like a business and less of a profession than it has been."[28] And these things will change the publics's understanding of the profession, with once-unthinkable results like throwing out the fee-schedule as if it were merely a device for price-fixing.

Willingness to represent clients who come along, indifferent (like English barristers) to the nature of their cause, is not the style of many young lawyers, who instead choose clients—lawyers who indeed chose the law itself—to advance causes, whose calling is to cause rather than profession.[29] Public interest practice aims to advance a certain kind of cause—blacks, women, trees—and the law is a mere tool among an arsenal. One wonders, while hoping for the best, if such selective attention to causes does not cost the profession stature gained in seemingly (if perhaps not actually) high-minded, idealistic commitment to "the law." In any event, the public may well come to view such lawyers, like their corporate counterparts, as "hired guns."

There appears to be decline along another dimension, too. A "learned profession" is more than merely trained, more than knowledgeable (although always that), more even than educated, but not necessarily scholarly (although always that for some and sometimes that for all). A "learned profession" has a body of knowledge which must be mostly learned by study, in contrast to the knowledge of the craftsman (*e.g.,* the carpenter) which cannot be much learned by study, despite the ludicrous curriculum of barber colleges, but needs doing instead. The higher aspects of the law have always eluded most students, even in the better law schools, and certainly in the "trade schools." But even with much of the curriculum and most of the concern of the student oriented toward passage of the bar examination, which tests a thoroughly practice-oriented body of knowledge, much of the most important knowledge seems to escape the student.[30]

The urgency of "continuing legal education," which while a credit to the profession and always pursued by some of its members, is an ironic acknowledgement of continuing legal ignorance. Unfortunately, the students in such courses (unless required, as in Minnesota) are the better lawyers to begin with rather than the ones who need it the most.

Underlying the proliferation of malpractice suits against lawyers is, among other things, a degree of incompetence so gross that other lawyers are finally willing to expose it and see it penalized. All of this suggests that the law is something less than a learned profession, even at the lower levels of knowledge, in spite of (and perhaps, paradoxically, because of) the quantitative explosion of knowledge confronting and learned by law students. As the profession devolves toward a trade, it will surely lose the prestige it enjoyed when the public perceived it as a learned profession.

The profession as calling, combined with its ethical and learned aspects, yields two more interrelated qualities, authority and independence, both in turn combining to yield yet another characteristic of a profession, its special privilege. Like other institutions, the legal profession is under attack and losing authority. The independence of lawyers is being eroded, too—by dependence on major clients, by the increasing incidence of employee status, and especially by the prospect of an extra 100,000 lawyers without law-jobs to occupy them. The status of employee, which ordinarily carries greater security than private practice, will be that of more and more lawyers, who will be less and less willing to give it up in a buyer's or client's market. The implications of this are unsettling to lawyers who prize an individual and collective prestige and privilege denied to "hired hands."

The authority and independence of lawyers have yielded a privileged status, which is manifested in protected territory and self-governance. But the territorial monopolies of lawyers are challenged today both horizontally and vertically and on several fronts. Some interests, like realtors, have successfully broken the monopoly in some areas, like the real estate sales contract. Already the Department of Justice's Antitrust Division has intimated that the "statements of principle," or accords between the legal profession and others, will have to go, thus opening up—and not leaving to lawyers and judges—the question of "unauthorized practice of law."[31]

At the same time that vertical lines promise to lop off privileged areas of authority and practice, a horizontal line is cutting through the practice of law, revealing those things a good many lawyers have traditionally done and which all lawyers do to some extent but which can be done by lesser-trained persons, or paraprofessionals.

The Antitrust Division appears to have its aim now on nothing less than the legal profession's privilege of self-definition, as indicated in the Division's view of the statements of principle; its ultimate target may be the profession's control of admission and discipline. Its self-governance is challenged today for the conspicuous failure of the bar to control its errant members. Although bar associations are beginning to attend to this, there is some likelihood that governance will nevertheless pass into public hands; some bar associations themselves have taken the first portentous step in that direction by placing laymen on the disciplinary bodies.[32] Moreover, as the once-voluntary bar associations become "integrated," that is, with all members of the bar belonging to the association, as in over half the states right now, the professions's association itself comes perilously close to the line between quasi-public and public agency.[33]

The Higher Stakes of Deprofessionalization

The legal profession's decline would bring with it somewhat lessened autonomy of lawyers, individually and collectively. If this were all, it would be of little concern except to lawyers. If a parallel decline, with loss of autonomy, occurred in other professions, it would likewise be of little concern except to their members. But there may be more to it than this. As more and more lawyers go into government and business, and as business draws closer into harmony (let alone symbiosis) with government, the affinity of lawyers for executive power that de Toqueville observed in the epigraph above would very likely flourish.

It would be likewise, and no doubt more so, with the professions which are emerging in (and from) that very milieu of bureaucracy. As that occurs, and as the legal profession's station in society sinks slowly, carrying down with it the promise professionalization once held for others, it may weaken in its capacity (and derivatively the capacity of its members) to resist the forces in and around the government of a democracy. The legal profession—and the others—might become an instrument of the state, like the clergy in times past, at grievous cost to itself and to its members in terms of freedom—but not just theirs: the community's and its citizens' as well. The professions, and the legal profession in particular, might be, as at least one lawyer likes to think they have been, a bastion of countervailing independence and authority in the mosaic of pluralistic powers that is the foundation of free government. But this only raises more questions: to what extent, if any, has free government in America (or elsewhere) been a function of plural and countervailing powers? of the professions? of their independence and authority? of the legal profession? of its independence and authority? of the professions' special privileges? of their self-governance in particular? Each profession, established and emerging alike, but especially the legal profession, has an interest in these questions and their answers—in the "higher stakes" of professionalization.

Notes

1. Tom Goldstein, *The New York Times,* May 17, 1977, p. 1, reporting figures from the Bureau of Labor Statistics, in a three-part series, May 16, 17, and 18, 1977. It may, however, be less grim: the forecast of jobs available has been increased by the Bureau of Labor Statistics, according to John Woytash, "Too Many Lawyers," *American Bar Association Journal* (January, 1977), p. 12.
2. Additional figures from the *1971 Lawyers Statistical Report,* published by the American Bar Foundation, are as follows: In 1970 there was a total of 355,242 lawyers. The ratio of population to lawyers was declining then, from 696:1 in 1951 to 572:1 in 1970, indicating more lawyers per capita. The percentage change for the general population declined steadily from 5.3 percent in 1951 to 3.2 percent in 1970. Meanwhile the change for lawyers, after holding even at about 9.0 percent until 1960 and dropping to 3.4 percent in 1963, jumped to 7.0 percent in 1966 and 12.1 percent in 1970. This percentage has presumably climbed even higher, and the ratio of population-to-lawyers declined accordingly, because of the influx of young lawyers since 1970, increasing the number of lawyers by 110,000 in the last seven years, while population has increased much more slowly. The number of lawyers in government has gone from 27,381 (or 13.4 percent of lawyers) in 1951 to 46,152 (or 14.3 percent of lawyers) in 1970, 1,498 of whom were women. In 1951 there were 7,471 of these lawyers in the judicial branch and 10,349 of them in 1970, 183 of whom were women, a slight decline from 3.6 percent to 3.2 percent of all lawyers. In the executive and legislative branches (which are combined in the compilation) there have been increases in those years from 19,910 (9.8 percent) to 35,803 (11.1 percent) overall, 1,315 of whom were women. A decline in the city/county sector of the executive-legislative category, from 8,019 (3.9 percent) in 1951 to 7,800 (2.4 percent) in 1970, 202 of whom were women, was offset by increases in the federal sector from 8,314 in 1951 to 18,710 in 1970, 713 of whom were women, and more steeply in the state sector from 3,577 to 9,293 in those years, 400 of whom were women. In percentages the state sector of the executive-legislative category showed increases in recent years: 1.8 percent in 1951, 1.6 percent in 1954, 1.7 percent in 1957, 1.7 percent in 1960, 2.6 percent in 1966, and 2.9 percent in 1970. The federal sector showed steady but lesser increases: 4.1 percent in 1951, 4.1 percent in 1954, 5.3 percent in 1957, 5.2 percent in 1960, 5.6 percent in 1963, 5.6 percent in 1966, and 5.8 percent in 1970.

   By comparison with the number of lawyers in government, 27,381 in 1951 and 46,152 in 1970, there were 176,995 lawyers in private practice in 1951 (or 86.8 percent) and 236,085 in 1970 (or 72.7 percent). In 1951 there were 11,274 lawyers in private industry (5.5 percent), a figure nearly doubled (per capita) by 1970, with 33,593 (10.3 percent) in this fastest-growing major segment of the profession. Likewise, the 1,213 (0.6 percent) in education in 1951 reached 3,732 (1.1 percent in 1970.
3. This is to say nothing of the legal profession's monopoly of the judicial branch of government, its hegemony in the legislative branch, and its disproportionate representation at the highest levels of the executive branch—two-thirds of the Presidents have been lawyers, a near majority of President Carter's cabinet are lawyers.
4. This is only one aspect in need of study. Olavi Maru, in *Research on the Legal Profession* (American Bar Foundation, 1972), sized up the work done so far in the following words: "While there has been in the past decade a substantial increase in studies on the legal profession, these studies have contributed less to our understanding of the profession than their number might suggest, and we still do not have a clear outline of the nature and functioning of the profession." (p. 47)
5. Little has been written about corporate "house counsel" and even less about its governmental counterpart. Harry C. Shriver's *The Government Lawyer* (Potomac, MD.: Fox Hill Press, 1975) contains reminiscences of government law-practice. Much more systematic but focusing on the litigating aspects of the governmental legal function is Donald Horowitz' *The Jurocracy* (Lexington: Lexington Books, 1977).
6. On these aspects—and most others—Martin Mayer's *The Lawyers* (New York: Harper & Row, 1967) is excellent. For the functions of lawyers, see his chapter two, pp. 27-70.
7. (Russell Sage Foundation, 1948), p. 84.
8. *Op. cit.,* p. 89.
9. "Special Issue: Government Intervention," *Business Week,* April 4, 1977, p. 47.
10. *Ibid,* p. 63.
11. *Democracy and the Public Service* (New York: Oxford University Press, 1968), p. 122. The converse is an equally interesting question: what is the effect of the bureaucracy on the thinking of the professional, of the lawyer in particular? There is a literature on the effect of working circumstances on the actor (see Jerome Skolnick's *Justice Without Trial* (New York: John Wiley, 1975), chapter three, and the litera-

ture cited there, applied to the "working personality" of the patrolman); but nothing has been done to discern the effect of public service—and bureaucratic service especially—on the thinking and other aspects of lawyers.
12. Quoted in Alexander Polikoff, "A Perspective on the Lawyer," *The University of Chicago Law Alumni Journal* (Fall, 1973), p. 7.
13. Quoted in Thurman Arnold, *The Symbols of Government* (New York: Harcourt Brace, 1962), p. 101.
14. Lest it be thought that these and later observations are unduly critical of lawyers, it should be said that any tilt in that direction is a function of the sentiment best expressed by Harrison Tweed: "I have a high opinion of lawyers. With all their faults, they stack up well against those in every other occupation or profession. They are better to work with or play with or fight with or drink with, than most other varieties of mankind." Quoted in Mayer, *op. cit.,* p. 3.
15. (Dobbs Ferry: Oceana, 1951) p. 101.
15a. *Idem.*
16. A more favorable view of first-year law students can be found in Alan N. Katz and Mark P. Denbeaux, "Trust, Cynicism, and Machiavellianism Among First-Year Law Students," *Journal of Urban Law* (February, 1976), pp. 397-412. But they conclude with a comment by Barry B. Boyer and Roger C. Cramton: "Although useful work remains to be done on law student motivation and selection, our zation process in law school and the early years of practice, and the economics of legal education suggests that these areas of research are more promising and urgent." "American Legal Education: An Agenda for Research and Reform," *Cornell Law Review* (January, 1974), pp. 221-297, at p. 235.
17. For example, Frederick C. Mosher, *et al, Watergate—Implications for Responsible Government* (Washington, DC: National Academy of Public Administration, 1974).
18. C. Normand Poirer, "The Federal Government Lawyer and Professional Ethics," *American Bar Association Journal* (December, 1974), p. 1541.
19. "The President's Report," *Third Biennial Report, 1973-1974,* Council on Legal Education for Professional Responsibility, pp. 7-20.
20. In *re Sanitary District Attorneys,* 351 Ill. 206, 184 N.E. 332.
21. Nicholas Henry, *Public Administration and Public Affairs* (Englewood Cliffs: Prentice Hall, 1975), ch. 2.
22. They put it this way: ". . . if legal education in the contemporary world is adequately to serve the needs of a free and productive commonwealth, it must be conscious, efficient, and systematic *training for policy-making."* "Legal Education and Public Policy: Professional Training in the Public Interest," *Yale Law Journal* (March, 1943), pp. 203-292, at p. 206; emphasis theirs.
23. Reprinted in E. F. Prichard, Jr., and Archibald MacLeish, eds., *Law and Politics* (New York: Harcourt Brace, 1962), pp. 238-249.
24. This and the foregoing quotation, *ibid.,* p. 247.
25. The course-offerings of the District of Columbia law schools are remarkable for their traditional private orientation.
26. George Steven Swan, "Today's Law Senior—Messiah or Moneychanger," *American Bar Association Journal* (March, 1973), pp. 277-278.
27. Marna S. Tucker, "Pro Bono Publico or Pro Bono Organized Bar," *American Bar Association Journal* August, 1974), pp. 916-919.
28. "Lawyers and Law Firms Look Ahead—1971 to 2000," *American Bar Association Journal* (October, 1971), pp. 971-975, at p. 975.
29. Comment, "The New Public Interest Lawyer," *Yale Law Journal* (1970), p. 1069.
30. For several aspects of the learning of law, see Francis A. Allen, "The Causes of Popular Dissatisfaction with Legal Education," *American Bar Association Journal* (April, 1976), pp. 447-450; "The Prospects of University Law Training," *American Bar Association Journal* (March, 1977), pp. 346-350.
31. "Justice Department Eyes New Bar Targets," *American Bar Association Journal* (March, 1977), p. 299.
32. "Lawyers—Can They Police Themselves?" *U.S. News & World Report* (June 6, 1977), p. 33.
33. If the voluntary American Bar Association is a quasi-public institution, as its President Leon Jaworski proclaimed, "The American Bar Association: A Quasi-Public Institution" (*American Bar Association Journal,* September, 1972, pp. 917-919), then there is little question about the integrated bar associations.

ECONOMISTS AND POLICY ANALYSIS

Steven E. Rhoads, *University of Virginia*

Ever since the great depression economists have been entering government service in increasing numbers. Most of these economists do technical work such as gathering and interpreting wage statistics in the Labor Department and forecasting future crop prices in the Agriculture Department. In recent years, however, an increasing number of government economists have been systematically analyzing and making recommendations about important questions of public policy. After a brief look at statistics on econo-

---

The author would like to thank Nechama Gancz for her research assistance, Mary Kay Tegard for her editorial and secretarial help, and James Ceaser, Darius Gaskins, Laurin Henry, Edgar Olsen, Diana Rhoads and the symposium editors for their valuable comments on an earlier draft.

Steven E. Rhoads is an associate professor of government and foreign affairs and director of the graduate program in public administration and public affairs at the University of Virginia. He served in the U.S. Bureau of the Budget in 1965-1966, and is currently engaged in research on the influence of normative economics in public policy analysis.

mists in government, this article will focus on the economists whose principal job is the analysis and evaluation of public policy. It is the work of these economists that is most likely to affect the scope and shape of public programs and thus the responsibilities of readers of this review.

Economists in Government

Good historical data are scarce, but recent National Science Foundation studies do give information on economists in government in the 1970's. These studies show that, compared to other social scientists, economists are disproportionately represented. While in 1973, 30 percent of the 32,773 social scientists in America with Ph.D's were economists, 43 percent of the 9,678 Ph.D. social scientists working for any level of government were economists. Below the Ph.D. level the proportion of all social scientists in government who were economists was higher still.[1]

We do not know precisely how many of these economists are involved with analyzing policy, but economists do hold positions which give them the potential to influence public policy decisions. According to Civil Service Commission data, in 1975, 74 percent of the 257 social scientists at the federal supergrade level (GS 16 and above) were economists.[2] And trends in cabinet level appointments show a rising influence at this still higher level. Table 1 lists the educational backgrounds of each administration's cabinet members and their principal deputies beginning with the second Eisenhower administration. Though lawyers appear most frequently in all administrations, the trend in the appointments of economists is clearly upward. In the Eisenhower, Kennedy, and Johnson administrations between 0 and 8 percent of all these office holders were economists; and in the Carter administration 21 percent are economists. Moreover, four of the five Carter appointees who were educated in economics head their departments. Looking at the 20 years as a whole, one notes that 62 percent of the cabinet secretaries and under secretaries who have held the Ph.D., have been students of economics.[3]

Though economists are well represented in government, it is difficult to know how much influence they have had on public policy. Economics stands more for a particular way of looking at policy alternatives than for particular policies. Moreover, public policies are influenced primarily by public moods and political factors, and thus, even when most economists support a particular policy approach or outcome and it is subsequently enacted, their support may not have been decisive. The volunteer army is a case in point. An overwhelming majority of economists preferred a volunteer army to the draft, but there were powerful political forces which might well have led to a volunteer army

TABLE 1
NUMBER AND PERCENTAGE OF CABINET MEMBERS AND THEIR PRINCIPAL DEPUTIES[a] BY DISCIPLINE OF HIGHEST DEGREE[b] FOR SELECTED ADMINISTRATIONS

HIGHEST DEGREE

Administration	Ph.D. in Economics	Masters in Economics[d]	Law Degrees J.D., LL.B. or LL.M.	Ph.D. Outside Economics		Masters in Bus. Admin.	Masters Outside Economics, Law or Business	B.A.[c]	B.S.	No. 4 Yr. Degree	Total All Appts
Carter[d]	3 (13%)	2 (8%)	9 (38%)	2 (8%)	Physics & Engr.	0 (0%)	0 (0%)	3 (13%)	2 (8%)	3 (13%)	24
Ford[e]	3 (10%)	1 (3%)	14 (45%)	2 (6%)	Pol. Sci. & Hist.	3 (10%)	0 (0%)	3 (10%)	1 (3%)	4 (13%)	31
Nixon	7 (13%)	0 (0%)	24 (44%)	3 (6%)	2 Geology & 1 Pol. S.	3 (6%)	0 (0%)	8 (15%)	2 (4%)	7 (13%)	54
Johnson[e]	2 (8%)	0 (0%)	14 (56%)	2 (8%)	Psych. & Hlth. S.	0 (0%)	3 (12%)	2 (8%)	0 (0%)	2 (8%)	25
Kennedy	0 (0%)	0 (0%)	17 (68%)	0 (0%)		1 (4%)	1 (4%)	3 (12%)	2 (8%)	1 (4%)	25
Eisenhower[c]	1 (3%)	1 (3%)	13 (38%)	1 (3%)	Pol. Sci.	1 (3%)	2 (6%)	4 (12%)	7 (21%)	4 (12%)	34
TOTAL ALL	16 (8%)	4 (2%)	91 (47%)	10 (5%)		8 (4%)	6 (3%)	23 (12%)	14 (7%)	21 (11%)	193

a. Individuals have been counted more than once if they held more than one office.
b. Where an individual holds two graduate degrees in different fields, both fields are entered in the table.
c. Two Eisenhower appointees with B.A.'s in engineering have been placed in B.S. column where most bachelors in engineering appear.
d. Includes one Carter appointee who completed two years of graduate work in economics but received no degree.
e. Where a new President took office through death or resignation of predecessor, appointees who continued to serve new President for a time but left office before the end of the new Presidency, have not been counted for the new Presidency.

Sources: *Who's Who in America, The New York Times,* Federal Register Compilation of Presidential Documents, U.S. Government Manual, Congressional Directory, Personal Correspondence with departments.

even without any economic input in the policy debate. On other issues, however, economic influence seems significant—for example, in the adoption of revenue sharing, in the small movement toward vouchers for low income housing dwellers and for students of higher education and in the likely enactment of some form of air transportation deregulation. As we shall see, there are other areas, such as pollution policy, where economists' recommendations have not been heeded.

Economists in Policy Analysis

Whatever the extent of their influence, economists' disproportionate representation in government suggests that those interested in public policy should understand their characteristic mode of thinking. This is particularly important because of the role of economists in the burgeoning "policy analysis" movement. In the last decade, Harvard, Stanford, Berkeley, Duke, Minnesota, Michigan, Texas, and other universities have established graduate schools or programs concerned with the systematic analysis and evaluation of public policies. Moreover, the number of policy analysts at all levels of government has grown. At the state and local levels some jurisdictions have separate policy analysis staffs, but most conduct analysis through the budget or planning units. At the federal level, however, most large departments have at least one separate, top level staff office which is principally concerned with analysis. These offices go by a bewildering variety of names, such as "Office of Planning and Program Review" and "Assistant Secretary for Policy, Evaluation, and Research." Some departments also have analytic units with their operating bureaus, and many analytic staffs are, in turn, composed of divisions broken down according to substance (elementary and secondary education, post-secondary education, etc.) or function (evaluation, planning, etc.).[4]

Though policy analysis is often called an interdisciplinary endeavor, it is generally acknowledged that economics has been the most influential discipline. A 1975 survey of eight of the leading schools of public policy found that economics was required in more programs than any other field and that it was the only discipline to have at least four faculty representatives at each school.[5] And in a recent study of policy analysts in the federal bureaucracy Arnold Meltsner, a political scientist, observed that "policy analysis continues to be dominated by economists or by those with an economic orientation."[6]

When the federal Planning, Programming and Budgeting System was at its height, federal level analysis clearly was dominated by economists, and this remains true today on some analytic staffs, such as the new Congressional Budget Office. Recently, however, the absolute dominance of economists has been challenged by the more frequent hiring of other social scientists and graduates of interdisciplinary programs such as the new schools of public policy. In part, this reflects a change in the political mood. As the emphasis has shifted from analyzing proposed new programs to evaluating old ones, psychology and other disciplines with long interests in evaluation methodologies have seemed important. But, more fundamentally, there is a growing recognition that the approach and methods of no one discipline are sufficient to determine good public policy in all areas.[7]

Still, economics can deeply influence analysis even when graduates from departments of economics are not involved. Economic thinking is making inroads not only in the interdisciplinary schools of public policy and public administration, but in other academic areas as well. Spurred on by economists' findings emphasizing the importance of considering costs and benefits from the point of view of the criminal, sociologists now focus more on the deterrent effects of punishment. And a path breaking book edited by two doctors and a statistician draws heavily on cost-benefit analysis and economic theory when assessing the *Costs, Risks and Benefits of Surgery*.[8] In interdisciplinary analyses economic theory usually supplies the analytic framework. In his recent book, *Analysis for Public Decisions*, E.S. Quade, the former head of the Mathematics Department at RAND, argues that analysis must be more than economics, but he also introduces his discussion of four of the most common forms of analysis (cost-benefit analysis, cost-effectiveness analysis, systems analysis and operations research) by noting that "all have economics as a core."[9]

Macro vs. Microeconomics

Non-economists usually associate economists and policy analysis with the macroeconomic questions of inflation, unemployment, and economic growth. This is understandable since macroeconomic issues are always in the news, and economists are generally thought to be the experts in this area. Nevertheless, this public perception of economists' policy interests is not accurate. For every governmental economist using macroeconomics when making policy recommendations, there are many others using microeconomics or related fields such as welfare or benefit-cost economics. These latter fields deal with "the allocation of scarce resources between alternative and competing ends." For years this was the usual definition of economics, and most mainstream economists still consider microeconomics to be the more solid of the two branches of the discipline. For our purposes it is also the most interesting because on microeconomic issues economists do not enjoy a monopoly of expertise, and their distinctive way of looking at the world is more easily seen when one can compare their policy advice with that of other experts in an area. Like lawyers, economists see themselves as policy generalists with a kit of concepts and tools applicable to all policy areas. The rest of this article will briefly introduce the reader to what is in that kit and to the assumptions that lie behind it.

Microeconomic Concepts

The resource allocation side of economics provides two types of policy guidance. The first type, guidance flowing from welfare and benefit-cost economics, is very ambitious. A belief in the principles of welfare economics has led economists to speak with conviction about subjects as grand as "the objectives of public programs effecting resource allocation"[10] and "The Appropriate Functions of Government in an Enterprise System."[11] Benefit-cost economics, the applied branch of welfare economics, goes even further and gives advice about how much money should be spent on justifiable objectives and functions. More will be said later about these two branches of economics.

The second kind of guidance derives from microeconomic concepts which are not meant to be so comprehensive or conclusive. They are instead things to be kept in mind—factors to be weighed against other relevant factors. Though these concepts are less ambitious, they are not necessarily less useful. One can reject the normative principles which lie behind welfare and benefit-cost economics and still learn from the three related concepts of opportunity cost, marginalism and economic incentives.

Opportunity Cost

Economists are sometimes defined as those who "know the cost of everything and the value of nothing." In their defense they point out that a concern with costs is really a concern with values because added costs lessen our ability to further values in other policy areas. This is the opportunity cost insight, the understanding that spending and regulatory decisions which use scarce resources or require their use incur costs in terms of foregone alternatives elsewhere.

This seems so obvious that one can wonder why it is worth discussing. Yet it is constantly ignored. Thus, when Congress proclaimed that the discharge of pollutants in navigable waters shall "be eliminated by 1985,"[12] it probably ignored the resulting costs in terms of more air pollution and solid waste disposal problems. Similarly, when government reports discuss environmental damage from off-shore drilling without *mentioning* tanker spillage of oil which would have to be imported if the drilling does not proceed, they are ignoring opportunity costs of a reduction in off-shore drilling.[13] And, when a local administrator explains that city recreation policy gives primary consideration to public welfare, but that cost considerations are also important, he suggests that costs are something other than public welfare foregone in other public programs and in the private sector.

Sometimes opportunity costs are far from obvious even to those used to thinking about them. Thus, Herbert Mohring has speculated that the more stringent interstate highway system design standards which were implemented in 1967 may have produced opportunity costs not only through foregone opportunities elsewhere, in education, health and such, but also in terms of an increase in highway deaths! The new design changes made roads safer, but they also raised the costs of building a mile of road by 13 per cent. These added costs have meant that fewer miles of interstate highway could be built with a given amount of money. Since U.S. interstate highways built *before* 1967 were already almost twice as safe per mile traveled as all other highways, some people traveling on non-interstate roads in the 1970's have died because relatively safer pre-1967 interstate highways have not been available to them.[14]

Marginalism

Marginalism involves looking at the details—understanding that most budgeting decisions concern spending a little more or a little less, not whether we should address a problem at all. It also involves renouncing the old proverb that anything worth doing at all is worth doing well. As we reduce our pollution, accidents, crimes, fires, and such, it becomes more costly to reduce them still further. At some point the marginal costs of program expansion will exceed the marginal benefits, and we will decide to do well what we do but not to do as much as interested professionals would think necessary if we were going to "really solve the problem." When our water is very dirty, we of course want to do something about the pollution problem. But if moving from a 99 per cent reduction of discharge to 100 per cent raises costs from $119 billion to $319 billion we may decide to settle for "slightly dirty" water.[15] Indeed, when budgets are tight and needs pressing elsewhere, we may quite rationally decide to do some things not well at all.

Marginalism can also help us see through self-serving interest group positions. In the late 1960's interest groups justified public subsidies for aviation facilities by a number of arguments, one of which was that the civilian aviation system strengthens national defense. Government economists countered in part by emphasizing the distinction between total utility and marginal utility. The general public does gain defense benefits from the civil aviation system just as it does from the electronics and steel industries. Thus, when individuals consume these goods and services, the *total* general public benefits of such consumption may be quite high, and in the absence of an extensive aviation system it might be in the public interest to subsidize its provision. However, where an extensive aviation system already exists, additional private consumption of aviation services will yield few, if any, defense benefits to the public at large. Therefore, a subsidized further expansion of aviation uses scarce public funds and yet provides negligible defense benefits to the public.[16]

Marginalism also may be used to assess certain aids for the allocation of public resources. Social scientists who are not economists sometimes recommend that a city's budget decisions be heavily influenced by poll results showing the public's ranking of the major problems facing the community. Such polls may be of some use, but the questions rarely indicate the real alternatives available. Perhaps a doubling of the local budget would have little effect on the "number one" problem while the third most important problem lends itself to dramatic improvement through spending a small additional amount. A similar problem appears in certain versions of the federal government's Management by Objectives System when firm output-oriented objectives, such as "reduce air delays by 25 per cent," are set before any analysis of the marginal costs and benefits of achieving these has been done.

Economic Incentives

Both theory and evidence have convinced economists that if the price of something valued goes up, some people will consume less of it and if the price goes down, some will consume more. Economists thus spend much time thinking about the public sector applications of simple supply and demand curves and then measuring those curves's slopes or elasticities. Because electricity users, air travelers, and tennis players respond to price signals, higher prices at periods of peak use can spread out demand and thus avoid expensive capital investment. Because flood protection projects and disaster relief programs reduce the costs of building on flood plains, the $7 billion dollars spent on flood protection projects since 1936 has not reduced total flood damages as many proponents of the dam building program had expected. Because employers have an economic incentive to react to laws requiring that they pay their employees certain wages or provide certain benefits, laws in these areas are unlikely to accomplish some of their important objectives. For example, "Economists generally believe that a payroll tax nominally paid by the employer is ultimately borne by the worker in the form of lower wages than he would otherwise receive or in higher prices for what he buys."[17]

In some areas, like pollution control, economists are nearly unanimous in their belief that current policies are wrongheaded because they ignore economic incentive insights. Current federal water pollution policy has two important elements: a subsidy program providing billions of dollars in matching grants for publicly owned waste treatment plants and a regulatory program giving authorities the power to impose effluent limits on individual waste dischargers. The subsidy is only for treatment plants when in fact changing industrial technology or raw materials or mechanically reaerating water at the end stage is often a cheaper way to reduce pollution. The federal program thus gives localities an incentive to clean up in an uneconomical way. Since the subsidy is only for the construction costs and some benefits go to other jurisdictions downstream, there is also no incentive for municipalities to operate their treatment plants efficiently, and in 1970 the GAO found that over half of the existing plants provided substandard service. Moreover, the matching grants reduce localities' capital costs which often lead to lower sewer charges for polluters and thus a reduced incentive for firms to clean up.

With respect to the effluent limits, economists note that there are about 62,000 sources of industrial water pollution. In setting limits the Environmental Protection Agency should take account of the costs of cleaning up for each firm since these costs will ultimately be paid by consumers. But, facing such a mammoth task, the EPA is dependent on the firms themselves, and the firms have every reason to exaggerate the costs and employment effects of more stringent pollution limits. Once limits have been set, the firms have an incentive to drag their feet and go to court so as to postpone making the costly changes. Once the firms have come into compliance, they have no incentive to make further improvements even when they could be made at small cost.

As an alternative strategy most economists recommend effluent charges. The charge could be set high enough to accomplish any desired degree of pollution control, and, as Kneese and Schultze note, the charge would give firms an incentive to seriously consider all changes which might reduce their pollution tax.

Each firm would be faced with different removal costs, depending on the nature of its production process and its economic situation. For any given effluent charge, firms with low costs of control would remove a larger percentage than would firms with higher costs—precisely the situation needed to achieve a least-cost approach to reducing pollution for the economy as a whole. Firms would tend to choose the lease expensive methods of control, whether treatment of wastes, modification in production processes, or substitution of raw materials that had less serious polluting consequences. Further, the kinds of products whose manufacture entailed a lot of pollution would become more expensive and would carry higher prices than those that generated less, so consumers would be induced to buy more of the latter.[18]

In a fascinating epilogue to their book Kneese and Schultze argue that one reason why the incentive approach is not popular in the public sector is because too many congressmen are lawyers. They note that lawyers learn to affect people's behavior by changing rights and duties, and law schools tend to neglect the economists' alternative method of affecting behavior: changing the channels of economic self interest.

Other economists think that the incentive approach must be applied to institutional arrangements before real improvements in government performance will be seen. These economists ask why one expects bureaucrats to attend to efficiency-oriented policy analysis when their pay, power and perquisites depend on a large and swollen bureau rather than a lean and efficient one. Those of this school usually argue for more voucher programs, for contracting out more public services, and for changing the incentives of administrators by increasing competition within government and by rewarding top managers for their success at achieving specified outputs at a reduced cost.[19]

Welfare Economics

Welfare economics rests on two fundamental normative assumptions: that societal welfare depends only upon individuals' subjective senses of satisfaction and that satisfaction is best achieved by letting individuals decide for themselves how to use their resources. If a society accepts subjective sense of satisfaction and consumer sovereignty as its standards, economists can show that it should be interested in achieving economic efficiency. In most cases economic efficiency is best achieved by letting a free market and flexible prices eliminate shortages and surpluses and allocate resources in accord with consumer demand.

Economic efficiency may, however, be served by government intervention when there are market imperfections—obstacles to the allocation of resources in accord with consumer valuations. Monopolies, powerful labor unions, and externalities (non-priced effects on third parties) are important examples of market imperfections. Economists find the externality concept particularly useful in determining or structuring debate about the role of government in a policy area.

Pollution is the classic case of an external cost which justifies government intervention. All of us are bothered by dirty air, but that cost to us is not paid by polluting firms. Thus profit maximizing firms and the market mechanism will not take adequate account of the "external" costs of pollution unless government intervenes in some fashion.

Without using the economists' terminology, aviation interest groups in effect used the positive side of the externality concept when they argued that benefits to the nonflying public justified continuing their aviation facilities' subsidy. Government economists could reject this argument by noting that external benefits *at the margin* were negligible and were balanced by the external costs of noise. Throughout the 1960's debate over air legislation, analysts in government looked to welfare for continued government subsidies, they supported increased aviation user charges so that consumers could make choices based on prices reflecting the opportunity costs of resources used in the various transportation modes.[20]

When externalities can justify government programs, economists then look at the geographical scope of the externalities to help decide whether federal, state, or local governments should take the lead. Most national defense benefits are shared by those in Pennsylvania and Virginia, and, thus, if given the responsibility, each state would be likely to buy less than an optimum amount and mix of defense since each would have no incentive to consider the external benefits which their defense purchases conferred upon other states; at the same time each state would be inclined to wait for other states to make purchases which would benefit them at no cost. On the other hand, though added police expenditures in Philadelphia may confer external benefits (if more area criminals are caught) or costs (if city criminals migrate to less vigilant environs) on surrounding jurisdictions, most of the added benefits and costs of such expenditures will go to the residents of Philadelphia; and it is not likely that such expenditures will have significant effect on criminal activity in Richmond. This suggests that the case for federal involvement with local police is weaker than the case for involvement in national defense.

Benefit-Cost Analysis

Benefit-cost analysis compares in dollar terms the worth of government programs and their cost. It rests on the same consumer sovereignty assumptions as welfare economics. Determining how much individuals are willing to pay for government goods and services is thus the crucial part of the cost-benefit analyst's task. But since citizens rarely pay directly for government services, discovering what they would be willing to pay rather than do without those services can be very difficult.

Still, over the years economists have developed a number of methods for operationalizing their theory. Where the government provides an intermediate good, such as irrigation water, its value can be estimated by looking at the value of the increased output (crops) less the cost of the other inputs needed to produce it. For job training programs one can look at the increase in future wages. For air and water pollution one can first estimate costs by looking at changes in relative property values after the appearance of a new expressway or factory. Once one has estimated the costs of pollution, one knows the benefits of programs which will eliminate it. When all else fails, economists sometimes conduct "willingness-to-pay" polls.

Criticisms of the Economic Approach

Application Problems

Most of the criticism of the economic approach to public policy analysis focuses on its most ambitious fields, welfare and benefit-cost economics. Some critics stress the application difficulties in benefit-cost analysis. None of the economists' methods for estimating benefits is perfect, and for many government programs no one has even attempted to place dollar values on program outputs. Still, one cannot intelligently reject benefit-cost analysis by stressing only the problems in application. If the normative principles on which it rests are good and sufficient ones, the sensible course is to value the benefits of government programs at our best estimate of the people's aggregate "willingness-to-pay" for them.

Materialism

Other observers criticize economists for only considering the materialistic side of man and thus stressing "economic" ends to the exclusion of social, environmental, and aesthetic ones. This criticism is based on a fundamental misunderstanding. Though certain applied studies do focus on output-oriented, narrowly construed "economic" benefits, in principle a welfare economist is concerned with anything that any individual values enough to be willing to pay something for. Fulfilling people's environmental, aesthetic, or educational desires is an economic benefit just as much as is an extra barrel of oil.

Equity and the Distribution of Income

A common cirticism which has more force is that economists' stress on economic efficiency produces neglect of questions of equity and the distribution of income. A program passes the benefit/cost, economic efficiency test if the gainers gain enough from the project so that they *could* fully compensate losers for their losses and still be better off with the project than without it. Who gains and who loses is irrelevant,[21] and it makes no difference whether the compensation is actual or hypothetical. A project yielding $100 worth of benefits for the rich is efficient though $99 of costs are imposed on the poor. Moreover, in the absence of psychic or other external benefits for the non-poor, a public health clinic costing $20 per visit of the poor is economically inefficient unless the poor would themselves be willing to pay the $20 per visit.

Many observers find inadequate a "willingness-to-pay" criterion which ignores differences in ability to pay. Economists must acknowledge that their efficiency criterion does this, but in their defense they generally make a number of points. First, for many projects, income distribution concerns are insignificant. When deciding whether to build a prison, state office building, or such, we can often assume that relative to their tax burden, the poor gain about as much as the rich. Second, where the rich gain more than the poor lose, why not require the rich to compensate the poor for all their losses? Then the equity problem disappears, and we need not forsake a project yielding net benefits. Third, as suggested above, when the poor are the program beneficiaries, but they would be unwilling to pay for the full program costs, we can add to the poor's willingness to pay that of the non-poor who feel benefits from programs for the poor.

Economists know that these arguments do not dispose of the issue. Actual compensation cannot always be arranged, and society may want the rich to help the poor more than they would freely agree to. Thus, economists acknowledge that efficiency calculations are not sufficient, and sometimes equity, not efficiency, should be controlling. But they also point out that welfare economics has always allowed for a government role in income distribution questions. Moreover, the discipline has been increasingly concerned with the distribution of the costs and benefits flowing from government programs and with assessing the "trade-off" between more equality and efficiency. Economists argue that they still spend most of their time on efficiency questions because that is where they can apply their expertise most usefully. They think others are as well equipped as they to answer the core value questions about problems of equity.

Externalities

The most fundamental criticism of the economic approach must look to areas where economists make claims rather than those where they do not. One such area is the economic concept of externality. As suggested by the aviation tax and pollution policy examples discussed above, the externality concept can be useful in pointing the way toward better public policy. Nevertheless, it is a very slippery concept. Externalities are everywhere. Crab grass, portable radios, mini-skirts, radical political speech and many other things produce them. No one wants government to take account of all externalities. But this very fact may lead to the neglect of important intangible ones, particularly when economists are trying to finish a complicated quantitative analysis or when the intangible externalities lead to questions unlike those that economists usually address. For example, Gordon Tullock criticizes the use of juries in certain civil cases without so much as acknowledging Tocqueville's view that the jury in civil cases is defensible not as a judicial institution but as a political one which produces better citizens by educating the people in the law and in their rights and duties.[22] On questions such as the one Tullock addresses, students of political thought or historians may be better able to identify externalities than are economists.

Another important question is whether we want to give public recognition to even all the significant externalities. In an upwardly mobile society almost every Cadillac bought brings psychic pain to some emulating friends and neighbors. And many racists and greedy heirs undoubtedly feel psychic and monetary pain when tax dollars fund sickle cell anemia research and medical programs for the elderly. Welfare economics makes no distinction among worthy and unworthy tastes, and thus there is no economic principle which would support treating the externalities of envy and malevolence differently from others. Indeed one welfare economist notes that for life-saving programs the economic calculus should treat external costs in the same way as other costs.[23] Even if beneficiaries of life-saving programs were willing to pay more than those who felt losses would need for full compensation, a decision to count psychic and monetary costs of racists or greedy heirs could still make a difference. Such programs would involve substantial direct, monetary costs beyond the external ones and thus counting the external costs could be enough to make costs outweigh benefits.

Consumer Sovereignty vs. Political Judgment

Questions about envy and malevolence lead to the heart of the matter. Does societal welfare depend only upon individuals' subjective senses of satisfaction, and is public policy best determined by "accepting as final only the individual's estimate of what a thing is worth to him at the time the decision is to be made"?[24] As the above section reveals, ethical standards may conflict with some consumers's tastes. Other problems may arise when consumers are not knowledgeable and thus may not know their own best interests. Paradoxically, economists in the main are the strongest spokesmen for consumer sovereignty, yet they constantly expose consumer ignorance about the real effects of popular policies and in their "free rider" theory[25] predict such ignorance and its intractability.

As Frederick Mosher has suggested, most economists seem to equate democracy with consumer sovereignty.[26] Even some of the best economists dismiss as elitists those who would quarrel with the consumer sovereignty assumption. By advocating that public policy be based on consumer "willingness-to-pay," benefit-cost economists silently assume the desirability of passive representatives. If political judgment or political leadership is needed, it is only to find the best tactical route for implementing the policy desires of today's consumers.

Alexis de Tocqueville is just one of many serious political thinkers who saw the sources of good democratic policy as more varied and complex. Tocqueville argued that strong public feelings should sometimes be seen as danger signals rather than guideposts for policy. He showed why the social and political constitution of a people naturally predisposes them to do well in some important areas and neglect others. His thought provides a striking contrast with welfare economics in the important role he saw for political leaders who educate and extend public tastes and encourage certain institutions and policies precisely because of the effect that they have on habits and tastes, and through these, on liberty.

Within the American tradition also many have supported a larger policy role for political representatives than welfare and benefit-cost economics would seem to allow. That support is found in the distinction made in *The Federalists Papers* between the inclinations and interests of the people, and in its wish for representatives who "refine and enlarge the public views."[27] It continues at least through John Kennedy's call for courageous congressmen who "on occasion lead, inform, correct, and sometimes even ignore constituent opinion" so as "to exercise fully the judgment for which they were elected."[28]

Of course, the economists may be right and Tocqueville, Madison, Hamilton and Kennedy wrong. Certainly economists would be quick to point out how often legislative and administrative departures from consumer preferences serve the reelection and other interests of those involved rather than high principle. One possibility worth further investigation is that consumer preferences point the way toward good policy in some areas but not in others where the consumer is less knowledgeable or ethical considerations seem important. In any case, the consumer sovereignty assumption is the crucial one for those would reflect on the roots of normative economics and the significance of its growing influence.

Notes

1. *Characteristics of Doctoral Scientists and Engineers in the United States, 1973, Appendix B,* NSF-75-312A, National Science Foundation, and *Characteristics of the National Sample of Scientists and Engineers, 1974, Part 2, Employment,* NSF-76-323, National Science Foundation. The N.S.F. classifies as "social scientists": anthropologists, sociologists, economists, political scientists, and a few other smaller disciplines. Psychology is not included.
2. From unpublished Civil Service Commission data tabulated by the National Science Foundation.
3. Not all those educated as economists, lawyers, etc. were actually employed in their professions prior to their government appointments. By focusing on educational backgrounds, the table may overemphasize the influence of the professions as opposed to, for example, the business community. On the other hand, in the case of economists, their influence may be underestimated by not considering their frequent appearance in important subcabinet positions with the Council of Economic Advisers and, since 1960, the Office of Management and Budget.
4. For more on the organizational context of analysis in the federal government, see Arnold Meltsner, *Policy Analysts in the Bureaucracy* (Berkeley): University of California Press, 1976), chapter 5.
5. William Dunn, "A Comparison of Eight Schools of Public Policy," *Policy Studies Journal,* Vol. IV, No. 1 (Autumn 1975), pp. 68-72.
6. Meltsner, *op. cit.,* p. 15.
7. At RAND, one of the most respected public policy research organizations, economists grew from 4 per cent (8) of the professional staff in 1948 to 16 per cent (92) in 1968, more than all other political and social scientists combined (13 per cent or 71). In 1976, however, economists had slipped to 14 per cent (75) of the RAND staff while the proportion of noneconomic social and political scientists increased dramatically to a total of 21 per cent (110).
8. John Bunker, Benjamin Barnes, Frederick Mosteller, *Costs, Risks and Benefits of Surgery* (New York: Oxford, 1977), see esp. p. xiii.
9. E. S. Quade, *Analysis for Public Decisions* (New York: Elsevier, 1975), p. 22.
10. These are the words of Jack Carlson, former Assistant Director for Program Evaluation at the U.S. Bureau of the Budget, as he lists a "summary" classification scheme. ("Statement" on "Guidelines for estimating the Benefits of Public Expenditures," *Economic Analysis and the Efficiency of Government, Hearings,* Subcommittee on Economy in Government, Joint Economic Committee, 1969.
11. This is the first and most theoretical part of a PPBS Compendium *(The Analysis and Evaluation of Public Expenditures: The PPB System, A Compendium of Papers)* put together in 1969 by the Subcommittee on Economy in Government of the Joint Economic Committee. All eight articles in this theoretical section were written by economists.
12. The 1972 Water Pollution Control Act Amendments as quoted and discussed in Allen Kneese and Charles L. Schultze, *Pollution, Prices, and Public Policy* (Washington: Brookings, 1975), esp. pp. 53, 78. Achieving zero discharge in all media simultaneously is impossible.
13. An example of this is discussed in "Executive Summary, Evaluation of OCS areas by the net Financial Benefits and Environmental Costs of Development," Office of Minerals Policy Development, Department of the Interior, October 1974.
14. Herbert Mohring, "Three Back-of-an-Envelope Evaluations of the Interstate Highway System," in James Miller ed., *Perspectives on Federal Transportation Policy* (Washington: American Enterprise Institute, 1975), pp. 169-171.
15. Kneese and Schultze, *op. cit.,* esp. pp. 21-22, 56.
16. For more on this see Steven E. Rhoads, *Policy Analysis in the Federal Aviation Administration* (Lexington, Massachusetts: Lexington Books, D. C. Heath, 1974), pp. 42-44.
17. Charles C. Schultze, Edward R. Fried, Alice Rivlin, Nancy Teeters, *Setting National Priorities: The 1973 Budget* (Washington: Brookings, 1972), p. 241 (N).
18. Kneese and Schultze, *op. cit.,* p. 89.
19. William Niskanen, "The Peculiar Economics of bureaucracy," *American Economic Review,* Vol. LVIII, No. 2 (May 1968), pp. 293-306; Richard McKenzie and Gordon Tullock, *The New World of Economics* (Homewood, Illinois: Irwin, 1975), pp. 196-210.
20. Rhoads, *op. cit.,* pp. 27-62.
21. By convention, economists consider only costs and benefits for citizens of the nation in question.
22. Gordon Tullock, *The Logic of the Law* (New York: Basic Books, 1971), pp. 84-90. Tocqueville says that the jury "invests each citizen with a kind of magistracy; it makes them all feel the duties which they are bound to discharge towards society and the part which they take in its government. By obliging men to turn their attention to other affairs than their own, it rubs off that private selfishness which is the rust of society." *Democracy in America,* I (New York: Vintage, 1955), ch. XVI, p. 295.
23. E. J. Mishan, *Cost-Benefit Analysis* (New York: Praeger, 1976), p. 313.
24. *Ibid.,* p. 318.
25. In this case the "free rider" is the person who does not find politics intrinsically interesting and does not inform himself because he realizes that his single vote is very unlikely to have an effect on public policy directions even though public policy itself may affect his welfare substantially.
26. Frederick Mosher, "Limitations and Problems of PPBS in the States," in *Public Administration Review,* Vol. 29, No. 2 (March/April 1969).
27. James Madison, Federalist #10 and Alexander Hamilton #71 in *The Federalist Papers* (New York: The New American Library, 1961), pp. 82 and 432.
28. John F. Kennedy, *Profiles in Courage* (New York: Cardinal, 1957), p. 14.

Selected Bibliography for Further Reading

Allen Kneese and Charles L. Schultze, *Pollution, Prices and Public Policy* (Washington: Brookings, 1975).

Richard Lipsey and Peter Steiner, *Economics* (New York: Harper & Row, 1975).

Douglass North and Roger Miller, *The Economics of Public Issues* (New York: Harper & Row, 1976).
Ezra Mishan, *The Costs of Economic Growth* (New York: Praeger, 1967).
Ezra Mishan, *Cost-Benefit Analysis* (New York: Praeger, 1976).
Charles Schultze, *The Public Use of Private Interest* (Washington: Brookings, 1977).
Neil Singer, *Public Microeconomics* (Boston: Little, Brown, 1976).
Gordon Tullock, *Private Wants, Public Means* (New York: Basic Books, 1970).

PROFESSIONAL ACCOUNTANTS IN GOVERNMENT: ROLES AND DILEMMAS

Ellsworth H. Morse, Jr. *Assistant Comptroller General of the United States*

No institution, be it in private enterprise or in public service, can operate properly without the assistance of accountants. Accountants fill a variety of management needs that are essential in all enterprises—keeping systematic financial records, preparing reports for managers and policy-makers, analyzing and interpreting financial and other data, providing financial management advice, and auditing.

These are commonplace and generally well-understood functions and professional accountants can be found in all government agencies. Government accountants are also involved in many other types of activities, bringing their technical skills to bear on a wider variety of operations than generally recognized.

The listing below provides some idea of the extensive use of professional accountants in the federal government. Counterparts for many of these functions will be found in state and local governments.

Role of Accountants

The primary functions of management accountants are (1) to assist the managers in carrying out their responsibilities effectively and economically, and (2) to provide a proper accounting for the use of financial and other resources that have been entrusted to the organization. These responsibilities are inherent in all managers whether in government, in private industry, or somewhere in between. Accountants who work in this framework are a part of the management system.

In contrast, there are the accountants who perform an audit function. They evaluate how good a job is being done by the management, including its accountants, in accounting for their operations and in reporting on them. This function may be performed by internal auditors or under contract by independent public accounting firms.

In some government organizations, an external type of audit function will also be found—for example, in the Internal Revenue Service with respect to taxpayers and in procurement agencies who must audit the books and records of their contractors.

In recent years the audit function has been greatly extended beyond concern with accountability for funds and other resources and financial reports. Particularly in government operations, this extension has taken the auditor into basic management responsibilities such as the efficiency and economy with which public resources are used and what is being achieved with those resources. These extensions of the auditor's role have been very marked in the federal government and are being extended in state and local governments.

In government regulation, professional accountants play an important role when they participate in the regulatory processes by developing, prescribing, and auditing financial and other data from private organizations subject to regulation. There are many regulated fields in which these skills are applied—raising capital funds, securities and commodities markets, communications, energy, and transportation.

Number of Professional Accountants

U.S. Civil Service Commission records show about 35,000 professional accountants in the federal government. Of this total, 14,000 are Internal Revenue agents in the Treasury Department. The other 21,000 are deployed in other agencies throughout the government, in the diverse functional fields listed above. More than 9,000 are in the Department of Defense and in the military services. Smaller concentrations are found in executive departments such as Agriculture; Health, Education and Welfare; and Treasury. In the legislative branch, the General Accounting Office has about 2,600 accountants out of a total of 4,100 professional staff members.

Ellsworth H. Morse, Jr. before his untimely death on November 29, 1977 was Assistant Comptroller General of the United States, responsible for the overall policy and program planning functions of the United States General Accounting Office. He was a graduate of Oberlin College, held an MBA degree from the University of Michigan, and was a certified public accountant. He was a member of the American Institute of Certified Public Accountants and the Association of Government Accountants, of which he was past national president. Since its inception in 1974, Mr. Morse served as editor of the *International Journal of Government Auditing*, sponsored by the International Organization of Supreme Audit Institutions. He was also chairman of the Board of External Auditors of the Organization of American States.

FUNCTION	WHERE FOUND
Internal management (Designing accounting systems, maintaining accounts, preparing financial reports, analyzing and interpreting financial data, making internal audits)	All agencies
Central Government management (Budget review and analysis, central accounting, overall financial reports)	Office of Management and Budget Treasury Department
Taxation	Internal Revenue Service
Procurement of goods and services	Procurement review groups, financial analysts, reviewers of pricing data
Renegotiation of contracts to eliminate excessive profits	Renegotiation Board
Establishing accounting standards	General Accounting Office (for Federal agencies) Cost Accounting Standards Board (for negotiated Government contracts)
Independent audit	General Accounting Office Defense Contract Audit Agency and contract or grant auditors of other Federal agencies
Regulation of private enterprise	Securities and Exchange Commission Federal Power Commission Interstate Commerce Commission Federal Communications Commission Civil Aeronautics Board (and similar agencies)
Investigation for law enforcement	Federal Bureau of Investigation
Congressional budget, authorization, and appropriation activities	Congressional committees
Investigation or oversight of executive agency operations	Congressional committees

The statistics on federal accountants also show that it is a male-dominated profession. Less than 10 percent are women, a proportion that is increasing slowly. Traditionally, women have not chosen accounting as a career.

The General Accounting Office (GAO)

Much of what is included in this article centers on the United States General Accounting Office. In part, this is because the GAO is where the author has spent most of his professional career. A more important reason is that it has played a prime role in the modernization and advancement of federal accounting and auditing, and it has one of the largest aggregations of professional accountants in the federal government.

It is an independent agency in the legislative branch with a broad charter of authority and responsibility to audit almost all federal departments and agencies, and to obtain and report information for the use of the Congress in carrying out its budget, legislative, and oversight responsibilities.

The staff of the General Accounting Office is not confined to accountants, however. Other disciplines represented include lawyers, economists, engineers, statisticians, and business and public administration specialists. The diversification of GAO professionals in the past 10 years has been a major change attributable to the leadership of the present Comptroller General, Elmer B. Staats.

Although the word accounting is an integral part of its name, the GAO does not maintain accounting records for federal department and agency financial operations. It did do this at one time, but accounting procedures have been modernized in the last 25 years so as to confine this basic management responsibility to the Treasury Department and the departments and agencies themselves where it belongs.

GAO does have certain statutory responsibilities that effect how federal agencies account for their affairs. The most important of these is to prescribe the accounting principles, standards, and related requirements to be followed by federal agencies. GAO is also charged with helping agencies improve their accounting systems, approving them when they are satisfactory, and then checking on how well they are working from time to time.

The term accounting cannot be understood solely in the narrow context of accounting records and financial reports; it also embraces the concept of accountability. GAO's biggest job is to audit and evaluate the programs and activities of federal agencies. In doing so, it is not concerned only with the reliability of accounting records and financial reports and with the effectiveness of management control systems. It is also concerned with evaluating how well assigned responsibilities are carried out and what is accomplished with financial and other resources made available to the federal agencies.

This broadening of the audit far beyond the traditional role of the auditor has led to a sharp decline in the time most GAO auditors devote to purely "accounting" matters. As one result, steps are now underway to change the Civil Service classification of most GAO staff members now classified as professional accountants to a broader category, like GAO professional auditor.

Evolution of Professional Accountant's Role

How the role of professional accountants evolved into a vital part of agency management systems in the federal government is a long and complex story. Until after World War II, this role was not highly developed because of antiquated concepts of financial management and control, including undue reliance on the ever present General Accounting Office to check everything.

The emergence of professional accounting services as an integral part of federal agency management systems really began after World War II. As has often been the case, farsighted legislation paved the way to this evolution. For example:

- The Government corporation control legislation of 1945 provided for much stronger congressional as well as budgetary and audit controls over the numerous federal corporations. This legislation led the General Accounting Office to employ professional accountants with experience obtained in the private sector to help the Comptroller General audit these entities. Later, they helped modernize how GAO carried out its accounting and auditing responsibilities with respect to all federal agencies.
- The Federal Property and Administrative Services Act of 1949 and the Budget and Accounting Procedures Act of 1950 made it clear, by law for the first time, that the heads of federal agencies had the primary responsibility for accounting and financial control over their affairs. These laws were largely an outgrowth of the studies and related recommendations of the first Hoover Commission, which severely criticized the antiquated financial system of the federal government.

The great significance of these legislative enactments in this relatively short period is that they pointed the way to a more modern system of financial control. The principles and objectives stated in these laws are still governing.

Up to this time, the private sector had progressed much more than government institutions in "professionalizing" the practice of accounting and auditing. Public accountants in the private sector were a recognized profession and government agencies looked to them for guidance and assistance. Professional accounting and auditing in the federal government owes much to the public accounting profession, in a way not often recognized.

In the case of the GAO, for example, this debt goes back more than 30 years when the Congress enacted the very significant government corporation control legislation of 1945, referred to above. A new organizational unit in GAO —the Corporation Audits Division—was established, headed by and staffed largely with Certified Public Accountants who were new to GAO. Their job was to audit the government corporations in accordance with the principles and procedures applicable to commercial corporate transactions. The techniques of the public accounting profession were thus introduced into GAO and their application in the environment of a governmental agency was successful. In turn, this experience helped to pave the way for the modernization of GAO's outmoded audit practices as they had been applied to the federal government's unincorporated agencies almost from the inception of its financial system in 1789.

These practices consisted of checking financial documents in detail at a central location, where all government agencies who spent public funds were required to send them. They were superseded with audit techniques by which auditors first reviewed the strengths and weaknesses of an agency management's procedures for making sure that everything was correct and legal. These techniques, included checking samples of transactions to see that the prescribed procedures were being followed in actual practice.

Also, it is important to note, these techniques were applied in the agencies' offices rather than at batteries of desks in a remote central location. Coupled with the 1950 legislative mandate that effective accounting procedures were each agencies' responsibility, this change in audit procedures has to be regarded as one of the most revolutionary changes in the federal government's financial system since its inception. This concept was well grounded in the public accountants' approach to auditing, and its crossover to governmental auditing practices provides an excellent demonstration of one way that the public accounting profession contributed constructively to the betterment of government operations.

Achieving Statutory Objectives

The objectives set forth for all executive agencies in the 1950 Federal accounting legislation were clear enough: full disclosure of financial results of activities; adequate financial information for management; effective control over and accountability for funds, property, and other assets; reliable financial information for use in budgeting and overall financial reports.

Much progress has been made toward these objectives, but they cannot be considered totally achieved. For example, in improving their accounting systems, the executive departments and agencies must comply with the accounting principles, standards, and related requirements prescribed by the Comptroller General of the United States. The Comptroller General first published the required accounting principles and standards in 1952 and clarified them in 1965. However, many federal agencies still do not have approved systems. For example, as of April 30, 1977, 333 agencies, or all but five, had their accounting principles and standards approved, but only 178 had approved designs for translating their principles and standards into effective, working systems. And the gap from an approved design to a good, workable system in day-to-day operation is wide.

There are many reasons why more agencies do not have approved accounting systems. Overall, they illustrate how federal management accountants do not—and cannot—fully control how and to what extent they carry out their responsibilities.

- Some agency managers are not much concerned with using accounting information to make decisions and control resources.
- Frequent turnover in top management positions interrupts continuity in interest, direction, and even concern with the problem.
- Sometimes there are not enough competent staff to develop and install better systems.

- Federal programs and activities have grown in size and have become more complex. New agencies, reorganizations, and new fields of endeavor have complicated orderly systems improvement.
- Agency management officials often fail to understand how accountants and the products of their accounting systems can assist in promoting efficient and effective management.
- The Congress through its committees seldom demonstrates much interest in improved accounting in the departments and agencies despite the excellent objectives set forth in its laws. There is much concern with budgetary problems and decisions and these occupy the bulk of the time and attention of concerned committees but their processes rely relatively little on department and agency accounting systems for information on what has happened to money previously appropriated.
- The Office of Management and Budget in the executive branch has shown little continuous, effective concern with either agency attitudes or with agency accounting systems or their products.

Relating these reasons why statutory objectives have not been fully achieved is not to say that professional accountants have not had an important impact on improving the quality of financial management systems in the federal government. Even though many individual systems do not meet the Comptroller General's high standards, and even though auditors continue to find problems, overall the federal government's financial system is vastly better than what it was 25 years ago when operations were smaller and programs less complex.

The foregoing round-up of reasons why specified statutory objectives have not been completely achieved also illustrates not only the complexity of the environment in which such improvements have to be made but they show, too, that others besides the accountants have a very important part to play—managers, budget officials, the Congress itself. All have to work in concert and agree on what should be done. The accountants have neither the stature nor the clout to do the job on their own. Whether this concert of improvement action will ever come about is an open question. In the meantime, with some GAO pressure, the struggle for systems improvement continues without it.

A Unique Cooperative Improvement Program

In working to modernize and improve accounting and auditing practices in the federal government, professional accountants have participated in a unique mechanism of legislative and executive branch cooperation. This mechanism, now know as the Joint Financial Management Improvement Program, began in 1948 when the General Accounting Office, the Bureau of the Budget, and the Treasury Department decided to work together, rather than in conflict, to bring about much needed changes in the government's financial system. The heads of these agencies at the time, Comptroller General Lindsay C. Warren, Director of the Budget James E. Webb, and Secretary of the Treasury John W. Snyder, signed a pact which launched this much needed cooperative effort which is still going on today.

This program has had a long and creditable history, but the full measure of its impact over nearly 30 years has never really been assessed. It has been an important catalyst for many major accomplishments, many of them highly technical. Not only has it contributed to better and simpler financial procedures, but it has saved large amounts of public money by eliminating duplication of effort and other unnecessary work, and by promoting efficient mechanical or electronic methods of processing the vast volumes of detailed information that government agencies handle.

A recent example of constructive work under this program was the push for tighter management of federal cash by agencies, particularly those whose programs involve granting large sums to state and local governments. By narrowing the gap between the time federal funds are advanced and the time they are actually needed by the recipients, U.S. Treasury borrowings from the public have been cut back and interest costs reduced. As a result of such improved procedures, savings in interest costs of nearly $200 million a year are now being realized.

The Joint Program can be expected to go on promoting better ways of carrying out the government's financial management responsibilities. The earlier concerns with accounting and financial reporting procedures will still demand attention. In addition, it has the capacity and flexibility of operation to tackle new problems.

A notable recent example is the development of techniques to measure productivity of the federal work force. The government now has for the first time a system of indexes of such productivity which are being published regularly, with supporting reports interpreting the changes in the indexes. Representatives of the Joint Program led the development of this system and they produced the first three annual reports on productivity in the federal government (through 1975). For subsequent years, this work will be performed by the National Center for Productivity and Quality of Working Life, a federal agency created by the Congress in 1975.

Selection of Accountants as Managers

Professional accountants are seldom selected for top management positions in the federal agencies. When they have been, more often than not they have been Certified Public Accountants who came from the private sector; e.g., T. Coleman Andrews, commissioner of Internal Revenue and Percival F. Brundage, director of the Bureau of the Budget, in the 1950s; Maurice H. Stans, deputy postmaster general and budget director, also in the 1950s, and later secretary of commerce (1969-72); Robert N. Anthony, assistant secretary of Defense (comptroller) (1965-68); and Charles A. Bowsher, assistant secretary of the Navy for financial management (1967-71).

The head of the GAO is the Comptroller General of the United States—a presidential appointee. Yet only one of the five comptrollers general since the GAO was established in 1921 has been a professional certified public accountant, Joseph Campbell who served from 1954 to 1965. Of the others, John R. McCarl (1921-36) was a lawyer and private secretary to a member of Congress; Fred H. Brown (1939-40) was a lawyer and a U.S. senator; and Lindsay C. Warren (1940-54) was a lawyer and a member of Congress. The present Comptroller General, Elmer B. Staats (since 1966) is an economist and political scientist, and had been a long-time Bureau of the Budget official. Moreover, all of the deputy comptrollers general—also presidentially appointed—have been lawyers, not accountants.

There are, of course, many instances where professional accountants from within the government have been assigned to highly responsible positions below the top agency management levels. Examples include: controllers, directors of internal or contract audit organizations and chief accountants of regulatory agencies.

The main reason that accountants are not chosen for general management positions seems to be that the work of the government accountant, essential though it may be, is regarded as too narrowly focused, too technical, or too specialized. The "debit and credit" image, which accountants have done a poor job of neutralizing, tends to eliminate them from selection for the "meaty" management jobs.

Impact on Accountants in The Private Sector

How professional accountants in the federal government can have a strong impact on accountants in the private sector is illustrated by the Comptroller General's standards for qualifications of independent public accountants to audit governmental activities. Although the General Accounting Office has no mandate to prescribe standards in this field, it took on the task of recommending the qualification standards that practicing public accountants should meet to make audits of governmental agencies. The recommended qualifications (first published in 1970) were that after December 31, 1975, such audits were to be made only by certified public accountants or by uncertified public accountants who had been licensed to practice in their states by December 31, 1970. This recommendation applied to all governmental activities where independent public accountants are engaged to audit accounts and financial statements. It did not extend to governmental audit work that went beyond such matters.

While developing this recommendation, GAO studied the possiblity of federal testing as a basis for establishing qualifications for such auditors. It concluded, however, that any such system would be costly and would partially duplicate the system of uniform CPA examinations in use in the states. The Comptroller General's recommendation is advisory and not binding on any federal agency. However, it is influential and most federal agencies subscribe to it.

Some Challenges

This brief review of the role of professional accountants in governmental operations has had to leave out many aspects of their work—their role in budgeting, in investigations of various kinds, in the regulation of private companies, in establishing cost accounting standards, in procuring goods and services, in contract auditing and internal auditing and, not the least by any means, in administering the tax laws. All of these roles have their own problems and characteristics which call for separate discussion.

This review has focused mainly on the role of federal accountants whose operations are directly related to the management of federal government activities. In concluding, it seems desirable to identify some of the challenges that face the practitioners of this profession.

1. *Refining federal agency accounting systems so that they do their job efficiently and provide useful financial information to managers, budget officials, and legislators in a usable way is a continuing challenge.* This calls for more than just devising a system of accounts and reports that meets the bare minimum of the Comptroller General's principles, standards and related requirements. The real need is to integrate such systems into management processes so that they become a vital part of those processes and at the same time achieve the statutory objectives of producing good information promptly as well as serving as an aid in exercising effective control over resources and operations.

2. *Auditing financial operations, including accounts and financial reports, is a large order in a conglomerated but fragmented institution with the vastness and diversity of the federal government.* The Budget and Accounting Procedures Act of 1950 assigned the head of each federal agency the responsibility to have adequate accounting and internal control systems including internal auditing. The challenge is that all such systems have to be worked on and tested continuously to make sure they are working properly. Responsibility for the first line of such testing is in the agencies themselves, particularly through their internal audit systems. As an independent auditor, GAO has the responsibility to evaluate the quality of the internal auditing and to test the performance of these systems from time to time on behalf of the Congress to see whether the legislative objectives are being achieved.

3. *Professional accountants need to do much more to demonstrate to management officials and legislators the usefulness of the financial data that they accumulate, summarize, analyze, and report.* It is an unfortunate fact that many of these officials do not have the necessary experience or background in using financial data as a management tool. Professional accountants must constantly strive to make their products as useful as possible and to demonstrate how the information they produce can be used.

4. *A most important challenge is to try to familiarize members of Congress with the important place of the accounting fuction in the federal government's systems of financial management control.* These systems include budgeting and reporting in financial terms on what is done with funds and other resources authorized. Accountants should also try to assist them in using the information produced.

5. The federal government grants to state and local governments huge sums each year ($60 billion proposed for 1978) for a variety of purposes. Good accounting and strong auditing systems in those governments have therefore become most important to federal agency managers and to the Congress that authorizes such grants. Both need assurance that such funds are properly used and accounted for and not wasted. For this reason, *professional accountants in the federal government need to work out better ways to stimulate effective and reliable accounting and auditing systems in the recipient governments to obviate the need for federal auditors to make comprehensive checks on how federal funds are applied.*
6. The preparation of college and university students for careers in government management is very deficient particularly in the treatment of public financial management concepts and practices. *Professional accountants in the federal government need to concern themselves more directly with improving academic training by (1) helping faculty members develop course materials and case studies and (2) on invitation, participating in college programs.*

Similar challenges face accountants in state and local governments. Issues such as these bring to mind observations of a well-known and articulate naval engineer who took occasion several years ago to needle accountants in the federal government about what it took to be a professional. This was Vice Admiral H. G. Rickover. He noted that a person does not become a professional just by getting a degree and went on to say:

"Professionalism requires one to maintain constant awareness and consciousness of all matters affecting his area of competence; it also requires continued application of one's capabilities to advance his chosen field."*

Such a commentary is especially applicable to government accountants who wish to be regarded as professionals. The art and skills they practice require not only education and training and "the exercise of discretion, judgment, and personal responsibility for the application of an organized body of knowledge" (to borrow the words of the U.S. Civil Service Commission). To progress and attract recognition as a profession, its practicing members must also step out and demonstrate by words and deeds how essential their services are to better management and better government.

Author's Note:

As this paper was being written, the Subcommittee on Reports, Accounting and Management of the Senate Committee on Governmental Affairs conducted hearings on a staff report on "the accounting establishment" that concluded that setting accounting standards for private companies can no longer be entrusted to accountants in the private sector and that the function should be exercised by the federal government. The ramifications of this highly debatable proposal are beyond the scope of this paper. But it can be observed that—at least in the eyes of the subcommittee staff and some members of Congress—a better and more trustworthy job of setting financial accounting standards can be done by accountants who are federal employees than by accountants who are not—an implied vote of confidence that will also be subject to much debate.

For Further Reading

"Accounting Reform in Washington," by John W. McEachren, *Journal of Accountancy,* Sept. 1955;

"Financial Management in the Federal Government—Are We Doing Less with More?" by Larry A. Jobe, *The Federal Accountant,* Dec. 1970;

"Evaluating the Effectiveness of Federal Social Programs," by Elmer B. Staats, *The Federal Accountant,* Dec. 1974;

"The Environment in Governmental Accounting in the Seventies," by Leo Herbert, *The GAO Review,* Fall 1972;

"The Challenge to Federal Accountants In Improving Congressional Control of the Budget," by E. H. Morse, Jr., *The Federal Accountant,* Sept. 1974;

"Current Significance of the Accounting and Auditing Act of 1950," by E. H. Morse, Jr., *The Federal Accountant,* Sept. 1975;

Standards for Audit of Governmental Organizations, Programs, Activities & Functions, by the Comptroller General of the United States, 1972;

Annual reports of the Comptroller General of the United States;

Annual reports of the Joint Financial Management Improvement Program;

Also see *Bibliography on Federal Accounting, Auditing, Budgeting, and Reporting 1900-1970* (annotated)—the most comprehensive bibliography on these subjects in existence (published in 1971 by the Association of Government Accountants, Arlington, Va.)

---

*Address on "Accounting Practices—Do They Protect the Public?" at Federal Government Accountants Association National Symposium, June 18, 1970—published in *The Federal Accountant,* December 1970.

THE PROFESSIONS AND GOVERNMENT: ENGINEERING AS A CASE IN POINT*

Richard L. Schott, *University of Texas at Austin*

Engineering, among the largest of the professions, has had a substantial impact on American government at nearly all levels. As the domain of government activity has increased and its programs become more complex, engineers have provided an important source of talent for the implementation and the management of wide-scale technical ventures. Engineering's oldest branch, civil engineering, has, since its beginnings, been closely associated with public technology; some of its newer branches, such as aeronautical engineering, depend heavily on governmental support. In this essay, I hope to provide a brief introduction to the engineering profession, examine some characteristics of engineering which influence its impact on government, and raise several issues which surround the role of engineers in the public service.

Engineering and Engineers

Engineering, with roughly one million practitioners, is among the largest of American professions. Second in size only to primary and secondary school-teaching (which is largely a public function), it is the largest "general" profession. Since there is no commonly accepted definition of "engineer," their exact number in the American workforce is a matter of contention. Numerous individuals who identify themselves as engineers in census data, for example, do not hold even bachelor-level degrees in engineering.** Although the 1970 census lists some 1,200,000 engineers, an analysis by the National Science Foundation suggests that the number is closer to 986,000.[1]

Engineering is predominantly a profession of white males from lower-middle and lower class backgrounds. Indeed, it is the traditional under-graduate profession for upwardly-mobile males, as nursing and school teaching have been for females. Women engineers make up less than two per cent of the engineering population, minority groups about one per cent.[2] Engineering offers a professional curriculum of four years' duration which has tended to attract students who cannot afford the extended preparation required by the more prestigious graduate professional fields such as law and medicine. During this century, there has been a tendency for engineering to recruit from increasingly lower socio-economic strata; and the percentage of students coming from blue-collar families has steadily increased.[3] "Clearly," one observer concludes, "engineering has become an avenue of upward mobility for the intelligent sons of working class families."[4]

Engineering is open, diverse, and pluralistic. Entrance to its ranks is subject to firm control neither by its practitioners nor by its institutions of education. Engineering is not a terminal profession: large numbers of its practitioners eventually leave technical engineering work for managerial and executive positions. Its knowledge base is fragmented into a variety of disciplines and subdisciplines, and it lacks legal recognition in the sense that registration or licensing are not a requirement for most engineering practice. It lacks a generally-accepted code of ethics as well as effective peer control over the activities of its members. Its commitment to society and its concern for social responsibility traditionally have been weak. Engineering has yet to develop a guiding rationale for ideology; and its organizations, as we shall see, are numerous and diverse. And due partly to its large size, it lacks an essential characteristic of the older general professions—a sense of community.[5]

Sociological studies of the engineer depict him as an intelligent, stable, self-sufficient, conforming individual, rather introverted but not personally introspective. Engineers appear to be energetic and goal-oriented and to place a high value on advancement and on tangible (especially financial) rewards. Two scholars who have surveyed the literature concerning the characteristics of the typical engineer suggest he is "an authoritative person with few intimate relationships, strongly work-oriented, competent and energetic, and preferring to deal with objects and things rather than with people."[6] Studies of the occupational values held by engineers indicate that they place a high emphasis on jobs that provide a comfortable income and in which work is judged on its merits, and a low emphasis on jobs which involve working with people rather than things and which make a contribution to society.[7]

The professional model of the independent practitioner does not apply to engineers. The vast majority of them, over 95 per cent, work in and for organizations. Their dependence on large organizations has proved an historical

---

*The author would like to thank Mary Ryan for her assistance in the final preparation of this essay.

**I recall an incident related to me by an engineering professor, who was helping his aged father-in-law fill out some forms related to his retirement. Asked by his son what he wished to put down as his occupation, the father-in-law, a draftsman for thirty years, thought for a moment, then with a twinkle in his eye, suggested "engineer?"

Richard L. Schott is a member of the faculty of the Lyndon B. Johnson School of Public Affairs at the University of Texas at Austin. He is the author of *Professionals in Public Service: The Characteristics and Education of Engineer Federal Executives; The Bureaucratic State: Evolution and Scope of the American Federal Bureaucracy;* and of several articles on the professions and government. His study of congressional-bureaucratic relations and oversight of administration, *Congress and the Administrative State,* will appear this summer.

impediment to full professional status, for it means that the organization rather than a client is the consumer of the engineer's services. And it also means that for the most part, the engineer's performance is judged by superiors in his organization rather than his colleagues. This being the case, one might assume that the engineer is an excellent example of the classic problem of the professional-in-the-organization—an individual frustrated by the restraints on professional activity which the organizational environment places on him. Empirical studies of engineers in a variety of settings, however, suggest that this is not the case. These studies have found that engineers place little importance on such traditional professional values as a collegial orientation, a sense of professional community, and the acquisition of knowledge. Such findings have led two scholars to suggest that the engineer is rarely in conflict with the demands of large organizations, but rather adopts them to his own advantage. "The B.S. degree engineer", they conclude, "is in many ways the essence of the organization man. For, although he is a professional, this is largely due to his occupation having status in the larger society."[8]

This seemingly symbiotic relationship between the engineering profession and the organizational environment in which it moves may help explain a phenomenon of particular interest to us—the tendency of engineers to move into management and administration. Those from engineering backgrounds figure prominently among the executive cadres of private industry and, as we shall see, of government. Surveys of engineers' career patterns suggest a pronounced tendency over time for them to move into supervisory and administrative work.[9] One study by the Engineers' Joint Council found that of the sample they surveyed, over a third had become managers of programs, departments, or whole organizations.[10] The seeming appeal of administration may reflect a certain congruence between the engineer's occupational values and the norms of large organizations, as well as the scope within such organizations for the application of "rational" management. But it may also reflect the potential of executive positions to help engineers realize such career objectives as advancement, a sense of power and control, and financial reward which are important to many of them. "For many career-minded engineers," one observer suggests, "the executive office rather than the senior engineer's office is the ultimate goal."[11] For such individuals, professional "success" means moving out of technical activities into administrative ones; the practice for which they were trained becomes not an end in itself but a stepping stone to executive careers.

Engineering Education

One can gain a good deal of insight into the engineering profession and its practitioners by examining its professional schools, for it is here that attitudes, values, and the context of professional activity are largely determined. Engineering, like a number of the newer or emerging professions, differs from such well-established professions as law and medicine. Whereas the established professions developed a graduate curriculum on a base of undergraduate liberal or pre-professional courses, engineering education has, since its beginnings in the nineteenth century, offered professional training at the undergraduate level in a period of four years. This has placed considerable strain on the content of engineering curricula, which attempt to cover basic and applied science, mathematics, engineering design and tool courses, and liberal studies in a relatively short period of time. The result is a curriculum of great density, few electives, and only scant attention (less than a year) to courses in the humanities and social sciences.

Much of the debate over curricular matters in engineering education has turned on whether to give greater emphasis to the science underlying engineering practice (the approach most often favored by Ph.D.-trained engineering faculty) or to applied and technical courses which prepare the student for immediate employment (the approach favored by most industrial employers of graduating engineers). As a result, the social science and humanistic components of the curriculum ("socio-humanistic studies" in the argot of engineering education) are lost in the shuffle. Indeed, since the introduction of engineering education on a large scale, stemming from the impetus of the Morrill Act in the 1860s, the average proportion of the curriculum devoted to liberal studies has fallen from a little over a year to one semester.[12]

From our perspective, the problem of socio-humanistic studies is pressing. They are often the only "general" education many engineers receive, offering the potential of expanding his horizons beyond the narrow confines of technical study to the social and political environment and to the ecology of the profession. In fairness, it should be noted that a number of engineering educators have been sensitive to this problem, and a number of self-studies have argued for greater attention to the socio-humanistic area. Recently, there has been a growing awareness of the role of such studies in giving the engineering student an appreciation of the social impact of his work. While traditional views of the engineer's societal role held that rational design and the "impersonal service" rendered by the engineer was sufficient, a recent self-study countered that "It is becoming increasingly clear . . . that this genial optimism is not well-founded. Solutions to problems often merely generate more problems, with no guarantee that the end result will be in the interests of mankind. . . . It is the background of urgency which constitutes the new challenge to engineering education and to the humanistic and social sciences as part of engineering education."[13]

Despite such affirmations by engineering educators of the importance of liberal studies, they have simply not grown substantially, if at all, within the engineering curriculum. One limiting factor, of course, is that the press of technical subjects forces them to take a back seat. A contributing reason may be the fact that only since the 1950s has the engineering accreditation process paid formal attention to the place of socio-humanistic studies. Though accreditation guidelines require that one-half to one year be devoted to such studies, there is evidence that a number of schools have not significantly increased the amount of liberal arts courses in the curriculum.[14]

A key factor, however, may be the attitudes of many

engineering faculty toward such studies. Analyses suggest that engineering faculty are often hostile or at best indifferent to the liberal arts, and reluctant to see them expand as a proportion of the curriculum. One study of the views of the liberal arts held by faculty in various professional schools found that of nine undergraduate-level professions, engineering faculty ranked lowest in favorable attitudes toward liberal studies.[15] (There appears to be a tendency on the part of many faculty, I have been told on several occasions, to dismiss liberal arts courses as "cultural b.s.") Moreover, a survey of engineering schools found that a majority of them were satisfied with the amount of socio-humanistic studies presently offered in the curriculum; only a minority felt more were needed.[16]

Of those liberal studies which *are* offered in engineering curricula, courses which would give the student an appreciation of the ecology of the profession often are neglected. Engineers tend to place greater emphasis on subjects such as English composition and speech which contribute directly to professional performance. The social sciences, including government and political science, appear to be at a particular disadvantage: those engineering educators who accept the role of liberal studies as a contribution to their students' intellectual horizons often stress humanities courses such as literature, philosophy, and history, rather than social science offerings.[17]

The Engineering Student

What of the students who pursue and eventually complete the demanding and highly-technical engineering curriculum? Most research tends to indicate that engineering schools attract more than their share of bright students who rank high on aptitude tests, especially those which measure quantitative ability. High school male graduates near the top of their class often choose engineering as their initial major. As one scholar has observed, engineering "has not lacked for capable students, at any level, especially when compared to other areas."[18]

Recruits to engineering schools share a cluster of values which distinguish them from those entering other fields. Freshmen engineers studied by the National Opinion Research Center ranked high on measures of desire for financial reward and on measures of originality and creativity, but quite low on measures of "people orientation" and service to society. Student engineers appear to enjoy ordering and systematizing knowledge; to be pragmatic, practical, and "thing-oriented;" and to have a rather low tolerance for ambiguity.[19] A number of these characteristics are especially typical of students from lower socio-economic backgrounds. One observer suggests that their social origins influence strongly the values held by many engineering students, whom he found basically anti-intellectual, contemptuous of middleclass values, and suspicious of liberal education. "These students believe in efficiency and hard work. The narrow, workmanlike and anti-intellectual attitudes held by so many engineers are in part a function of engineering education [and] in part a function of social recruitment to the profession. . . ."[20] As I will note later, these characteristics of engineering students and the curriculum they pursue may have serious implications for the ability of engineers to grapple with the policy and administrative roles many assume at the upper levels of the public service.

Engineering Organizations

Engineering organizations, like the engineering profession itself, are diverse; the various national groups number well over one hundred. There is within engineering no one organization or society that can claim to speak for, or to represent, the engineering proession as a whole—certainly not in the sense that the American Bar Association, for example, claims to speak for the bulk of the legal community. Some engineering organizations serve engineering disciplines and technical specialities; others serve its institutions of learning; still others like the National Society of Professional Engineers (NSPE) attempt to increase the professional status of its members. In addition to these organizations there have appeared groups which have tried to act as "umbrella" organizations for the engineering profession as a whole.

The earliest, and still among the most influential discipline-oriented engineering organizations are the four "Founder" societies, formed around the dominant disciplines of the nineteenth century—the American Society of Civil Engineers (ASCE), the American Society of Mechanical Engineers (ASME), the American Institute of Mining, Metallurigical and Petroleum Engineers (AIME), and the Institute of Electrical and Electronics Engineers (IEEE). The numerous disciplinary and technical societies which exist today are spread over a spectrum which ranges from the highly-professional (in the sense of an orientation toward the individual, practicing engineer) at the one end, to those that are basically business or industry-oriented at the other. One clue to a particular society's place on this spectrum is the kind of membership which it allows. Those which admit only individual members fall toward the professional end; those which admit individual *and* institutional members somewhere in the middle; and those whose members are solely institutional toward the business or trade-association end. Another clue is the qualifications necessary for full membership. The more "professional" organizations stipulate that full members be qualified in engineering *design,* a requirement which limits full membership largely to practicing engineers. Other societies require that a full member be only in "responsible charge" of engineering activities—a term broad enough to include most managers and executives. A last category of membership requires only that members be engaged on interested in a particular field of engineering.

Two engineering organizations—the American Society for Engineering Education (ASEE), and the Engineers' Council for Professional Development (ECPD)—serve the interests of engineering education and its educators. The ASEE, formed in 1893 as the Society for the Promotion of Engineering Education (SPEE), was the creation of engineering educators. Its founding gave expression to a need for greater cohesiveness and planning among engineering schools and curricula and as well to a feeling that the existing technical societies seemed disinclined to give the educational process sufficient attention. The early members of the ASEE were educators, not practitioners, representatives of a newer "school culture" which gradually gained control over curriculum content and admissions standards for a majority of engineering schools.[21]

The Engineers' Council for Professional Development, formed in 1932, was a response to pressures for the formal accreditation of engineering curricula, generated largely by members of the "school culture." The ECPD was formed originally from members of the four Founder societies plus the American Institute of Chemical Engineers; the (then) SPEE, and the National Council of State Boards of Engineering Examiners—organizations representing the professional, educational, and legal aspects of engineering. Today, the ECPD accredits curricula leading to the first degree in engineering, usually the B.S., as well as programs in engineering technology, considered sub-professional.

A special role in the professionalization of engineering has been played by the National Society of Professional Engineers (NSPE). With membership open only to individual engineers, NSPE was formed in the early 1930s in support of then-current attempts to enact strict provisions for the registration and licensing of engineers. NSPE has since attempted to promote greater professional competence among engineers by encouraging them to take and pass examinations for registration. And as it has promoted registration at the upper levels of engineering practice, it has also attempted to combat unionism at its lower levels and has campaigned actively to defeat engineering unions.[22]

Though the engineering profession has proved too diverse and perhaps simply too large to enable the growth of a single, unified professional group representing all engineers, it has been successful in creating a succession of umbrella organizations made up of technical society, institutional, and trade group members. The current engineer umbrella organization, the Engineers' Joint council (EJC), was formed in the 1940s and today includes some two dozen member societies and associates. Since 1967, it has allowed the affiliation of industrial corporations as well (a move which led one of the Founder societies, the IEEE, to withdraw). The EJC, in the eyes of one of its critics, has demonstrated a special concern for the "interests of employers of engineers." It helped to fight the growth of engineering unionism in the 1950s, has generally supported increasing the number of engineers to ensure an adequate manpower pool for employers, and has worked to keep engineering "open" by supporting less restrictive registration and licensing laws.[23]

The newest arrival on the scene is the National Academy of Engineering (NAE), which received a charter from the National Academy of Sciences in 1964. Its establishment represented a counterweight to what many engineers considered an over-emphasis, institutionally, on pure science at the national level. Among the Academy's activities is the provision of advice to the federal government on the application of engineering techniques to problems encountered by government agencies. And its Commission on Education has paid a good deal of attention to new developments in engineering education, especially those related to an enhanced appreciation of the social role of engineering.

The organizational picture of the engineering profession is thus one of great diversity—a melange of technical and special interest groups, some looking toward the individual practicing engineer, some toward engineering education, others toward engineering as a profession, and still others to business and industrial interests. No single organization speaks for all of engineering, and few even for the majority of those they claim to represent. Historically and functionally, engineering organizations are as diverse as the engineering profession itself.

The Engineering Profession and Government

Engineering has a substantial influence on governments at many levels. Its practitioners perform not only a variety of technical tasks but also form an important managerial cadre at the upper echelons of the public service. Recent data indicate that roughly 16 per cent of employed engineers work for federal, state, or local government with the vast majority, some 73 per cent, employed by private business and industry. The balance are in college teaching or non-profit organizations. There is considerable variation, however, among the various branches of engineering. Government employs about 43 per cent of all civil engineers, for example, but only six per cent of chemical engineers.[24] Though the percentage of engineers working in government is small compared to their total population, the fact that engineering is such a large profession helps explain why its members constitute such a large segment of all professional employees of government. In the federal government, engineering—with some 84,000 of its practitioners employed in professional positions—is far and away the largest single professional group. Indeed, engineers account for nearly one-third of all professionals in federal employment.[25]

There is evidence that the engineering profession, as a whole, denigrates government and government employment, and that its sympathies lie with the private sector. Support for this assumption comes in part from the Kilpatrick studies of the image of the federal service, which included sample groups of engineers in industry and business, in college teaching, and in public service. Attitudes toward government and public service among the sample from business and industry (which employ the vast majority of engineers) were found to be quite negative. Business engineers, for example, rated their present job much higher than the same job in the federal government. Asked how their families would feel should they go to work for government, the majority of engineers who said it would make a difference indicated that their families would see such a move as "down the ladder." Engineers in business saw government employment as restrictive, involving red tape, wasted motion, lack of self-determination, and rigid supervision. And they tended to have unfavorable views of federal employees in general, seeing them as security-conscious and lacking ambition.[26] (Such feelings were also reflected in the observation made to me by the head of an engineering professional organization that only the bottom members of his graduating class went to work for government.) Engineers in federal employment, however, do not share these negative views of themselves and their work. They prefer their present job in the federal service to the same job in the private sector, and view government work overall as more appealing. They are attracted to the fact that government employment offers greater security, but agree with their colleagues in the private sector that business organizations provide a better opportunity to become "really successful."[27]

In the federal government, engineers are employed in large numbers by those agencies whose missions are closely associated with applied science and technology. The Department of Defense is the single largest employer of engineers, followed by the National Aeronautic & Space Administration (NASA), the Department of Transportation, the Department of Interior, the Environmental Protection Agency, and the Department of Agriculture. Engineers are found in substantial numbers at the middle and upper levels of the federal service, their *median* grade being GS-13.[28]

Of greatest interest to us are not primarily those engineers (the bulk of the federal engineering population) who are journeymen pursuing technical work, but rather those—like many of their colleagues in the private sector—who have moved upwards into administrative and executive positions. It is these individuals through whom the influence of the engineering profession on government is most likely to be translated. Exact estimates of the number of engineers in the federal executive population (defined as GS-15 and above by the U.S. Civil Service Commission) are difficult to make, since those from engineering backgrounds hold a proportion of the jobs in the category "administration," and as well in the "public law" group. But sources suggest that the number of engineers and engineers-turned-administrators in the federal executive population is probably as high as 25 percent.[29] It is, however, interesting that during the past few years, the number of engineers in the engineering occupational category has been steadily decreasing, due at least in part to retrenchment in NASA, traditionally a large employer of engineer executives, and in the Navy. The legal profession, by contrast, has shown a corresponding growth over this same period, reflecting perhaps the growing influence of the legal profession at the highest levels of the federal service as the national government has placed more emphasis on regulation and less on the development of technology.[30]

A study of federal engineer executives conducted several years ago addresses a number of the concerns raised earlier in our discussion of the engineering profession.[31] Based on a sample of engineers in NASA, the Corps of Engineers, and the Federal Highway Administration, the study found that by the time engineers in these agencies reached grade GS-14 and higher (including thus a grade lower than the Civil Service definition of the federal executive population), their work had already shifted substantially from technical activities into administration and management. More than 80 per cent of the sample reported that their work was at least half administrative in nature, with over a quarter reporting that it was primarily or exclusively so. And as he advanced in rank, the engineer's work focused increasingly on administration.[32]

These federal engineers, as administrators, are working in areas far removed from their formal education, which, as we have seen, has little relevance to administration and broad policy concerns. This group of engineers were well aware of this situation, and disagreed almost unanimously that their engineering curriculum had done little to prepare them for the broader executive roles they had assumed. In looking back on their education, they favored increasing substantially the portion of their curricula devoted to socio-humanistic studies, especially the social sciences. Had these engineers known they would have ended up in their present positions, they would have (as before) done undergraduate work in engineering; but of those who went on to graduate work, nearly half would not have continued in engineering, but would have taken degrees in public or business administration. Though they felt their continuing, in-service education had contributed substantially to their ability to cope with their new roles, more than half expressed a moderate-to-strong need for additional training in such areas as human relations, public administration, and personnel management.[33]

The sensitivity which these federal engineer executives display toward their educational needs is triggered, at least partly, by the demands of jobs for which they were not well-prepared. But why did they opt for administrative and executive positions? One answer may be found in the occupational values—financial reward, increased responsibility—discussed earlier in connection with the proclivity of engineers to move into management. However, a seminal study of the transition from professional to administrative positions made by engineers (and scientists) in several federal agencies suggests other factors also may be important. This study found that engineers fall into several different groups, depending on how they view the prospect of moving from technical to administrative positions. One group included those whose motivations and values were consistent with moving into management. A second group was comprised of those who were reluctant to do so, but who grew to enjoy administrative responsibilities. A third were inclined against such a move, and remained strongly opposed. But over two-thirds of those studied fell into the first group,[34] thus suggesting that the federal executive engineer cadre is drawn largely from those with an inclination to assume executive roles—an inclination no doubt buttressed by the values which appear to permeate the engineering profession.

Concluding Observations

It is impossible in an essay of such brief compass to assess in any comprehensive way the impact of the engineering profession on government. There are, however, a few central themes or questions which can be raised. As we have seen, the engineering profession is oriented in the main to the private sector, its major employer. The need to produce engineering graduates for immediate employment in industry and business is reflected in the engineering schools, where the humanities and social sciences, not to mention the study of government and the "political" are given short shrift. In spite of some pressure for reform from within, engineering education remains a narrow, technical curriculum which allows the student little time for reflection or for exposure to vast domains of human knowledge. It is doubtful that this narrow training does much to broaden or inform the public service by those engineers—often second-class citizens in the eyes of their colleagues—who end up working for government. Granted, however, that the relationship of engineering to government varies with the field concerned. Civil and environmental engineering, for example, have generally demonstrated a deeper appreciation of public sector problems through their close association with government than have such branches as industrial and mining engineering, which traditionally have been closer to the private sector.

A second question concerns the *kinds* of individuals who traditionally have been recruited to engineering. As we have seen, they have come predominantly from lower socio-economic backgrounds and tend to share the provincialism and authoritarianism often typical of upwardly-mobile individuals. One long-time student of the engineering profession suggests that the social origin of engineers has foreclosed the development of a service ethic in the profession and has kept it from becoming concerned with human welfare and broad social goals.

As the importance of engineers has increased to the point where major segments of the society are dependent upon their expertise, we have also observed a corresponding decline in the possibilities for the development of engineering as a service profession committed to the service of man. . . . The social origins and consequent mobility experiences of persons entering engineering lead to the reinforcement of business rather than professional values, thereby inhibiting the emergence of a service ethic which focuses upon human welfare. . . .[35]

Given what appear to be rather clear sets of characteristics of engineers and the lack of a social ethic among them, their impact on the social and human dimensions of government activity is quite possibly a negative one.

A special problem is created by the proclivity of engineers to move into management and executive positions. Such positions generally require a broad approach to analysis and decision-making and substantial interaction with the policy and political environment of the program or agency concerned. One must question whether government is necessarily well-served by placing in its highest career echelons individuals of rather provincial and technical backgrounds. It is likely that continued reliance on engineers for the highest administrative cadres will contribute to the narrowing tendencies which professions often have on public service—in the words of Frederick Mosher, "gradually but profoundly moving the weight toward the partial, the corporate perspective and away from that of the general interest."[36] Though one of the antidotes to such influence offered by Mosher is a reform of professional education, one cannot be sanguine about the possibility of such developments in engineering.

One should bear in mind, however, that the technical expertise of engineering has been invaluable to the number of complex tasks that governments have undertaken over the years: From water and roadways in the early nineteenth century, through sanitary engineering accomplishments in the rise of the cities later in that century, through the successes of the Manhattan Project in the 1940s and the Apollo space program in the 1960s, to the most recent developments in protecting the environment and developing new sources of energy. Engineering, moreover, had a certain rationalizing effect on the early development of a public service which was shaking off the vestiges of the spoils system, and has played a major role in designing information and other control systems which have contributed greatly to the administration of vast and complex public organizations. But the injection of engineers into the commanding heights of these organizations continues, justifiably, to give pause.

Notes

1. U.S. Bureau of the Census, *1970 Census of the Population*. Vol. 1, *Characteristics of the Population: Summary Data* (Washington: USGPO, 1973), p. 1-718; U.S. National Science Foundation, *The 1972 Scientist and Engineer Population Redefined* (Washington: NSF, 1975), p. 5.
2. U.S. Bureau of the Census, *op. cit.,* pp. 1-718, 1-739.
3. Carolyn C. Perrucci, "Engineering and the Class Structure," in Robert Perrucci and Joel E. Gerstl, eds., *The Engineer and the Social System* (New York: John Wiley and Sons, 1969), pp. 282-284.
4. Robert L. Eichhorn, "The Student Engineer," in *Ibid.,* p. 144.
5. For an elaboration of these themes, see Robert Perrucci and Joel E. Gerstl, *Profession Without Community: Engineers in American Society* (New York: Random House, 1969).
6. Donald E. Super and Paul B. Bachrach, *Scientific Careers and Vocational Development Theory* (New York: Teachers' College of Columbia University, 1957), pp. 66-67.
7. See, for example, William K. LeBold *et al.,* "The Engineer in Industry and Government," *Journal of Engineering Education,* Vol. 56, No. 7 (March, 1966), p. 727.
8. Perrucci and Gerstl, *op. cit.,* pp. 118-119; 137; 161. It should be noted that there are variations in the degree of professional orientation among engineers, and that the level of professional activity as well as the importance of professional values appear to increase with a higher level of education. This relationship may show either that advanced education leads to more "professional" jobs or that professional values are imparted during the longer professional socialization which advanced study entails. *Ibid.,* p. 123.
9. See LeBold, *op. cit.,* p. 245.
10. Engineers' Joint Council, *A Profile of the Engineering Profession* (New York: EJC, 1971), p. 11.
11. Laure M. Sharp, *Education and Employment: The Early Careers of College Graduates* (Baltimore: The Johns Hopkins Press, 1970), pp. 54, 79.
12. Society for the Promotion of Engineering Education, *Report of the Investigation of Engineering Education, 1932-1929* (Pittsburgh: Lancaster Press, 1930-34), Vol. I, p. 552; American Society for Engineering Education, "Liberal Learning for the Engineer: Report," *Journal of Engineering Education,* Vol. 59, No. 4 (December, 1968), pp. 303-342.
13. American Society for Engineering Education, *op. cit.,* p. 310.
14. See *Ibid.* pp. 332-333.
15. Edwin J. Holstein and Earl J. McGrath, *Liberal Education*

15. *and Engineering* (New York: Teachers College of Columbia University, 1960), pp. 97-103.
16. William K. LeBold, Robert Perrucci, *et al.,* "Educational Institutional Views of Undergraduate Goals of Engineering Education," *Journal of Engineering Education,* Vol. 56, No. 6 (February, 1966), p. 218.
17. Holstein and McGrath, *op. cit.,* p. 44.
18. Paul Heist, "The Student," in National Society for the Study of Education, *Education for the Professions* (Chicago: NSEE, 1962), p. 222.
19. James A. Davis, *Undergraduate Career Decisions* (Chicago: NORC, 1965), p. 180; Perrucci and Gerstl, *Profession Without Community,* p. 51.
20. Martin Trow, "Some Implications of the Social Origins of Engineers," in U.S. National Science Foundation, *Scientific Manpower: 1958* (Washington: USGPO, 1959), p. 72.
21. See the discussion in Monte A. Calvert, *The Mechanical Engineer in America, 1830-1910: Professional Cultures in Conflict* (Baltimore: Johns Hopkins Press, 1967), p. 48.
22. Joel Seidman, "Engineering Unionism," in Perrucci and Gerstl, *op. cit.,* pp. 225-226.
23. Edwin C. Layton, Jr., *The Revolt of the Engineers: Social Responsibility in the American Engineering Profession* (Cleveland: Case Western Reserve Press, 1971), pp. 249-252.
24. U.S. National Science Foundation, *1972 Scientist and Engineer Population Redefined,* Vol. 2, *Detailed Statistical Tables* (NSF76-306) (Washington: NSF, 1976), p. 2.
25. U.S. Civil Service Commission, *Occupations of Federal White-Collar Workers, October 31, 1974 and 1975* (Washington: USGPO, 1976), pp. xiv, 5-6.
26. Franklin Kilpatrick, *et al., The Image of the Federal Service* (Washington: Brookings Institution, 1964), pp. 71-75, 221-237, 321-337. One should temper these findings by noting that the data were collected in the early 1960s before such projects as Apollo brought additional glamour to government engineering and also before the substantial salary increases of the middle and late 1960s.
27. Franklin Kilpatrick *et al., Source Book of a Study of Occupational Values and the Image of the Federal Service* (Washington: Brookings Institution, 1964), pp. 71, 75.
28. U.S. Civil Service Commission, *Occupations of Federal White Collar Workers,* pp. 38-41, 86-89.
29. U.S. Civil Service Commission, *Executive Personnel in the Federal Service: October, 1976* (Washington: USGPO, 1976), p. 6; sources in the Bureau of Executive Manpower, U.S. Civil Service Commission.
30. U.S. Civil Service Commission, *Characteristics of the Federal Executive* (Washington: USCSC, 1969), p. 5; U.S. Civil Service Commission, *Executive Manpower in the Federal Service* (Washington: USGPO, 1971-1975); U.S. Civil Service Commission, *Executive Personnel,* p. 6.
31. Richard L. Schott, *Professionals in Public Service: The Characteristics and Education of Engineer Federal Executives* (Beverly Hills: Sage Publications, 1973).
32. *Ibid.,* pp. 16-24.
33. *Ibid.,* pp. 31-40.
34. James Bayton and Richard Chapman, *The Transformation of Scientists and Engineers into Managers* (Washington: National Academy of Public Administration, 1971), pp. vi., 103.
35. Robert Perrucci, "Engineering: Professional Servant of Power," in Eliot Friedson, ed., *The Professions and Their Prospects* (Beverly Hills: Sage Publications, 1973), p. 121.
36. Frederick C. Mosher, *Democracy and the Public Service* (New York: Oxford University Press, 1968), p. 210.

SCIENTISTS AND GOVERNMENT: A CASE OF PROFESSIONAL AMBIVALENCE

W. Henry Lambright, *Syracuse University*
Albert H. Teich, *George Washington University*

Introduction

One of the most important developments of the 20th century has been the growing interaction of science, technology, and society. The reciprocal relations of science with technology, and of both with society, had been ongoing long before this century. However, the rapid movement from basic scientific discoveries to the building and use of an atomic bomb made clear to all that these relations could have awesome consequences. Sputnik and the ensuing Apollo moon landing were equally spectacular examples of the power of science and technology. Today, science and technology are called upon to cope with a host of earthbound problems—energy, pollution, famine. Indicted often as a cause of societal problems, science and technology invariably are asked to provide tools for the amelioration of these problems. When governments throughout the world spend billions of dollars on research and development, the centrality of science and technology to societal needs is no longer a subject of debate.

As science and technology have become a self-conscious matter for government and societal concern, so also have scientists. Scientists—mainly "pure" natural scientists drawn from the university—developed the atomic bomb, and thereafter sought to influence the course of atomic energy development in the policy arenas of Washington. Their knowledge proved relevant to the economic and political concerns of officials in government. The consequence has been the growing participation of scientists in a variety of roles other than their traditional role in the research community.

Many scientists have viewed their rise to the status of an "elite" in government decision-making with some ambivalence. One reason is that they are merely one professional group among many vying for influence in political decision-making. Another is that the more successful they may be in government, the less they are likely to have time to be scientists in their laboratories.

Working for the government is not uncommon among scientists. A significant number are employed in government laboratories and in administrative positions in federal agencies. In fact, the federal government is the third largest sector of employment for scientists, employing 12 per cent of the 663,000 persons in the U.S. labor force classified as "scientists." Business and industry are the largest employers with 37 per cent followed by educational institutions with 27 per cent.[1] The percentage of *doctoral* scientists and engineers working for the federal government is somewhat smaller; only 8 per cent of a total population of 227,000 (statistics for doctoral scientists are not available separately). The greater part (59 per cent) of this most highly trained segment of the scientific community is employed in educational institutions. A few other facts about federally employed scientists and engineers are worth noting. Nearly one-third (33.1 per cent) of those holding doctorates are life scientists; slightly less than one-fourth (23.4 per cent are physical scientists; 15.2 per cent are engineers; 11.2 per cent environmental scientists, and 8.2 per cent social scientists.[2] Three-quarters of all government scientists and engineers work in just four agencies: the Departments of Defense (45 per cent), Agricultural (15 per cent), and Interior (8 per cent); and NASA (7 per cent). The Departments of Commerce & Health, Education & Welfare each employ about 4 per cent, while the remaining 16 per cent are split among all other federal agencies.[3]

Despite the large numbers of scientists employed by the federal government and the growing technical orientation and involvement of many federal agencies, a career in government still poses some difficult value conflicts and barriers to policy influence for a scientist. The most important direct policy role for scientists thus appears to be not full-time employment in government, but a part-time advisory relationship. However, even the power of the science advisor has waxed and waned in different circumstances over the years. The fact that he is close to power, yet does not ordinarily possess power himself, is one ingredient among many that makes for ambivalence in the scientists' attitude toward government service.

The reasons for ambivalence go deeper, however. Scientists are professionals in the same manner of the other groups in the essays of this symposium. However, they are a peculiar species quite different from, say, lawyers or social workers. Scientists have a difficult time gauging their "professional" responsibilities vis-a-vis society and government. Ironically, scientists, who have been around a long time and are among the more prestigious groups in society, are in some sense "emerging" professionals. That is, their traditional training (unlike that of lawyers and doctors) does not equip them for the "professional" role that society and government expect of them. The scientist as a professional is a person under tension—pulled one

---

W. Henry Lambright is professor of political science and public administration, the Maxwell School, Syracuse University, and director of the Science and Technology Policy Center, Syracuse Research Corporation. He is the author of a book, *Governing Science and Technology* (Oxford University Press, 1976).

Albert H. Teich is associate professor of public affairs and deputy director of the Graduate Program in Science, Technology, and Public Policy at George Washington University. He is the editor of *Technology and Man's Future* (St. Martin's Press, 2nd edition 1977) and *Scientists and Public Affairs* (MIT Press, 1974).

way by what he feels he is supposed to do as a *scientist*, pulled another way by what society needs from him as an *expert*. How this tension is resolved by the individual scientist determines his own view of his professional calling.

Scientists and Professionalism

What is a scientist? Why is there a tension between his role as a scientist and as a "professional"? The central role for scientists *qua* scientists is research, the pursuit of knowledge either for its own sake (basic research) or for the sake of practical application (applied research). Over the years, those scientists engaged in basic research have developed an intense sense of community surrounding their work, a set of norms governing their participation in that community, and a particular reward structure emphasizing recognition by their peers.[4]

The most important social aspect of the scientific profession is the orientation of scientists toward their work and peers. They are science- (i.e., discipline) oriented and scientist-oriented. They work in accordance with the internal logic of their discipline. The greatest rewards for scientists come from making the most important contributions to knowledge in their fields of science. These produce the Nobel prizes, the National Academy of Sciences memberships. Decisions as to who wins these awards are made primarily by other specialists in a scientist's field. If the nature of a scientist is such that he is primarily interested in his discipline and what others in his field—who share his orientation—think of his performance therein, then it follows that it is less important what non-scientists, including other social institutions of society, think. A scientist is trained and socialized to science, not to society. Indeed, he is taught to believe that he serves the *long-run* interests of society by ignoring its immediate demands in his scholarly endeavors.

He may be correct, but in the short-run there is a problem. As Price and others have pointed out, the essence of professionalism is *society-oriented*.[5] The scientist seeks to advance knowledge for its own sake. He chooses problems that are amenable to solution in *scientific* terms, i.e., those that are deemed high on the priorities of his discipline. This "ivory-tower" perspective gives time for reflection and intense labor on discrete subjects that make scientific progress possible.

But society needs applications. Particularly when government is providing the funds, the major concern of society is practical problem-solving, not knowledge for its own sake. From this derives the professional orientation. Price carefully distinguished "professionals" from scientists. He saw professions such as engineering and medicine, as having the purpose "of taking abstractions of science (or other systematic knowledge) and applying them to the concrete and practical affairs of men." Said Price: "Science can insist on ignoring questions of purpose in order to be objective and precise; the professionals cannot."[6]

What Price says *science* can do, *scientists* no longer can. Society, particularly government, and the internalized sense of responsibility of many scientists force scientists to confront societal issues. Price spoke of two other estates in addition to those of the scientific and professional. These were the administrative and the political estates. The administrative generalist relates to organizational, not professional, purposes. Thus, he draws on professional knowledge but must deal with a multitude of problems beyond any professional base of understanding. Politicians, of course, are even further removed from the precision of science. "The men who exercise legislative or executive power may make use of the skills of administrators and engineers and scientists, but in the end they make their most important decisions on the basis of value judgments or hunch or compromise or power interests."[7]

If only scientists would stay within their estate-role, or if only society would let them, all would be simple. The fact, of course, is that scientists play a variety of other roles in government, and therein lies the tension. The role of scientists as professionals (i.e., scientists applying their skills toward societal purposes) is ambiguous and uncharted. Since there is no profession called "the society-oriented scientist," the scientist who finds himself playing this role must define his own course. He finds increasingly that he cannot escape doing so whether he is in the scientific estate in the laboratory, the administrative estate in Washington, or serving elected political officials as an advisor. Indeed, from the time, thirty years ago, when atomic scientists lobbied for civilian control of the atom, through the recent efforts of some biologists to place limits on DNA experimentation, scientists have played the direct political role—lobbying, as other interest groups, for policies they favored. Whatever role they play, scientists feel the tension between their science-oriented values and those that might be called society-oriented. The scientific professional is being forced to cope with the conflict between these perspectives, and he will have to do so to an increasing extent in the future.

Scientists in the Laboratory

The scientist in the laboratory, particularly the academic laboratory, most closely approximates the classical image of scientific professionalism. No doubt, there are many scientists who, in conjunction with one or two graduate students, pursue their research with little or no outside funding. Such scientists are increasingly rare, however. The nature of most scientific fields has changed dramatically over the past three decades, and the changes have made science and scientists more and more dependent upon, and thus responsive to, government. Scientific research itself has become technology-intensive. Nuclear physicists need particle accelerators; astronomers need giant telescopes in both optical and radio frequencies; biomedical researchers need laboratories with sophisticated instrumentation, and all branches of science need computers. Such technology makes possible an acceleration of scientific research, but it is often extraordinarily expensive.

The impact of big technology on science has been to change the organization and style of scientific research in many fields from the aforementioned lone investigator with one or two disciples, to an effort involving teams of researchers backed by squadrons of graduate students and technical assistants. In some fields, such as high energy physics and astronomy, scientific teams must travel from their homes in universities to the sites of the big machines on schedules designed to optimize efficient use of the technology.

Thus, the era of big technology has paralleled, and in many cases has been an imperative to, the growth of big science. Big science is inevitably government-supported science. Before World War II, only a minor share of the nation's basic scientific research effort was government supported. By 1953, the federal government was sponsoring more than half (52 per cent) of all basic research in the United States. This proportion reached nearly two-thirds (62 per cent) in the mid-1960's and has remained at more or less this level since that time (in 1977 it was 68 per cent). Government supports science for practical purposes—or, at least, in the faith that the results will be ultimately useful. The scientist knows this and, thus, as the price he must pay for doing modern scientific research, he becomes a "grantsman." His grant proposals feature the latest "buzz words" current in Washington. Increasingly, they are "relevant" to current government priorities. Try as he might to avoid it, the scientist, as grantsman, is skewing his values to those deemed important by social institutions.

This may be good, or it may be bad. Probably, it is inevitable. As a consequence, government pulls the scientist toward its interests—even though the scientist often promises more relevance in his proposals than he actually delivers in his work. The nature of government funding and increasingly stringent management practices have the effect of moving the scientist, to a greater or lesser extent, toward values reflecting societal orientation.[8] The scientist may not always do so willingly, but, in seeking research funding, he adapts.

The Scientist as Administrator

Like their academic colleagues, some government scientists who are affiliated with such outstanding facilities like the National Institutes of Health or the National Bureau of Standards, devote their efforts to science-oriented basic research. More frequently, however, scientists in federal agencies are engaged in applied research and in monitoring research performed under contract in universities and industry, since 70 per cent of the money the government spends on R&D is contracted. Because of these monitoring duties and the hierarchical nature of government organization, an ambitious government scientist seeking to reach the highest salary levels and the highest levels of professional responsibility generally finds it necessary to move into management and administration. Thus, over a period of time, the career patterns of governmental scientists tend to diverge from research achievement and lead more and more into administrative positions.[9]

As the scientist in the laboratory is increasingly a person under professional tension, so also is the scientist in executive suite. Whether in private or public life, the scientist who chooses to become an administrator rather than strictly a researcher faces a dilemma. As an administrator, he must make decisions that are in the organization's interest. As a scientist, he has scientific values and peers in the scientific community whose approval and support he desires. What happens when organizational and scientific interests diverge, particularly in the governmental context?

The higher the administrator's level in government, the more likely it will be that his organizational and scientific interests will be at odds. Because simpler issues are usually resolved at lower levels, issues at higher levels of government are more complex and must take into consideration more variables. Perhaps the position that symbolizes the dilemmas of the scientist as administrator most vividly is that of the bureau chief.[10] Beginning with the Department of Agriculture in the nineteenth century, scientists have risen in the civil service to positions where many head technical bureaus in large federal organizations. They are low enough in the hierarchy to feel the pressures of their own technical staffs as well as of their peers in the scientific community. Yet, they are sufficiently high in administration to be fully cognizant of a political environment involving values far beyond those of the scientific community. Such administrators have had important roles in the interface between science and government over the years. The National Academy of Sciences has always had a number of scientific administrators in its ranks. Indeed, the absence of an administrative class in the United States similar to that in England has encouraged the rise of specialists, including scientists, to top administrative positions in government bureaus and some independent agencies.[11]

The problems of the scientist as administrator are illustrated vividly in the case of the chief of the Weather Bureau in the early years of weather modification technology which constituted a span of approximately a decade, from 1946 to the mid-1950's. Weather modification, which involves the seeding of clouds to accomplish such ends as enhancing precipitation, suppressing lightning, and blunting hurricanes, emerged from the work of Vincent Schaffer and Irving Langmuir of the General Electric Company in the early 1940's. Neither of these individuals was a meterologist. Langmuir, however, was a physical chemist with a Nobel prize. He began making claims for the technology of cloud seeding that most meteorologists found incredible. The most powerful meteorologist in the country at that time was the chief of the Weather Bureau. From his perspective, Langmuir was making claims that could not be verified in terms of the current state of knowledge in meterology. The Weather Bureau chief also saw Langmuir as legitimating the activities of a band of nonscientific commercial "seeders" who were putting into practice the emerging cloud-seeding technology in the drought-stricken west and who many meteorologists regarded as charlatans. The problems of the chief of the Weather Bureau as a scientist were complicated by his role as an administrator. There were agencies in the federal government with strong interests in weather such as the Department of Agriculture and The Department of Interior. These agencies wanted the Weather Bureau to take the lead in developing the technology that would aid them in accomplishing their missions and satisfying their constituencies. At the same time, there were some persons within these agencies who would just as soon have seen their own organizations become vehicles for the development of the new technology. There was, therefore, some bureaucratic rivalry with respect to what was perceived as a possible new scientific and technological mission regarding weather modification.

The Weather Bureau chief, whatever his scientific reservations with respect to Langmuir and the seeders, saw the bureaucratic stakes quite vividly. What was the Weather Bureau chief to do? What he *did* was to speak out forcefully against Langmuir and the commercial seeders. This activity brought a response from the other side. The debate escalated and polarized, and all parties were driven into extreme positions. In the end, the Weather Bureau chief found himself defending meteorologists' claims against a host of outsiders.

The field of weather modification was set back by the debates of the late 1940's and early 1950's. At the same time, the bureaucratic interests of the Weather Bureau were severely damaged. In 1958, when Congress established a National Weather Modification Research Program, it deliberately chose not to give the mission to the Weather Bureau. Wary of the Weather Bureau because of the position it had taken in the preceding decades, Congress gave the mission to the National Science Foundation, which did not really want it. To this day, the successor agency to the Weather Bureau, the National Oceanic and Atmospheric Administration, has had difficulty reassuring supporters of weather modification of its enthusiasm for the field. Memories are long in the bureaucracy and in Congress. The scientific administrator who wishes to be a developer of a new technology may find that, as an administrator, it is difficult to speak for what his scientific peers believe to be the truth.[12]

The conflicts that engulfed the Weather Bureau chief are not unlike those experienced by other scientific administrators. In this case, there was an agency that was concerned with developing and using technology involving weather. In the case of regulatory agencies, where the control of technology is at issue, similar matters invariably arise. Results of scientific tests and experiments suggest that there may be risks of harmful effects to those exposed to certain technologies; for example, an increased probability of developing cancer. If the scientific administrator goes along with the technical community to which he relates, he may find himself opposed by various interests and responsible for causing considerable disruption in the parts of the economy affected by regulatory ruling. Disruption of the economy invariably leads to criticism of the agency. Recent cases involving cyclamates, saccharine, and the fire-retardant chemical, TRIS, are cases in point. How certain does the scientific administrator in a regulatory setting need to be of the scientific facts before issuing a ruling? How serious do the disruptions in the economy have to be before the risks are outweighed by the economic costs? To what peer group should the scientific administrator in such circumstances defer? Where do bureaucratic stakes enter? Where do personal stakes become critical? In a famous controversy over the efficacy of an automobile battery additive, which took place some years ago, a scientific administrator (the director of the National Bureau of Standards) defended a particular technical judgment against his superior, the Secretary of Commerce. The Secretary found the NBS director's technical judgment to be against the pro-business policies he was trying to promote. As a result, the scientific administrator was fired. An intense lobbying effort by leaders of the scientific community got the order reversed, but the lesson for scientific administrators is fairly clear.[13] Scientific administration involves a rather tortuous task of balancing scientific, bureaucratic, and personal interests. Correct professional behavior, under certain circumstances, cannot be defined in terms of the usual scientific norms.

There are, in fact, indications that, as the relationships between science and government grow and become more routinized, this lesson is being learned. Scientific reaction to the recent firing of U.S. Geological Survey Director Vincent McKelvey by the Carter administration is one sign. Although the Geological Survey is primarily a scientific bureau and has hitherto been regarded as non-political, the administration made no attempt to hide the fact that McKelvey was fired because of policy differences. Yet, in contrast to the NSB case, which took place during the 1950's, McKelvey's firing has stirred no great outcry from the scientific community. The Geological Survey may be a scientific agency, but the policy impacts of its activities (for example, in energy resources) mean that it must be treated as an integral part of government.

The Scientist as Policy Advisor

Few scientists rise to top policy posts in the sense of becoming presidents or members of Congress. In rare instances, a scientist such as Defense Secretary Harold Brown, may become a cabinet secretary, but such appointments are exceptional. Scientists generally achieve policy posts at the middle, or administrative, levels of government. The main opportunities for scientists to relate to what would usually be called "national" policy issues are in the role of advisors.[14] In such roles they may be called upon to provide guidance relating to scientific or technical matters in broader issues of policy ("science in policy"), or relating to policy questions on the planning or exploitation of scientific research ("policy for science").

One might suspect that professional ambivalence would be less a problem for scientists in advising than in administration. After all, one could argue that the scientific advisor can tell the decision-maker the facts, leaving value judgments to him. It does not work that way in the "real world."[15] Most of the time, the questions that policy-makers want to pose to their science advisors are of the type Weinberg has called "trans-science."[16] They are questions that involve an amalgam of facts and values or that require the application of seasoned judgment. They are, in a fundamental sense, beyond the power of science to answer. Furthermore, they are usually questions about which expert scientists disagree, questions such as those concerning the safety of civilian nuclear reactors. Presidents and congressmen are usually more interested in questions of science in policy than those relating to policy for science. Both kinds of questions are value-laden, but the former are infinitely more complex. They generally get the scientist into questions of national defense, the economy, and such inherently controversial matters as ABM and SST.

Issues of professional responsibility inevitably arise in matters of controversy. What does the scientific advisor do when the decision-maker fails to heed his advice? In particular, what is an appropriate relationship between science advisors and presidents?

Science advice to the president became an institutionalized feature of American government in 1957 as a result of Sputnik. Prior to this, relations were episodic, although not necessarily unimportant (e.g., the interaction of Vannevar Bush, head of the Office of Scientific Research and Development, and Franklin D. Roosevelt during World War II.) However, Sputnik caused President Eisenhower to elevate an existing Executive Office science advisory body to the presidential level and to appoint the first presidential science advisor. Other science policy innovations followed, and staff was provided for this advisory function.

As is usually the case, the decision-maker, not the advisor, determines the power of advice. The consensus seems to be that, during the Eisenhower and Kennedy administrations, science advisors had effective access to the president. The relationship between Lyndon Johnson and his science advisor was more distant. In part, this was a result of personality; in part, it was because of the changing nature of issues on the national agenda. Scientists were obviously critical of the space and missile technology decisions that dominated the concerns of Eisenhower and Kennedy. They were less relevant (at least, they were so perceived) to a president bent on building a Great Society at home and fighting a guerilla war abroad. Indeed, the attacks by academic scientists on the Vietnam War angered Johnson, and, undoubtedly, this ill feeling affected his relations with the academic men who made up the majority of his Science Advisory Committee.

The low point of the relationship of a president and his science advisor was reached during the Nixon years. Prior to this, scientists followed the rule of keeping confidential their advice to the president. When President Nixon opted in favor of the SST against the advice of his Science Advisory Committee, one member of the committee felt that he had an obligation to take his position to Congress. This violation of the traditional, confidential nature of the president-science advisor relationship contributed to Nixon's decision to rid himself of his science advisory apparatus. "Who do those science bastards think they are?" one Nixon aide demanded.[17]

Under President Ford, the White House science advisory apparatus was restored on a statutory basis. Congress, meanwhile, had asserted itself by forming its own vehicle for acquiring scientific advice: the Office of Technology Assessment, established in 1972. Scientists now, presumably, have institutionalized access not only to the president but also to Congress.

At this time, the relationship between President Jimmy Carter and his science advisors appears relatively sound, if not cozy. He had an opportunity to drop the science advisory machinery as part of an Executive Office reorganization and, instead, opted to keep its primary units, particulary the science advisor. All evidence about Carter points to a president uncommonly interested in and knowledgeable about science and technology. The current science advisor, Frank Press, reportedly sees Carter easily and has no difficulty providing advice. Whether this advice is taken or not is another matter, of course. Problems remain, however, in the fundamental relationship between the scientist with his norms and the politician with his necessities. As long as scientists retain a professional orientation in which truth, as they see it, is valued as highly, or more highly, than political loyalty, there will always be the potential for tensions and occasional violations of bureaucratic and hierarchical norms. Advice is not neutral; it is a potential weapon that the user may deploy in the unending struggle between president and Congress, between president and bureaucracy or between various other factions involved in the policy process. Whatever the producer of advice may wish, the receiver will seek to use the advice in his own best interests, and those interests may involve releasing it selectively or keeping it to himself.[18]

The Scientist as Citizen and Lobbyist

Professional norms apart, the willingness of scientists to engage in overt political activity through lobbying on specific public policy issues has grown substantially in recent years. In years past, scientists successfully asserted their preferences on behalf of civilian control of certain technologies such as atomic energy and space technology. More recently, they have fought for and against deployment of ABM and the United States SST.[19] They have also increasingly been among the leaders in the environmental movement.

To a large degree, political activity among elite scientists is *ad hoc,* issue specific, and unorganized. Leading scientists take stands on matters of the day, often irrespective of their expertise in a particular area. To the extent that there is organization, it tends to be through an "old-boy" network in which the Cosmos Club in Washington, D.C. is the meeting ground for the generals and the telephone the means for recruiting the troops.

The longest standing issue on which scientists have lobbied persistently and consistently is arms control. It is here, also, that organized interest group activity with all its symbols and paraphernalia can best be seen.[20] Possibly, the oldest organized scientific interest group in this field is the Federation of Atomic Scientists established in 1946. The predecessor organization launched the *Bulletin of the Atomic Scientists,* a journal famed for its doomsday clock. Pictured on its front cover, the clock's minute hand moves toward or away from twelve o'clock in accord with the threat of nuclear war.

As the science-based issues facing the country have changed and broadened, so also has the orientation of the *Bulletin* and the Federation. The Federation now publishes a monthly newsletter called the *Public Interest Report.* The masthead reads:

The Federation of American Scientists is a unique, nonprofit, civic organization, licensed to lobby in the public interest, and composed of 7000 natural and social scientists and engineers who are concerned with problems of science and society.

Indeed the Federation may be unique in terms of scale and longevity among organizations of scientists concerned solely with influencing public policy. But, it is not the only such organization. David Nichols' survey, conducted several years ago, lists nine scientific groups which fit his criteria of organized public activism, national in scope and aimed at changes in policy.[21] They range from moderate organizations, like the Federation and the Scientists' Institute for Public Information, to such radical bodies born in the turbulence of the late 1960's, as Scientists and Engineers for Social and Political Action and Computer People for Peace. Primack and von Hippel document the activities of a variety of organizations and individuals engaged in what they term "public interest science."[22] Some, such as the Union of Concerned Scientists (UCS), have had remarkably large impacts on policy issues (on nuclear power in the case of UCS) with little more resources than a name, a post office box, a mimeograph machine, and the ingenuity of a couple of enterprising scientists.

Most other organizations of scientists, from the American Association for the Advancement of Science to the numerous disciplinary professional associations representing physicists, chemists, biologists, engineers, and others adhere generally to the rule that professional organizations do not overtly lobby. They are more prone than they once were to issue pronouncements on particular issues such as human rights for scientists in repressive regimes, but the wording of such pronouncements often reflects the ambivalence of their memberships as well as the members' divided views.

The record suggests that the vast majority of scientists are not especially active in public affairs. However, a vocal minority is extremely active on issues such as arms control and environment; and a growing segment, particularly among younger scientists, is aware of and willing to face the many realms of science-society interaction. Many of those scientists who do take to the political lists do so in the belief that they have a special responsibility as scientists to aid the public in dealing with issues that have a heavy scientific or technological content. Do they see themselves and their policy positions as "objective"? How about their colleagues or opponents? Cahn's study of scientists in the ABM debate suggests a realistic assessment by many scientists of the value-laden nature of their own positions and those of other scientists.[23] The norms of science demand a certain insulation from worldly concerns to protect the fundamental research process. Few would maintain any longer, however, that that insulation or the nature of scientific expertise make the *policy* preferences of a scientist any closer to "truth" than those of a non-scientist.

Conclusion

This paper has sought to illustrate various facets of the professional ambivalence of scientists in relation to government. Whether as academic researchers on campus seeking funds for basic research, as scientific administrators heading technical or regulatory agencies, as advisors to the President and Congress in the national policy arena, or as lobbyists outside government, scientists face a common dilemma. They are trained to think and act in one set of norms. In relation to government, they must adapt their behavior to a very different operating environment. Scientists face professional ambiguity; they face ambivalence, and there are no easy resolutions. The energy crisis and predictable future resource scarcities indicate that scientists and government will grow closer, rather than more distant, in the years ahead.

The vision of four estates, articulated more than a decade ago by Price, seems insufficient as a model for appropriate scientific behavior. If the Price model does not hold, what does? Is it possible to develop a new set of principles for professionalism in science akin to those for lawyers and doctors? And, if such codes were formulated, who would be the enforcers? Clearly, there is room for much serious thinking here. There is also an urgency. As the controversy over recombinant DNA research suggests, what scientists can do can affect us all, and what they say about what they do affects how governments treat them and their work. More often than not, neither politicians nor scientists seem to understand each other, and the general public loses faith in both. The scientific estate requires a new model, a model of professionalism that realistically blends public purpose with disciplinary needs. Unless scientists create such a model for themselves, society ultimately will do so in their stead.

Notes

1. U.S. National Science Foundation, *U.S. Scientists and Engineers: 1974* (Washington, DC: USGPO, 1977), NSF 76-329, p. 5.
2. U.S. National Science Foundation, *Characteristics of Doctoral Scientists and Engineers in the United States, 1973* (Washington, DC: USGPO, 1975), NSF 75-312, p. 15.
3. U.S. National Science Foundation, *Science Indicators, 1974*, Report of the National Science Board, 1975 (Washington, DC: USGPO, 1976), p. 126.
4. See Warren O. Hagstrom, *The Scientific Community* (New York: Basic Books, 1965); Normal Storer, *The Social System of Science* (New York: Holt, 1966). For an up-to-date review of this subject area see T. J. Mulkay, "The Sociology of the Scientific Research Community," in Ina Spiegel-Rosing and Derek de Solla Price, *Science, Technology and Society: A Cross-Disciplinary Perspective* (Beverly Hills, Cal.: Sage Publications, 1977), pp. 93-148.
5. Don K. Price, *The Scientific Estate* (Cambridge, Mass.: Harvard University Press, 1965).
6. *Ibid.*, pp. 122-23.
7. *Ibid.*, p. 134.
8. W. Henry Lambright, *Governing Science and Technology* (New York: Oxford University Press, 1976), pp. 137-40.
9. See Simon Marcson, "Research Settings," in Saad Z. Nagi and Ronald G. Corwin, eds., *The Social Contexts of Research* (New York: Wiley-Interscience, 1972), pp. 161-191.
10. For a broad discussion of sociological aspects of scientists' participation in government, see Simon Marcson, *Scientists in Government* (New Brunswick, N.J.: Rutgers University Press, 1966). Also see A. Hunter Dupree, *Science in the Federal Government* (Cambridge, Mass.: Harvard University

Press, 1957), and Stuart Blume, *Toward a Political Sociology of Science* (New York: Free Press, 1974).
11. Don K. Price, "The Scientific Establishment," in Robert Gilpin and Christopher Wright, eds., *Scientists and National Policy Making* (New York: Columbia University Press, 1963).
12. W. Henry Lambright, "Government and Technological Innovation: Weather Modification as a Case in Point,"*Public Administration Review,* January/February 1972.
13. Samuel A. Lawrence, "The Battery Additive Controversy," *The Inter-University Case Program #68* (New York: The Bobbs-Merrill Company, Inc., 1962).
14. Gilpin and Wright, *op. cit.*
15. The extensive literature on this subject is reviewed in Albert H. Teich, "Objectivity and Advocacy in Scientific Advice," paper presented at the annual meeting of the American Association for the Advancement of Science, Boston, February 1976.
16. Alvin Weinberg, "Science and Trans-Science," *Minerva,* Vol. 10, No. 2 (April 1972), pp. 209-222.
17. Lambright, *Governing Science and Technology,* p. 131.
18. Joe Primack and Frank von Hippel, *Advice and Dissent: Scientists in the Political Arena* (New York: Basic Books, 1974).
19. See, Anne H. Cahn, "American Scientists and the ABM: A Case Study in Controversy," in Albert H. Teich, ed., *Scientists and Public Affairs* (Cambridge, Mass.: MIT Press, 1974), pp. 41-120.
20. David Nichols, "The Associational Interest Groups of American Science," in Teich, ed., *op. cit.,* pp. 123-170.
21. *Ibid.,* pp. 124-126.
22. Primack and von Hippel, *op. cit.*
23. Cahn, *op. cit.,* pp. 101-102.

CONFLICT & CONVERGENCE: THE MENTAL HEALTH PROFESSIONAL IN GOVERNMENT

Saul Feldman, *National Institute of Mental Health*

In the 200 years since the first mental hospital was opened in Williamsburg, Virginia, the mental health field has grown substantially, both in size and complexity. While this growth has been uneven, and at times chaotic, it has nonetheless transformed what was once a "cottage industry" into an enterprise that costs nearly $20 billion a year and provides employment for more than one-half million people in 4,500 organizations.

As with all such endeavors, it is difficult to identify with any precision the causal factors associated with the growth of the mental health field. It is clear, however, that the need to care for the mounting "casualties" of an increasingly complex society, a more enlightened and receptive "zeitgeist," and the development of new and more effective treatment methods all played an important part. Perhaps of even greater importance has been the activity of powerful advocates both within and outside of government who are strongly committed to the need for and expansion of mental health programs.

Prominent among these advocates are mental health professionals in the four major fields of psychology, psychiatry, psychiatric social work, and psychiatric nursing as well as in a variety of others—occupational therapy, rehabilitation, counseling, art therapy, and the like. Singly, as employees of mental health facilities, and as members of professional organizations, they constitute both the substance of the mental health field and the principal mechanism through which it is sustained. The membership of these professional organizations reflects the growth of the field—the American Psychiatric Association today has 23,000 members; there were under 6,000 in 1950. In 1975 the American Psychological Association had 45,000 members; in 1960 there were 18,000 and in 1950 about 7,000. Other professional organizations in mental health have grown apace.

Role of Government

Unlike general health care with its dependence on the private sector, the development of the mental health field largely has been the result of government action. State governments alone spend about $7 billion annually on mental health care and in many of the states, mental health is among the largest budget items—about $1 billion in New York State alone. Today, every state has a mental health authority—some in departments reporting directly to the governor, others as part of an "umbrella" human services agency and still others located elsewhere in the state bureaucracy.

Stimulated by the availability of state matching funds, local governments also have become heavily involved in mental health. City and county mental health programs abound throughout the country and with the increasing emphasis on the decentralization of state functions, they are growing both in resources and responsibility.

The federal government entered the mental health scene relatively late. It was not until 1946 with the enactment of

---

Saul Feldman is director of The Staff College at the National Institute of Mental Health and serves as a visiting lecturer at a number of universities and training programs. He has written many articles, and his latest book *The Administration of Mental Health Services* has recently been published. He is the founder and editor of the journal, "Administration in Mental Health." He is a faculty associate at the Johns Hopkins University School of Hygiene and Public Health and a visiting professor of psychiatry and behavioral science at the State University of New York, Stony Brook.

the National Mental Health Act and the subsequent creation of the National Institute of Mental Health that significant federal interest was expressed—first in research and training and later mental health services in the 1960's. From a relatively modest beginning, the current annual budget of the Alcohol, Drug Abuse, and Mental Health Administration (in HEW) is approximately $1 billion. And this amount is dwarfed by the expenditures of other federal agencies directly providing or purchasing mental health care for the military, veterans, and beneficiaries of federal aid programs.

In 1976, nearly 150,000 mental health professionals (full-time equivalent) were employed in facilities providing mental health services, including psychiatric hospitals, residential treatment centers, outpatient clinics, and community mental health centers.[1] To a very considerable extent, these facilities are either owned, funded, or regulated by some level of government. In addition, a substantial number of mental health professionals are employed in academia, health and social service organizations, private practice, and administrative positions with government agencies.

The role of government as a major employer of mental health professionals is illustrated by a study of 10,000 mental health professionals whose training during the years 1948-1968 was supported at least in part by the National Institute of Mental Health. The data indicate that 32 per cent of the psychiatrists, 60 per cent of the psychologists, 58 per cent of the psychiatric social workers, and 60 per cent of the psychiatric nurses listed government as their principal employer. In addition, a large number of others worked for government part-time and/or were employed in private nonprofit organizations funded by government.

In essence, mental health professionals whose careers have not been profoundly affected by government in some way are very rare. The graduate departments in which they seek degrees, the licensure requirements governing their practice, the research they pursue, and the organizations in which they work are all beneficiaries (or victims) of government funding and regulation. Many of these programs would not exist were it not for government support.

This dependence of the mental health field upon government is not reflected in the graduate education of mental health professionals. The training of psychologists, psychiatrists, psychiatric social workers, and nurses does not include course work designed to enhance their understanding of the governmental system, particularly those aspects of it that will affect them most directly—government grant programs, legislative and regulatory processes, and intergovernmental relations.

This lack of knowledge does not appear to inhibit mental health professionals from expressing their displeasure at government actions with which they do not agree. The rhetoric at professional meetings and other settings in which mental health professionals gather, is frequently marked by sharp (if not vituperative) criticism of government actions—budget cuts, increases that are too small, misplaced priorities, restrictive policies, excessive regulation, and a general criticism of government as not sufficiently sensitive to the need for and value of mental health training, research, and services.

At least in part, this recurrent dissatisfaction is a function of too little knowledge and too much isolation from the political/governmental processes in which priorities are determined and budget decisions are made. As Connery has pointed out, changing government priorities is very complex and results from a "continuing process of bargaining, pressuring, inducing, bribing, supervising, demonstrating, harrassing, encouraging, and publicizing."[2] Mental health professionals frequently do not have the knowledge or tolerance for so arduous a process, one in which a large number of well-informed and sophisticated advocates for other worthy programs are involved. For those mental health professionals employed in community mental health centers, hospitals, and other facilities owned or funded by government, this often results in dissatisfaction with the level of services they are able to provide, salary scales, and physical facilities. For others in administrative/program development positions with government agencies this lack of knowledge about the functioning of the bureaucracy, the governmental system, and organizational behavior puts them at a decided disadvantage.

To compound the problem, the training and professional socialization processes in which mental health professionals are involved seem to result in personal and professional values that may be at variance with, if not alien to, the ethos of the government bureaucracy. While some of these values appear to be associated with professionalism in general, others seem more specifically related to the mental health field.* In either event, they result in attitudes and behavior that represent points of tension between mental health professionals and the government agencies in which they work. Depending upon the circumstances, these tensions may enhance or impede the functioning of those agencies.

Autonomy

Webster defines autonomy as "functioning independently without control by others." It is among the values most highly cherished by mental health professionals, particularly those with doctorates. In the professional training of psychiatrists and psychologists, for example, autonomy is frequently defined and communicated, at least implicitly, as the ability (or divine right) to be free of most external controls. The idealized role model is that of the private practitioner who may consult with colleagues, but whose sovereignty is inviolate.

Omnipresent in the graduate training of mental health professionals, the sanctity of this self-image is consid-

---

*It should be noted here that, for the sake of the argument, all the major mental health disciplines—psychology, psychiatry, psychiatric social work, and nursing—are being endowed with a common set of values. To deal with the differences between them is beyond the scope of this paper. Besides, there seems to be evidence that the differences between the various professional disciplines are not quite as real as was once believed. See esp. Bernard L. Bloom and Howard J. Parad, "Professional Activities and Training Needs of Community Mental Health Center Staff," *American Journal of Community Psychology*, in press; and William E. Henry, et. al., *The Fifth Profession: Becoming a Psychotherapist*, (San Francisco: Jossey-Bass, 1971).

erably reinforced by the nature of the "doctor-patient" relationship. Patients with emotional problems or those who are mentally ill may, in the course of their treatment, become highly dependent and endow mental health professionals with virtues they do not always possess. While well-trained clinicians recognize and are able to cope with this process, it may inflate their self-image, strengthen their feelings of autonomy, and affect their relationships with the "nonpatient world." Within hierarchical government organizations, it may be manifested as an unwillingness to comply with orders, a need to have everything explained so that "reasonableness" is assured, hurt feelings, and an insistence upon being involved in all decisions.

As H. G. Whittington has written, the mental health professional "frequently receives enormous ego gratification from patients who see him as all powerful. It is difficult to move from a position of such great authority and status—to a position as an employee of an agency. The mental health professional simply does not want to fit into a system. . . ." In effect, his work with patients "reinforces and encourages his strivings toward independence and special status."[3]

On the other hand, feelings of autonomy are often accompanied by a willingness to take responsibility, a tendency not always found in the "native bureaucrat." It may also breed a capacity for creativity and the development of new and innovative program ideas or unique solutions to chronic problems. This inclination of the professional to challenge the conventional wisdom, a quality found too infrequently in government, may, under certain conditions, stimulate others to do the same. And the need to understand a particular decision or mode of behavior and be convinced of its "correctness" can considerably lessen the unfortunate inclination in government to "follow the leader," even to the margins of legality.

Organizational Loyalty

Professionalism, almost by definition, requires adherence to a set of standards and values that delineate acceptable and/or desirable modes of behavior. These values are instilled throughout professional training and reinforced afterwards through relationships with colleagues, continuing education programs, and most significantly, membership in professional organizations. In addition to their other roles, these organizations are often the originators and enforcers of professional standards. For mental health professionals in government, they also provide a source of external support and continuing validation of one's professionalism.

As a result, mental health professionals often become strongly identified with the values of their profession and sympathetic to its needs. This professional loyalty may not always be consistent with the needs and objectives of the government agencies in which they work. According to Blau and Scott, "a professional orientation is inversely related to organizational loyalty." They conclude that "professionals tend to assume a 'cosmopolitan' orientation and a willingness to move from one employer to another, whereas only those less committed to professional skills are usually 'locals' with strong feelings of loyalty to their organizations."[4] Similarly, in a study of mental health professionals, Wagenfeld and his colleagues found that "agency policy is seen as expendable to professional standards."[5] In the event of a real or imagined conflict between the two, professional standards would dominate.

These conflicting loyalties may manifest themselves in several ways. Without even being aware of it, the mental health professional in government may be reflecting the views of his profession in policy discussions and other activities—views that may more closely reflect the needs of the profession than the intended beneficiaries of the government program. Where proposed government policy is viewed as a clear threat to the profession, then more conscious and direct actions may result. For example, a shift in government policy might be proposed which would, if implemented, transfer funds from training grants in psychology to research. Such a shift presumably would be viewed with alarm by many graduate departments of psychology. Given what we appear to know about the conflict between professional and organizational loyalty, psychologists within the government agency responsible for such programs might be tempted toward a variety of behaviors—passive resistance, overt opposition to the change, or covertly working with the affected outside constituency group to defeat it. In our system of government, the timely and effective mobilization of such a group can be very effective.

It is important to recognize that if this behavior occurs, it is likely to be impelled by the best of intentions, i.e., a strong conviction that graduate training in psychology is essential to the mental health of the nation, rather than by overtly self-serving or nefarious motives. In an arena where "truth" is elusive, where values are more compelling than facts, and where professionalism is likely to have a significant impact on the perceptual context in which beliefs are developed and decisions made, the boundaries between propriety, disloyalty, personal beliefs and the public interest are not easily defined.

As with all such phenomena, the extent to which organizational loyalty may have positive or negative effects is highly situational. Is dissent disloyal and the refusal to "go along" insubordinate? Under what conditions is it proper or even essential to work against the objectives of one's own organization?

These are difficult issues with which society has struggled for some time, issues unlikely to be resolved easily, if at all. But it does seem clear that in the government bureaucracy, "organizational loyalty" has a powerful positive valence and behavior that appears to deviate from it is generally unwelcome. Dissent is not popular nor easily expressed and the organizational reward system strongly reinforces the "go along to get along" syndrome.

In this sense, organizational disloyalty can be constructive if it promotes an adversarial process that results in the critical scrutiny of government policy and an opportunity to express diverse points of view, including the self-interest of outside groups. While it complicates the decision making process, professionalism can substantially improve the quality of the product. Rarely loath to express a point of view and never lacking the verbiage to do so, mental health professionals are particularly well suited for this adversarial process, particularly on issues affecting their own profession.

Collegialism

Closely related to professional loyalty, collegialism represents its more personal and fraternal aspects. It is manifested when mental health professionals in government develop policy, write regulations, and monitor grant programs. In effect, they are prescribing and monitoring the behavior of their colleagues with whom they share a professional, and, not infrequently, a personal bond. The problem here is quite apparent: how to reconcile the need for affection or a least acceptance by one's colleagues while at the same time critically reviewing thier behavior and making decisions that affect their welfare. The problem is sharpened when such behavior appears to warrant a decision to terminate or not renew a government grant.

The collegial bonds between mental health professionals within government and those outside also may erode the quality of site visits and other compliance mechanisms. In effect, the regulators become more identified with the needs and values of the regulatees than with the public interest—a not uncommon occurrence. No wonder then that such processes as peer review tend to be less than effective instruments to ensure the quality of professional performance.

A not dissimilar process exists with regard to the promulgation of rules and regulations. Here the mental health professional is sensitive, not always consciously, to how these will affect friends and associates. There may be a tendency to make them "acceptable" and as a result gain or retain the admiration of colleagues. The dilemma here is a classical and perhaps timeless one for government—how to maximize the effectiveness and objectivity of needed professional expertise while eliminating or at least reducing the dysfunctional aspects of the process through which such expertise is acquired and retained. Gouldner has described this dilemma as the "tension between an organization's bureaucratic needs for expertise and its social-system needs for loyalty."[6]

Frustration Threshold

Mental health professionals, particularly those with terminal degrees, have a great deal of occupational mobility. While the employment market varies with the state of the economy, the demand/supply ratio is generally in their favor. This lack of a "captive" status or dependence on government employment seems to have several effects. Within government, mental health professionals may be treated more benignly than their real value warrants because they are not easily replaced. Perquisites such as attending conferences and flexible work hours may be more readily available to them than to others, with a resulting decrement to the morale of the organization. Further, their tolerance for frustration is likely to be substantially lower than that of their colleagues whose options are fewer.

While adequate pay, satisfying work and good working conditions are important contributors to employee satisfaction and, therefore, to tenure, the perception that other desirable jobs exist elsewhere and are attainable is a powerful motivator of job change. As a result, mental health professionals are likely to endure less frustration than other government employees before deciding to resign. While comprehensive studies comparing the turnover rate of mental health professionals with others in government do not exist, the rate does appear to be higher.

Of course, within an organization, mental health professionals are not easy to please. They appear to have a strong (if not overdeveloped) sense of entitlement stemming from long years of study and sacrifice as well as a keen sense of the privileges attached to the title "doctor." As such, they may be impatient with routine, highly selective about the activities in which they choose to engage, resistant to supervision and invariably alert to their "special status" in other ways as well.*

Administrative Style

For the mental health professional who is also an administrator, there are several special attitudinal issues. Mental health is a helping profession in which the values of caring, support and therapy are dominant. These values are often inconsistent with the exercise of power—the directive and perhaps authoritative stance sometimes necessary for successful administration.

As a result, mental health professionals are not always comfortable with the use of power in organizations. As Levinson and Klerman have indicated, "Often the clinician-turned executive is hindered in the exercise of authority by his feeling that an interest in power is intrinsically immoral; that it is antithetical to truly noble interests in being a healer or a scientist. Indeed, the predominant view of power . . . in the mental health profession is much like the Victorian view of sex. It is seen as vulgar, as a sign of character defect, as something an upstanding professional would not be interested in or stoop to."[7] This reluctance to use organizational power contrasts with the "professional" power derived from special expertise in the "doctor-patient" relationship discussed earlier. One is expressed as a disinclination to *exercise* control; the other as an aversion to *being* controlled.

This anxiety about power may lead mental health professionals in governmental administrative positions to an overemphasis on collective decision making or participatory management and a hesitancy to make decisions. It may also cause them to avoid jobs in which the exercise of power is required. On the other hand, a sensitivity to the psychological needs of employees and the value of a supportive environment may improve the psychological "climate" of an organization and result in improved performance. The mental health professional in government who is able to blend the use of power with an understanding of human needs is likely to be an extremely effective administrator.

---

*I have coined the term "M.Deity" to describe this attitude although it is certainly not limited to physicians.

Points of Compatability

Mental health professionals come from personal and educational backgrounds that are seldom compatible with the responsibilities they assume in government. The values to which they ascribe, i.e., autonomy, professional loyalty, and collegialism are at least superficially dissonant if not alien to the ethos of the government bureaucracies in which they are employed. Yet, federal, state, and local governments attract and retain a significant number of well-qualified mental health professionals who have been responsible for the creative programming and vitality of many government sponsored mental health programs. This operational congruence of seemingly incongruent values seems to result from several factors.

First, mental health professionals have adapted relatively well to government work despite their lack of preparation for it. Their intelligence, tolerance for ambiguity, understanding of human behavior, and ability to cope with complexity have been valuable assets in negotiating the government system.

Second, mental health professionals have become much more aware that government is the major instrument through which large scale and significant changes in the mental health field can take place. Those who are committed to such change can hardly find a better vehicle for it. As individuals they are learning that their influence is more profound and their impact on mental health care far broader in government than elsewhere.

Third, on a more pragmatic level, government service has become more financially attractive to mental health professionals and more highly valued as a phase in their lives and as a career. Particularly at the federal level, recent salary increases have caused government jobs to become more competitive with those in community agencies, hospitals, and academia.

Fourth, in their unhappiness with government policies, mental health professionals have not infrequently reacted like the ostrich, by burying their heads. They have now begun to discover that in the process, they have exposed a significant part of their anatomy. This heightened sense of vulnerability is resulting in a somewhat greater inclination to participate in the policy making process, either through involvement in a constituency group or a period of government service at federal, state, or local levels.

Finally, mental health professionals frequently do well in government because the most basic value, if not the *raison d'etre* of both, is caring for people who need help. Whether this caring is manifested by improved facilities for the mentally ill, more community mental health centers, improved housing, or better schools it is the bond that transcends and helps neutralize the value differences between government and the mental health professions. This commonality of purpose has become more explicit as the community mental health movement has developed. Mental health professionals increasingly have become aware that substandard schools, poverty, urban decay, and other social problems for which government has responsibility all have a marked impact on the mental health of the nation.

Conclusion

To a significant extent, the vitality of the mental health field, if not its very existence has rested upon its intimate relationship to government. While this basic dependency is not likely to be altered substantially, at least in the short term, there do appear to be some changes on the horizon. For example, the advent of national health insurance and/or other increases in third party payments for mental health services could shift the funding bases of these services away from government. The seeds of this approach already are contained in the increasing interest of the federal government in helping community mental health centers maximize third party payments as a possible mechanism to reduce government funding. With sufficiently broad insurance coverage, the private sector could become much more important and bring with it the investment of private capital into the mental health field on a scale unprecedented in this country.*

Shifts in the support of graduate education for mental health professionals appear to be taking place as well. The Department of Health, Education, and Welfare has proposed a phaseout of all federal support for such education and, if implemented, it would drastically reduce the training opportunities in the mental health field and slow down or halt what has been a very rapid growth in the number of mental health professionals. Even if federal support for training should continue, it will likely deemphasize the training of the core mental health professionals toward more multidisciplinary approaches.

There is little evidence to suggest that either the content of the graduate training received by mental health professionals or the personal values resulting from that training will change substantially, at least in regard to knowledge and attitudes about government. Although mental health professionals, particularly those in community settings, have become more sensitive to the importance of understanding government processes, this is not likely to be reflected in curricula changes within academia. The relative impermeability of academic prerogatives is more likely to result in the development of new nontraditional training programs such as the National Institute of Mental Health Staff College. The College provides continuing education to mental health professionals in the public sector as well as those employed by facilities supported, at least in part, by government funds. A major emphasis of the training is on the interface between government and the mental health field, particularly the implications of government funding and regulatory requirements for mental health practice.

While the future role of government in mental health is unclear, it is clear that mental health is coming out from behind the desk, off the couch, and into the mainstream of society where it belongs. The traditional retreat behind mysterious language, remote treatment facilities, and the walls of academia is giving way to a new era, one in which

---

*In that event, the nature of governmental involvement in mental health care may shift to a lesser emphasis on direct funding and a greater role in the development and enforcement of standards, quality control and the like.

close cooperation and understanding between mental health professionals and government is essential. Mental health professionals are beginning to respond, perhaps mindful of John Gardner's observation that a "subtle exit from the grimy problems of the day is to immerse yourself so deeply in a specialized professional field that the larger community virtually ceases to exist. This is a particularly good way out because the rewards of specialization are very great today, so that you may become rich and famous while you are ignoring the nation's problems."[8]

Notes

1. National Institute of Mental Health, "Staffing of Mental Health Facilities in the United States 1976", Series B, #14, 1977.
2. Robert H. Connery, et al, *The Politics of Mental Health*, (New York: Columbia University Press, 1968), p. 588.
3. H. G. Whittington, "People Make Programs: Personnel Management," Saul Feldman, (ed.), *The Administration of Mental Health Services*. (Springfield, Ill.: Charles C. Thomas, 1973), p. 64.
4. Peter M. Blau and W. Richard Scott, *Formal Organizations*, (San Francisco: Chandler Publishing Company, 1962), p. 69.
5. Morton O. Wagenfeld, Stanley S. Robin and James D. Jones, "Structural and Professional Correlates of Ideologies of Community Mental Health Workers," *Journal of Health & Social Behavior*, 15: 199-210, (1974), pp. 199-210.
6. Alvin W. Gouldner, "Cosmopolitans & Locals," *Administrative Science Quarterly*, 2 (1957-1958), p. 466.
7. Daniel J. Levinson and Gerald L. Klerman, "The Clinician-Executive Revisited," *Administration in Mental Health*, (Winter, 1972), pp. 64-67.
8. J. W. Gardner, *No Easy Victories*. (New York City: Harper and Row Publishers, 1968), p. 34.

Professions in Public Service

Frederick C. Mosher, *University of Virginia*

This symposium and the one preceding it[1] have discussed a dozen different professions and their relations to government in the United States, their respective impacts upon public policy and the ways in which it is carried out. They have ranged from among the least to among the most "professionalized" of governmental occupations—from the police to the lawyers. The ones discussed are far from a 100 per cent sample; indeed, some of the largest and most influential—the teachers, social workers, nurses, doctors—are not included. It would be difficult to summarize them in a single essay, and it is probably unnecessary. Instead, I undertake in these paragraphs to make some observations (or present hypotheses) which seem to me relevant to the consideration of professions in general. The topics, which are fairly discrete though related, include: the means whereby individual professions influence public policies and their execution; the sources of differences among the professions; their common attributes; and some of the problems which are confronting all of them. My examples are based largely upon the professions treated in the symposia, and most of the references are to articles in the symposia.

Channels of Professional Influence

In a recent meeting of scholars from a variety of fields, when the subject of the influence of individual professions on public policy was raised, the immediate, and almost the sole, response concerned the activities of the larger professional associations, such as the American Bar Association and the American Medical Association, in behalf of the interests of some or many of their members. Most of the speakers cited examples where, in their view, those activities were against the public interest—such as the AMA resistance to medical insurance or ABA's opposition to no-fault automobile insurance. This kind of reaction was not, in my experience, either unique or particularly unusual. Yet it seemed to me somewhat naive. One need not deprecate the power of private professional associations—though those in some fields pack very little punch in government—to suggest that there are other means whereby professionals may initiate or modify or veto policy proposals, or affect them in their execution. In fact, one of the most significant trends in recent decades has been the growing dominance of those within government in the

---

The author is indebted to a number of people who have read and criticized an earlier draft of this paper. They include Dwight Waldo, Jeffrey Jacobs, Richard J. Stillman, co-editor of the symposia, and the authors of several of the articles in them: William I. Bacchus, Ellsworth H. Morse, Jr., Edith K. Mosher, Steven E. Rhoads, William J. Taylor and Laurin Wollan.

Frederick C. Mosher is Doherty Professor of Government and Foreign Affairs at the University of Virginia. He is currently working on a study of the U.S. General Accounting Office, its development and its role. He has written a number of books and articles concerned at least in part with professions in government, including particularly *Democracy and the Public Service*.

framing, the shaping, as well as the carrying out of public policies and programs. In the words of Professor Samuel H. Beer, ours is an era of "technocratic politics" in which specialists with training and experience in depth in differing fields of governmental endeavor have assumed, or have had thrust upon them, the initiative for charting the course of governmental programs. Beer recently wrote: "I would remark how rarely additions to the public sector have been *initiated* by the demands of voters or the advocacy of pressure groups or the platforms of political parties. On the contrary, in the fields of health, housing, urban renewal, transportation, welfare, education, poverty, and energy it has been, in very great measure, people in government service, or closely associated with it, acting on the basis of their specialized and technical knowledge, who first perceived the problem, conceived the program, initially urged it on president and Congress, went on to help lobby it through to enactment, and then saw to its administration."[2] The "people in government" about whom Beer writes are approximately the professional specialists like the ones who are treated in these symposia.

Certainly, private business, including government contractors, organized labor, sectional interests, and other segments of the private sector are exerting significant influence on public policies as they have in the past. Equally certain is that the "technocrats" within government have joined with, or coopted, or have been coopted by their professional colleagues in the foundations, universities, and other profit and non-profit organizations, in pursuit of common goals. Yet, the influence of the specialists within government today is probably greater than it has ever been before in peacetime. And though their influence is sometimes enhanced—and occasionally resisted—by professional associations, such organizations are surely not the only or even the major channels of professional expression.

This situation has led me to try to identify and to classify the principal mechanisms and channels whereby professionals within government individually or in concert do indeed influence the course of governmental action. They seem to me to fall primarily though not exclusively in five major categories, each of which is briefly discussed below.

The first and most obvious is through *election or appointment of professionals to high political or judicial office*. Here one profession is predominant at state and federal levels and has been for most of American history—the law. As pointed out by Laurin Wollan, the legal profession has monopolized the judiciary, accounted for a majority of legislators above the local level, provided nearly two-thirds of American presidents and probably an equal proportion of state governors, and accounted for a plurality of top political officials in the executive branches. Another profession which has been significant is the academic group—often in-and-outers selected more for their reputation in their field of study than for their political importance. At one time, a majority of President Johnson's cabinet were former professors. Among those who come from the academic world or have advanced academic education, other than lawyers, the most numerous are economists, as pointed out in the article by Steven E. Rhoads. At the local level, the city manager profession falls in this category, as do school administrators.

The imbalance of professional representation in political or quasi-political positions is tremendous. Many professions whose numbers far exceed the lawyers are totally excluded from the judiciary and go virtually unrepresented in legislatures and top levels of the executive branches—teaching, medicine, military, engineering, science, accounting, and others. The reasons for the legal dominance probably have grown principally from our historical and social traditions. I am not persuaded that there is very much in legal education—or experience in legal practice—which is particularly useful or necessary for most political offices, any more than most other education and experience. In fact, some of the legal background would appear dysfunctional. Yet some young people study law for the purpose, specific or vaguely perceived, of getting into politics. Few enter any other professional field with this in mind. And the bias of most professional education—probably even the legal—is against politics, even against government.

A second pathway to professional influence on public policy is through the effective control, often a near monopoly, of the *significant managerial and operating positions of administrative agencies* by individual professions—usually at the second, third, or fourth levels of administrative organization. Here we find perhaps the most potent influence of professionals on public policy, but in segmented governmental programs. In such agencies—and they are a majority—professional goals, perceptions of the world, skills, and methods roughly equate with those of the agencies which they inhabit.

Examples of this phenomenon are rife in big governments: military bureaus and services and military officers; the State Department and the Foreign Service; educational agencies and educators; public works agencies and engineers, and many others. Most of the well known professions have at least one agency somewhere in the executive branch to crystallize or to make or change or prevent change in policy, and to channel their goals and views to other, higher-level decision-makers. In fact, since a large share of new or changed public policy is generated within such agencies, this pathway of professions to policy is probably the most important of all. Professional and organizational goals tend frequently to reenforce each other—despite the often discussed sociological concern about conflicts between the professional and the bureaucratic models. That such conflicts do exist in some fields is well illustrated in some of the articles in these symposia, especially those by Saul Feldman on the mental health professions and by W. Henry Lambright and Albert H. Teich on scientists. In contrast, Richard L. Schott suggests that among engineers, conflicts between organizational and professional demands and standards are rare, that there is a "symbiotic relationship between the engineering profession and the organizational environment."

A third kind of channel is through *professionals who operate within agencies which they do not dominate* and which may in fact be largely controlled by another profession. Thus, most large agencies have their own legal counsels or advisers, accountants and auditors, and budget and personnel officers. Many have their resident policy analysts (usually economists), planners, scientific advisers (both physical and social), and others. These kinds of professionals contribute to policy by: collaborating in its development; analyzing and evaluating policy and performance; reviewing, auditing, and advising; modifying, and sometimes vetoing. Many of them have a professional "home base" on which they can draw for support: a department of justice, or a central budget office, or a civil service organization, or a government-wide office of policy analysis.

A fourth vehicle of professional influence is through the *bringing of ideas, modes of thought and pressures upon political executives and legislative bodies and their appropriate committees by professionals* through indirect extragovernmental channels. These include the use of the media, the mobilization of outside experts, professional associations and labor unions, and many others. The strength of this kind of influence is often enhanced by the formation of coalitions with other groups having common or related interests—as the military with veterans' organizations or business contractors, lawyers with bankers, corporate executives, or labor unions, and many others.

The fifth channel of professional influence I would mention is a somewhat special case. It is *the influence of professionals at one level of government on the operations and policies of another level* through, or in alliance with, their counterpart professionals at that other level. It is usually associated with the administration of categorical grants-in-aid from higher levels to lower, but it can also operate in the other direction with the lower level bringing influence to bear on their counterparts at the higher level to help resolve their problems or indeed to obtain grants. Most of the larger fields of domestic governmental activity are replete with examples: health and mental health, education, highway engineering, law enforcement, the National Guard—to name a few.

The accompanying chart undertakes to estimate the relative importance of these five channels of influence for each of the twelve professions treated in these symposia. The estimates are of course subjective and judgmental, unsupported by empirical evidence. It is hoped, nevertheless, that they are suggestive. The practice of law in government and the military appear to be the only professions utilizing all five channels; and the control of a specialized professional agency is the most frequent, and probably most important, channel of professional influence.

Origins of Uniqueness of Individual Professions

It is tautological that every profession is in some ways different from all the others; otherwise, we could hardly refer to them separately as professions. The converse of this observation is that there are some elements and attributes within each profession that are common to most or all of its members. This does not necessarily mean that all the members of any profession agree with each other, or that they are all alike. Some, like lawyers, are paid to disagree. But, in the case of lawyers particularly, the idea of advocacy and of adversary procedures to resolve problems

Channels of Influence of Different Professions on Governmental Policy and Conduct

	Top Political Office	Professional Agency Control	Professionals Operating in Other Agencies	Professional or Other Interest Group	Inter-Governmental
Military	X	XX	X	XX	X
Foreign Service	X	XX	X	O	O
Education Administration	X	XX	O	XX	XX
City Management	XX	O	O	X	X
City Planning	O	XX	X	X	X
Police	O	XX	O	X	X
Law	XX	XX	XX	XX	X
Accounting-Auditing	O	X	XX	O	X
Engineering	O	XX	X	XX	XX
Economics	X	X	XX	O	O
Mental Health	O	XX	O	XX	XX
Sciences	O	XX	X	X	X

Key: XX = strong or frequent channel of influence
 X = moderate or occasional channel of influence
 O = weak or rare channel of influence

is pretty well ingrained in the underlying thinking of the profession. Those within each profession—or many of them— have some common ways of perceiving and structuring problems and of attacking and solving them; they are likely to share their views of the world and of the place of their profession in it; they are likely also to share a common, and more or less unique, bundle of techniques, skills, knowledge, and vocabulary.

One must distinguish between professional attributes and the popular stereotypes of the well-known professions. Probably all of us bear a baggage of stereotypes about professions in general and about a number of individual professions. Occupational stereotypes seem largely to come out of the past but are modified by individuals in the society, by current events in the news, and by personal acquaintance and experience—or the absence thereof. Some of the current social science literature about the professions reinforces a popularly held stereotype about the "model" professional: that he or she is autonomous in his or her work; that the primary motivation is service to others on a one-to-one basis rather than personal gain or prestige or power; that the services are paid for by the recipient through a fee; that the professional is rational, unbiased, and non-political. Few if any of the professions discussed in these symposia (or any others) would qualify as professionals according to such definition. On the other hand, most of them suffer under another kind of stereotype: as "bureaucrats".

Not long ago a psychologist facetiously described the accountant as the "most likely to straighten a picture in a house where he was a visitor, and most likely to play a practical joke. And, after bankers, most likely to beat his children for disobeying. Compared with others, the accountant is also seen as most likely to run away and join a circus."[3] Most stereotypes are less amusing. The accountants still suffer from the stereotype of the green eye-shade bookkeeper, industrious, unimaginative, and dull.[4] A few examples of popular stereotypes of other fields are suggested by certain words and phrases:

military: the "military mind"; profession of violence; authoritarian;
foreign service: cookie-pusher; dilettante; Ivy League;
city planners: visionary; socialistic;
economists: materialistic; rational; negative; the "dismal science";
psychiatrists: "head-shrinkers"; listeners at the couch.

Not all of the stereotyped attributes are unfavorable, and some of them are actively fostered by the professions themselves. None would openly disavow being rational and nonpolitical, not even legal and academic groups although they have an unofficial license to go into politics when they choose and return without sacrifice. As Richard J. Stillman suggests, the popular strength and acceptability of the city managers' success has been built in part on their image as even-handed, non-political, efficiency-oriented administrators.

Granted that many professional stereotypes are dimly related to, often inaccurate caricatures of, the reality, they still have some impact upon the reality. They no doubt have some bearing on the kinds of people who opt to enter the different professions, their posture after entry—often of defensiveness, sometimes of conceit—and the expectations of them held by their associates, colleagues, clientele, and the general public.

This leads to an underlying question: If each profession is different from the others and if most or all within a given profession share some of the same attributes as professionals, how did they come to be that way? What makes a school superintendent a school superintendent? an engineer an engineer? a physicist a physicist? a policeman a policeman? Although these questions could be addressed in a great variety of ways, I would suggest three key processes: self-recruitment, educational preparation and socialization in school and college and particularly in professional training, and socialization on the job and within a given organization or series of organizations.

What kind of young man or woman applies for West Point, Annapolis, or Colorado Springs and what leads him or her to do it? What kind of person majors in international relations with the intention of joining the foreign service, or majors in government as a preliminary to law school? What kind of person goes to business school and majors in accounting, and why? Are there significant differences among these beginners in their perceptions, values, and social-economic status at the time these initial decisions are made, and if so what is their nature? It is no doubt true that a good many delay these decisions while they proceed through college and some, perhaps an increasing proportion, drop out and change their career directions in mid-stream. But it is probably still true that most of them decide on their career occupations at a fairly early age—frequently in high school or earlier—and that it becomes more and more difficult and expensive to change as one's investment in time and money devoted to professional preparation mounts. Very likely, many of those early and crucial decisions are products of ready opportunity and chance, of the career preferences of relatives and cohorts, of parental advice (which sometimes works in reverse), and of counseling and guidance.

But there is good reason to believe that certain professions (or commonly held stereotypes of them) tend to attract certain kinds of people and discourage others. This is crudely illustrated by the career choices of women and minorities in the past. Few aspired to enter the more prestigious professions. It is interesting to note that the great majority of virtually all the groups treated in these articles (excepting the psychiatric nurses and social workers) are white males, although the proportions of new entrants who are non-caucasian and women is gradually rising. This is despite the fact that a very substantial percentage (40 per cent in 1970) of all professionals are women. Most of these are in professional but non-administrative jobs—school teachers, nurses, librarians, social workers. For example, while 71 per cent (in 1970) of elementary and secondary school teachers are women, more than 99 per cent of school superintendents are male.

Another element of self-recruitment is a choice between public and private sector employment. Most of those who opt for public service professions are automatically making this choice when they make their initial career decision—though some may not be fully aware of it. On the other hand, the chances are that most of those opting for the general public-private professions are deciding in favor of private sector employment—the accountants, psychiatrists, engineers, lawyers, police—though some are no doubt leaving the question open.

Space does not permit more than superficial discussion of the impact of professional education upon those who opt for and are admitted to one or another professional school, but three observations seem particularly relevant. First is that while the purported intent of professional education is the transmission of knowledge, techniques, and skills, a major element, perhaps *the* major element, is the orientation of neophytes to the "thinkways", workways, attitudes, and philosophy of the professional community. It is the beginning of professional socialization. As Jencks and Riesman put it: "The primary role of the professional school may thus be socialization, not training."[6]

Second is that, under the pressure of university academism in the last several decades, professional education has generally grown more and more theoretical and research-oriented and more and more fractionated into sub-specialties, at the same time that it is less and less directed to the practice of the profession. These trends may have been halted, even reversed, in some fields and some schools since the student disturbances of the sixties and their loud demands for "relevance." But many practitioners still complain that university training does not provide much that is useful to effective practice.

A third observation is that little of professional education is directed toward imbuing the neophyte with a sense of public dedication and responsibility. Politics and government are viewed as outsiders to the profession, often as interferers or nuisances, sometimes as antagonists. This is particularly true of the general professions like law or economics, engineering or science. It is even true of some predominantly public service professions, like education. Some professional education virtually ignores the existence of government in its teaching, even when education, research, and credentials are in substantial degree made possible by government contracts, subsidies, and delegations of authority. Where the traditional ethos of individual autonomy and independence remains strong (law, accounting, medicine in some degree), the antipathy extends to bureaucracy and organization in general—public or private. It should be noted, however, that in *some* professional schools in virtually all the fields, and in education for most of the public service professions, the idea of dedication to public service is an important element of the educational process.

The third influence which shapes the professional—the way he thinks and works, the values and standards which guide him—is his socialization in his work setting and in his organization. This operates through a variety of mechanisms: formal and informal training and indoctrination; daily association and friendship with professional colleagues; peer review and criticism of his work against official or informal standards of performance; voluntary or involuntary separation of those who do not fit or do not measure up; perhaps most important, the speed of promotion to higher levels of responsibility and accompanying rewards, usually determined by professional superiors in the organization. The input of organizational socialization is probably strengthened when

- a single profession clearly dominates an organization, as the Department of Justice with lawyers, the Bureau of Standards with scientists, and the Council of Economic Advisers with economists;
- there is a policy of relatively frequent transfers of professionals within an organization so that individual professionals work for temporary periods in different subprofessional specialties, under different professional supervisors, and in different offices;
- there is emphasis on generalism vs. intra-professional specialism, the generalism approximately equating with the scope of the larger professional organization;
- there is a career system of employment and most entrants come in at an early age and are expected to spend most of their working lives in the profession.

There have been relatively few solid studies of the process of organizational socialization—or resocialization—of professionals, but my impression is that it is a powerful shaper of people in many different fields.[7] Its importance grows if, and to the extent to which, professional education becomes distant and irrelevant to organizational practice. The degree to which a professional organization can reshape persons of diverse backgrounds and education in its own image has been repeatedly demonstrated, especially in the military services.

Common Attributes of Governmental Professions

Although each profession is unique unto itself, and it is therefore difficult to generalize, there are nonetheless some features which most of them hold in common. For example, most of them have stressed their linkage with specialized higher education, and the pressure has been to make educational requisites ever higher and more specialized. Most of them went through similar stages of educational preparation: on-the-job experience, apprenticeship, proprietary school, and finally university. Within the universities, they have proceeded, or, in some cases are proceeding, from separate professional courses to separate majors to separate and often higher degrees to separate organizations—academic departments, or preferably, semi-autonomous schools.

Following the development of post-secondary professional education came the business of accrediting educational programs, normally by groups from the concerned professions themselves. And with it, provision for credentials to authorize the graduates of professional education programs to practice the profession. In the more advanced fields, credentials came to require passage of examinations, usually given on a state-wide basis, in a few cases, national. Both the accreditation and the credentialing, including the writing and grading of examinations, are in fact conducted by representatives of the appropriate professions themselves and teachers thereof, whether or not acting in the capacity of government boards or as agents of professional associations.

Some time along this route, usually very early, associations of professionals were created to form a nucleus of the professional community, often beginning on a local basis, then coalescing at the state and finally national levels. They, in varying, but usually growing degrees shaped the profession through journals and other publications, meetings, support of research, issuance of standards and codes of ethics, and policing the practice of the profession, not only for those within it but also by preventing the intrusion of those outside it. To the more successful of the associations were delegated governmental powers, to control not alone the educational process and its requirements, but also admissions to practice and exclusion of those who failed to meet its standards.

Law, civil engineering, and medicine (from which sprang the elite sub-professions of mental health and psychiatry) were among the first along these routes to full-scale professionalism. The majority of the others treated in these symposia got their start in the late nineteenth and early twentieth centuries and have moved along the way at varying speeds. The latest comer, police, probably still has the furthest distance to go, as indicated in Richard A. Stauffenberger's article. And the public service professions generally have progressed somewhat differently from those that operate in both the public and private sectors although the outcomes are not essentially different. The city managers constitute a somewhat special case since, by the nature of the city manager plan wherein they are appointed and removable by a political body, it is difficult for any central professional organization to enforce standards of admission, advancement, and behavior.

Problems of the Professions

The traditional path toward the professional "model" with attendant goals of exclusiveness, eliteness, and self-government may well be in process of fundamental change. The article by Laurin A. Wollan, Jr. about lawyers, who have very nearly run the whole route, suggests that even they are changing directions. One senses from all these articles that there is a general malaise among the professions. William C. Baer suggests that urban planners must retreat from the utopian aspiration of master planning to the role of midwives—inducing, evoking, and suggesting. The educational administrators are described by Edith K. Mosher as "anxious, hard-pressed, and defensive", and these adjectives might be applied to a good many of the others—the Foreign Service, the city managers, even the accountants. Some feel that they are under-recognized and under-utilized in government or are submerged by politicians in a political sea—city managers, planners, police, economists, and scientists. All are being forced to change and some are threatened by changes that are occurring in the society—some of those changes encouraged or wrought by the professions themselves. These social changes are interrelated and merge into one another, but it may be useful to attempt to enumerate the more important ones.

Most obvious, and trite, are science and technology. They have transformed, and are continually enlarging, the knowledges and the techniques of most of the professions. To some they have been a great help—the military, the police, the accountants, the economists. To some, they have reduced much of what used to be the professional core to machinery and automation, with the effect of either elevating the sights of the professionals to higher and more challenging pursuits or raising a question as to whether the vocation involved merits being considered a profession—or a little of both. They have given rise to a bundle of new professions or semi-professions, some of them challenging the older ones. One may safely generalize that they are greatly complicating our vocational systems both in and outside of government.

A second change is the erosion of the line between what is properly the role of the expert, the professional, and what is the role of the politician, the generalist, the amateur representative of the people. The line has become a vague zone with shifting boundaries. Its cloudiness is partly a product of the professions' increasing involvement in controversial matters, partly of citizen and politician suspicion or dissatisfaction with the products of professional judgment. This professional role confusion applies to every profession treated in these symposia although somewhat differently to the lawyers, who have lived with it for many, many decades. One classical manifestation of it is such expressions as "we can't afford to leave military policy to the military"; but as pointed out in Col. William J. Taylor's article, the military has become more and more involved in policy matters. The same could be said about the Foreign Service, the educators, the planners, the police, the accountants, the engineers, the scientists, the mental health professions, and the economists.

A related development has been the growing demand, starting in the mid-sixties, for direct citizen involvement in making and executing domestic policy. This has been a direct challenge not alone to the established institutions of government, but also to the presumed expertise of a number of professions, well exemplified in education, city planning, police, and health.

Citizen participation is but one manifestation of a larger movement toward equal rights and equal opportunities for the poor as for the rich, the women as for the men, the minorities as for the WASPs. Indeed, the demand for equality of opportunity in education and employment may, in the long run, prove the gravest of all threats to the traditional customs and to the elitist and exclusive aspirations of the professions. Their standards and criteria for entrance, credentials, and advancement are already under challenge, and the courts have made it clear that the relevance of the criteria to the jobs to be done must be proven. As suggested earlier, those criteria are in many cases doubtful and hard to defend. The egalitarian push in education and employment is likely to have particular impact upon professions such as those treated in these symposia, since their members have been predominantly white males. The professions long have been a major, perhaps *the* major, channel for the middle and lower middle strata of society aspiring to climb higher. But the more prestigious professions have, until recently, generally narrowed the reservoir of aspirants by effectively excluding most of the poor, the minorities, and the women.

Another important social change for the professions has been the growth and growing militancy of unions in the public service. Many of these are unions of professionals themselves or products of the conversion of professional associations into what amount to unions—such as the National Education Association or the American Foreign Service Association. Even those professions which have not and may not become unionized, such as the military and city management, have increasingly to deal with other groups who are. On one side or the other of the table, or on both sides, professionals are involved in collective bargaining, an unfamiliar posture for them at the very least. Some of the pure in heart feel that unionism is an outright denial of the spirit of professionalism, and certainly it would have been fifty years ago. Without making any precise predictions, one may safely generalize that unionization is bringing about changes in the nature of professionalism and promises to bring more in the future.

A whole set of problems for the traditional professions has been posed by three more or less simultaneous developments: the tremendous growth of knowledge about our condition and about methods of improving it; the recognition or the hope, but certainly the demand that the society do something about it; and the tendency, however reluctant, to turn to government to find and effect solutions. But public problems have little respect for professional boundaries. Few significant ones can be handled adequately within the "turf" of any given profession, even when the problem seems central to the core content of the profession in question—as crime and police, mental health care and the psychiatrists, foreign affairs and the foreign service, or policy analysis and the economists. Increasingly this writer has heard from professionals in a variety of fields that their training and the lore of their profession are only marginally related to the kinds of tasks and problems they confront day by day; and this impression is confirmed in a number of the papers in these symposia.

The professions, and particularly that fraction of them in government, have responded to this situation in a variety of ways. One has been to broaden and reorient the professional boundaries and to absorb new elements and techniques. The city managers began as civil engineers concerned primarily with the physical facilities and services of the city; they developed into generalist managers of going concerns; they seem now to be moving toward policy-initiators, civic leaders, and politicians. School superintendents have followed a somewhat parallel course, as have the military, some of the scientists, and many others. Such professionalism frequently, if not usually, involves the invasion of someone else's occupational territory. As indicated by Ellsworth H. Morse, Jr., the auditors, who constitute a major segment of the accounting fraternity, increasingly have moved from their traditional financial concerns into management reviewing and now into the analysis of program results, a territory already peopled by economists, some engineers, systems analysts, political scientists, mathematicians, and others.

A second response is to develop sub-specializations within the profession, capable of coping with those aspects of problems that are beyond the reach of the core professional. This has already occurred to a major degree in most of the professions, and further fragmentation appears inevitable. Another kind of response is working with representatives of other professions on a problem-oriented, inter-disciplinary and inter-professional basis. This is being accompanied, though in a rather slow-footed way, by the development of inter-disciplinary education.

How long and how effectively the traditional concepts about our time-honored professions—semi-autonomous, self-governing, self-disciplining—will be able to stand up to this kind of fractionalization and cross breeding is a nice question. Certainly the professions have changed, are changing, and will change more in the future. Possibly, the changes will amount to a complete transformation. The article by William I. Bacchus dealing with specialists in foreign affairs describe them as "professionals without professions." According to some, we already have professional schools without professions, such as those in business and public administration. There must already be a good many in the public service whose linkage to any given profession or to any given type of professional education is tenuous. Maybe this is the prospect for the future; professional schools and professionals without professions.

Notes

1. *PAR*, Vol. 37, No. 6, (Nov.-Dec. 1977).
2. See Beer's Presidential Address before the American Political Science Association, "Federalism, Nationalism and Democracy in America," *American Political Science Review*, Vol. LXXII, No. 1 (March, 1978).
3. Selwyn W. Becker "The Accountant as Others See Him", *The Newsletter of the Graduate School of Business, University of Chicago,* Spring, 1969.
4. In contrast to the stereotype, a recent study of personality attributes of accountants and a number of other professions and occupations (measured through the California Personality Inventory) indicated that accountants compared favorably with most other professions. Compared with architects, they were seen as more "enterprising, competitive, honest, obliging, practical, self-denying, cooperative, outgoing, organized, conventional, stereotyped in thinking, hardheaded, masculine and impatient with delay, indecision, and reflection." Don T. DeCoster and John Grant Rhode "The Accountant's Stereotype: Real or Imagined, Deserved or Unwarranted", *The Accounting Review,* October, 1971, pp. 651-664.
5. There has been a good deal of research relevant to this question (and the paragraphs that follow) with respect to individual professions, and the authors of many articles in these symposia have summarized some of it. See particularly Richard L. Schott's discussion of engineers. But there is not very much comparative treatment of different professions.
6. Christopher Jencks and David Riesman, *The Academic Revolution,* Doubleday and Company, Inc., 1968, p. 206.
7. Probably the best to this date is Herbert Kaufman, *The Forest Ranger, A Study in Administrative Behavior,* Johns Hopkins Press, 1960.